MW00808611

POSTAL HISTORY
of
John Butterfield's Overland Mail Co.
on the Southern & Central Routes
including
Butterfield's Pony Express
1858-1864

by Bob Crossman

To learn about the STAGECOACH LAND ROUTE across Arkansas,
see Bob Crossman's 2021 book (266 pages):
*"Butterfield's Overland Mail STAGECOACH Route
Across Arkansas: 1858-1861"*

To learn about Butterfield's use of STEAMBOATS across Arkansas,
see Bob Crossman's 2022 book (460 pages):
*"Butterfield's Overland Mail Co. use of STEAMBOATS
to Deliver Mail and Passengers Across Arkansas 1858-1861"*

To read the history of Butterfield from the newspapers of the time,
see Bob Crossman's 2023 book (632 pages) :
*"Butterfield's Overland Mail Co. as REPORTED in the
Newspapers of Arkansas"*

First Printing • September 2023
Ingram Spark Press

John Butterfield, President, Butterfield Overland Mail Co.

Photo courtesy of Silver Dollar City, Branson, Missouri
The original stages only had "Overland Mail Co." on the side, without "Butterfield."

978-0-9996578-9-8 - Hardback

© 2023 Robert O. "Bob" Crossman

Cover Art: Stagecoach image by Nathan A. Wright from Pixabay.

TABLE OF CONTENTS   Page

1. The Overland Mail Company
  Collection of Stagecoach Images.. 5
  Background 27
    Butterfield Travel Diary of Rev. Thomas M. Johnston 48
    Rebecca Yoakum's Story of Riding the Butterfield Stage 51
  End of the Southern Route.. 71
  Move to the northern Central Route 73
  Overland Mail Company's Pony Express 95
  First Hand Report of Telegraph Line's Construction 122
  Wells Fargo & Co.. 124

POSTAL HISTORY

2. Postal Rates During Butterfield's Years 132
  Mail Delivery in the Gold Fields.. 137
3. Pre-Butterfield Mail... 143
  Ocean Steam Ship Mail 145
4. Butterfield Mail on the Memphis to Fort Smith Route 153
  Overland Mail Co. Mailbags & Overland Mail Co. Shotgun 165
5. Butterfield Mail on the St. Louis to Fort Smith Route 167
  Butterfield Mail NOT marked *"via overland"* 185
  One of the Last Covers Carried on the Southern Route........ 205
6. "Butterfield" Mail on the Central Route, 1861-1864 207
  Overland Mail Co. Bible on Central Route 232
7. Mail on the Central Route After Butterfield's Contract Ended 233
8. US Postal Service Remembering the Butterfield 237

APPENDIX

Appendix A - Photographs of the Postmaster Generals.................. 243
Appendix B - Report of the Postmaster General, Dec. 1, 1857 244
Appendix C - Articles of Association of the OMC, 1857 270
Appendix D - Report of the Postmaster General, Dec. 4, 1858 279
Appendix E - Postmaster 's Handwritten Journal, 1858, 1864 280
Appendix F - Report of the Postmaster General, March 3, 1859 281
Appendix G - Report of the Postmaster General, Dec. 3, 1859 293
Appendix H- Butterfield Employee Record Book, 1859 295
Appendix I - Report of the Postmaster General, Dec. 1, 1860 313
Appendix J - List of Various Postal Routes to the West, 1860 318
Appendix K - Report of the Postmaster General, Dec. 2, 1861 321
Appendix L - Original Contract of March 2, 1861......................... 324
Appendix M - Modified Contract of March 12, 1861 325
Appendix N - Sub Contract of March 16, 1861................................ 326
Appendix O - Financial Report from the Central Route, 1861-2 328
Appendix P - Report of the Postmaster General, Dec. 1, 1862........ 333
Appendix Q - Report of the Postmaster General, Oct.31, 1863........ 334
Appendix R - Report of the Postmaster General, Nov. 2, 1864 336
Appendix S - Summary of All Contracts with OMC 1857-1864 337
Appendix T - Report of the Postmaster General, Nov. 15, 1865 345
Appendix U - Report of the Postmaster General, Nov. 26, 1866 346
Sources 347
About the Author 349

Purpose

Purpose: To show covers (envelopes) and letters carried by Butterfield's Overland Mail between September 1858 and March 1861 on the Southern Ox Bow Route, and beginning in July of 1861 on the Central Route. Also, to include additional information and artifacts from US transcontinental mail carried immediately before and immediately after the existence of Butterfield's Overland Mail Co.

Preface

This book greatly expands my three previous books on Butterfield's Overland Mail Co. In most instances within the previous three books, I focused primarily on Butterfield's land and water routes across central Arkansas. This volume, by contrast, expands to focus on the POSTAL HISTORY along the entire route of the Butterfield from San Francisco to the Mississippi River.

By contrast, instead of only focusing on the Southern Route (1858-1861) this volume focuses the entire time period of the Overland Mail Company's contract with the postal system from 1858-1864.

Also, this book is the first time the author has reported on The Overland Mail Co.'s 1861 relationship to the once privately operated famous Pony Express from St. Joseph, Missouri to Placerville, California.

The purpose of my research of the Overland Mail Company was to satisfy my personal curiosity as a resident along the old route. Hopefully this collection of my research will also make a contribution to Butterfield's Overland Mail Company's new status as a National Historic Trail.

Acknowledgements

I am so appreciative of Dr. Gordon Nelson, professor at Florida Tech in Melbourne, Florida. He has made excellent suggestions, corrections and additions to this research. He is a true asset to the Western Cover Society.

Any remaining errors that may be in this book are the responsibility of the author, and not Dr. Nelson.

I must acknowledge and recommend the authoritative resource on the postal history of the Pony Express: the 2005 book by Richard C. Frajola, George J. Kramer, and Steven C. Walske entitled *"The Pony Express: A Postal History."*

I also express my appreciation and give credit to Wikipedia where I was able to discover biographical information on many of these cover's recipients, and find descriptions of the sending and receiving locations.

This is the only photograph in existence of a Butterfield owned Overland Mail Company stage.
Butterfield used two types of stages: a Concord Mail Stage and this lighter Celerity stage.
The driver of this Celerity shown above in the 'ten gallon hat' was David McLaughlin.
This copy of a 1861 daguerreotype image is courtesy of the
Nita Stewart Haley Memorial Library at Midland, Texas.

"The Overland Mail - The Start from Fort Smith, Arkansas for the Pacific Coast – First Coach Driven by John Butterfield, Jr. " Frank Leslie's Illustrated Newspaper, Vol. VI, Oct. 23, 1858 pg. 325-328. Lithograph, hand colored; 15 $^3/_4$ x 10 $^3/_4$

THE OVERLAND MAIL—PASSING A BIVOUAC OF EMIGRANTS IN WESTERN ARKANSAS.

"The Overland Mail — Passing a Bivouac of Emigrants in Western Arkansas"
Frank Leslie's Illustrated Newspaper, Oct. 23, 1858, pg. 325-328.
lithograph, hand colored; 15 3/4 x 10 3/4 in.

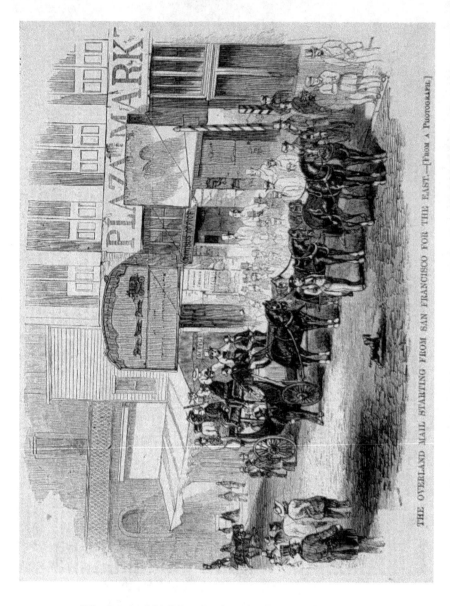

"The Overland Mail Starting from San Francisco for the East,"
[FROM A PHOTOGRAPH] – *Published in Harper's Weekly, December 11, 1858*

Crossing the River by Ferry
"Beyond the Mississippi: From the Great River to the Great Ocean,"
by Albert D. Richardson, American Publishing, 1867, page 35

THE OVERLAND MAIL CROSSING A STREAM AT NIGHT.

"The Overland Mail Crossing a Stream at Night"
At night it was not unusual for a rider with a lantern to lead the stage.
Frank Leslie's Illustrated Newspaper, Oct. 23, 1858, pg. 325-328.
lithograph, hand colored ; 15 3/4 x 10 3/4 in.

"The Overland Mail – Changing Stage-Coach for Celerity Wagon"
Frank Leslie's Illustrated Newspaper, Oct. 23, 1858, pg. 325-328.
lithograph, hand colored ; 15 3/4 x 10 3/4 in.

"Overland Stage Route - Comet, Arizona, 1858" by William Hayes Hilton
This is no doubt Donati's Comet, observed from June to November, 1858 with the naked eye. This comet will not be seen on Earth again for another 1,600 years. The artist of this sketch and those on the next six pages was a passenger in 1858 on Butterfield's Overland Mail Co. stages across California, Arizona, Nevada, and Mexico. His nine sketchbooks, from 1850 to 1870, are at The Huntington Library.
Source: Huntington Library, call number mssHilton Book 3, San Marino, California.

"Alamo Mucho Station" by William Hayes Hilton
Note the Celerity stage headed down a steep embankment on left side of sketch.
The artist entitled this sketch 'Alamo Mucho Station.' He misspelled name of Alamo Mo-
cho Station, which was one of the original Butterfield Overland Mail stations. The Alamo
Mocho Station is located south of the Mexican border, in Baja California.
Source: Huntington Library, call number mssHilton Book 3, San Marino, California.

"Guadalupe Pass, 3rd View" by William Hayes Hilton

Guadalupe Pass is a mountain pass in Culberson County, Texas.
It is located just outside of Guadalupe Mountains National Park, Texas

Source: Huntington Library, call number mssHilton Book 3, San Marino, California.

"Tucson Desert and the 'Picacho' - view from the south" by William Hayes Hilton

Picacho Peak (Picacho is Spanish for "Big Peak") is located in Arizona between the cities of Phoenix and Tucson. Gerald Ahnert locates the Picacho Stage Station near the peak at GPS 32.6545. -111.3962. The image shows saguaro cacti which are endemic to the Sonoran Desert.

Source: Huntington Library, call number mssHilton Book 3, San Marino, California.

"Celerity Stage Passenger Shooting Antelope for Pleasure" by William Hayes Hilton
Legend has it that Wells Fargo Co. rules for stagecoach passengers in the 1870's included:
"... Firearms may be kept on your person for use in emergencies. Do not shoot them for
pleasure or at wild animals as the sound riles the horses. In the event of runaway horses,
remain calm. Leaping from the coach in panic will leave you injured, at the mercy of the el-
ements, hostile Indians, and hungry wolves. Forbidden topics of discussion are stagecoach
robberies, Indian uprisings, politics, and religion..."
Source: Huntington Library, call number mssHilton Book 3, San Marino, California.

"Crossing Boggy River, Texas, 1859" signed by William Hayes Hilton
This sketch by William Hays Hilton that he entitled, "Crossing Boggy River, Texas, 1859"
clearly shows that there were times that fording a creek or river was difficult.
This may be the Boggy Creek about 15 miles northwest of the Butterfield Route that
passes through Fort Belknap, Texas. The other possibility is that he was sketching one of
the three sites that actually are on the Butterfield Route: North Boggy Creek,
Middle (Muddy) Boggy, or Clear Boggy in Indian Territory (Oklahoma).
Source: Huntington Library, call number mssHilton Book 3, San Marino, California.

*"Coast Range, Marysville Butte from West, Cherokee, Nevada Co." by Wm H. Hilton
Cherokee, California (60 miles north of Placerville) was not a Butterfield Route, but may
have been on a Pioneer Stage Line route. Its unclear what mountains he is referring to.
Source: Huntington Library, call number mssHilton Book 3, San Marino, California.*

"Overland Mail Stage, Arizona, 1858" signed by William Hayes Hilton
In 1858, passenger Waterman Ormsby wrote, "The mules reared, pitched, twisted, whirled,
wheeled, ran, stool still, and cut up all sorts of capers. The wagon performed so many evolu-
tions that I, in fear of my life, abandoned it and took to my heels, fully confident that I could
make more progress in a straight line, with much less risk of breaking my neck."
Image Source: Huntington Library, call number mssHilton Book 3, San Marino, California.

"Overland Mail-Coach Crossing the Rocky Mountains - Scene in Guys Gulch"
Sketch by Theodore R. Davis, 1868

Harper's Weekly Journal of Civilization, New York, Saturday, February 8, 1868, page 88

"The Overland Mail - First Meeting of the Coaches in Guadalupe Pass"
Frank Leslie's Illustrated Newspaper, November 27, 1858, page 407
Courtesy of The Internet Archive: Digital Library

"The Overland Mail Coach from Arizona as it is Crossing the Country"
Published by Hiram C. Hodge, 1877, etching artist unknown

*The images below are **NOT** Butterfield Overland Mail Co. stagecoaches, however they may help visualize what many of the swing stations looked like, the clothing of employees and passengers, and what a four or six horse stagecoach actually looked like.*

This very sharp detailed photo is the Hundley Stage line to Cripple Creek, Colorado ca. 1892-1893.

Ben Holladay's Overland Stage Company at Idaho's Boise City, Post Office Source: Idaho State Historical Society.

"Corn Exchange Hotel" by local artist Cliff Donaldson

George Hackler writes, *"In 1858, Mesilla was the largest settlement on the entire route; there were some 3,000 people living in the area at the time. This was a designated meal stop, so passengers had time to rest and satisfy their appetites. The Butterfield station in Mesilla was just south of the El Patio bar on Main Street. The road out of the Mesilla passed in front of San Albino's Church, made a sharp left turn, and then turned right on Calle del Norte"*

Image compliments of LaPosta de Mesilla Mexican Restaurant, Mesilla, New Mexico

Pioneer Stage Company: from Sacramento to Virginia
by George Holbrook Baker, American, lithographer

The 1861-1864 Central Route postal contract covered the distance from St. Joseph, Missouri to Placerville, California. The Pioneer Stage Company had the postal contract to carry the mails west from Placerville. It is interesting to note that the Pioneer Stage Company used river steamboats to carry the mail between Sacramento and San Francisco for 19 months from April 3, 1860 to November 20, 1861. The horse and rider were on the boat and would gallop off at the dock. The steamers saved 5½ hours off using a stagecoach over that 100 mile distance.

"Potts Tavern" by Gloria McHahen, 1984
Print 83 of 500 in Bob Crossman's collection.
Kirkbride Potts, postmaster and station agent, built this home in 1858 for his family.
This building also served as an official Butterfield Overland Mail Co. home station.
This magnificent structure is open for tours Wed-Sat. 10-3pm in Pottsville, Arkansas.

CHAPTER ONE
Background

The population of California tripled in size in less than a decade in large part due to the discovery of gold and the Gold Rush that resulted. In response to that growth, Congress received official requests from California and New Mexico for improved mail service.

There were many attempts to provide a mail route to the west coast. **[see 1860 List of Routes in Appendix J]** Among the attempts, Butterfield's contract was the most efficient and successful.

California's Official Request

Several resolutions from California were sent to Congress requesting improved mail service. For example, a joint resolution of the California State Legislature, approved March 18, 1854, requested that its Senators be *"instructed"* and its Representatives *"requested"* to advocate that Congress provide a weekly mail service to California.

Texas also sent a joint resolution to the US Senate in Washington D.C. on December 17, 1853 specifically requesting improved military and post roads to California as *"absolutely necessary for the preservation of the lives and the property of the emigrants who wish to settle within our borders."* [Source: "Resolutions of the Legislature of California," Senate Miscellaneous Documents, 33rd Congress, 1st Session, No. 49; and 34th Congress, First and Second Sessions, No. 2 and No. 57, pages 1-2.]

New Mexico's Official Request

The council and house of representatives of the Territory of New Mexico wrote to Postmaster General Campbell, December 29, 1855: *"...respectfully request, that the people of this Territory has suffered for many years for want of a semi-monthly mail between this Territory and the United States. Our geographical position, being in the center of the American continent without navigable rivers or means of communication by railroad, renders our situation through mail facilities as the Sandwich Islands* [the old name of the Hawaiian Islands] *...The least time in which a reply can be had to any communication from this Territory, is three months, and only then by prompt attention being given to it, and* *we seldom get a reply from the eastern cities under four months... We think that we deserve, and know that we need..."* [Source: "Laws of the Territory of New Mexico, 1855-1856, Santa Fe, 1856, pages 142-144.]

During 1855 and 1856 multiple bills were introduced in Congress to establish such a transcontinental mail line, but could not secure enough votes. Finally, on March 3, 1857, a bill was passed to establish a six year contract. After reviewing multiple bidders, Postmaster General Aaron Brown awarded Postal Contract number 12578 to John Butterfield's Overland Mail Company.

[See Postal Contracts in Appendix B, F, L and M.]

[See the original "Articles of Association of the Overland Mail Company, 1857" in Appendix C]

Oath For Contractors & Carriers
(Source: Letter from the Postmaster General, December 16, 1868)

John Butterfield, along with all contractors and carriers of the mail were required to take an oath shortly after accepting the contract. Upon swearing the following oath, a certificate was filed in the General Post Office:

"I _____ _____, do swear (or affirm, as the case may be) that I will faithfully perform all the duties required of me, and abstain from everything forbidden by the laws in relation to the establishment of the post office and post roads within the United States."

The above oath, first instituted by Congress March 3, 1825, was extended in light of the Civil War by an act of Congress on July 2, 1862 and March 3, 1863:

"I, _____ _____, being 'employed in the care, custody, and conveyance of the mail' on route No. _____, from _____ to ___, State of _____, do swear that I will faithfully perform all the duties required of me, and abstain from everything forbidden by the laws in relation to the establishment of post offices and post roads within the United States; and that I will honestly and truly account for and pay over any moneys belonging to the said United States which may come into my possession or control; and I further solemnly swear that I have never voluntarily borne arms against the United States since I have been a citizen thereof; that I have voluntarily given no aid, countenance, counsel, or encouragement to persons engaged in armed hostility thereto; that I have neither sought, nor accepted, nor

attempted to exercise the functions of any office whatever under any authority or pretended authority in hostility to the United States; that I have not yielded a voluntary support to any pretended government, authority, power, or constitution within the United States hostile or inimical thereto. And I do further swear that, to the best of my knowledge and ability, I will support and defend the Constitution of the United States against all enemies, foreign and domestic; that I will bear true faith and allegiance to the same; that I take this obligation freely, without any mental reservation or purpose of evasion; and that I will well and faithfully discharge the duties of the office and which I am about to enter: So help me God." (Source: Letter from the Postmaster General, December 16, 1868)

The contract allowed some flexibility on the exact route, but did require John Butterfield's Overland Mail Company to carry the mail overland in four-horse stagecoaches from St. Louis and Memphis to San Francisco in twenty-five days or less.

Butterfield's Overland Mail Company stagecoach service operated on the Southern Ox Bow Route from mid September 1858 to mid March 1861, carrying U.S. Mail and passengers between the Mississippi River and California to fulfill the U.S. postal contract number 12578.

Simultaneously the Overland Mail left San Francisco, St. Louis and Memphis. Stations were built every 15 to 20 miles for a change of horses for this day and night, almost non-stop 23 day transcontinental journey. Having two eastern starting points, Memphis and St. Louis, was an attempt of the Postmaster General to appease both the southern and northern sympathizers.

The two eastern terminus, Memphis and St. Louis began the westward journey by train. From St. Louis the train traveled 168 miles to tracks end at Tipton, Missouri. From Memphis, the train traveled 24 miles to tracks end 12 miles east of Madison, Arkansas. Transferring from the trains, the two stagecoaches traveled westward from Tipton, Missouri and Madison, Arkansas to merge at Fort Smith. In late 1858/early1859, when the Missouri railroad reached Syracuse, it succeeded Tipton as stage terminus.

From Fort Smith the Overland continued in a single stagecoach westward toward the terminus at San Francisco.

Twice a week, from San Francisco, the stagecoach headed east to Fort Smith, where the mail and passengers were divided, based on their ultimate destination, into either the St. Louis or Memphis stagecoach to continue their journey eastward.

On the first trip, about 100 miles east of El Paso, on September 28, 1858, passenger Waterman Ormsby reported on the dramatic moment when the very first east bound and first west bound stages passed each other in route.

SOUTHERN OX-BOW ROUTE 1858-1861

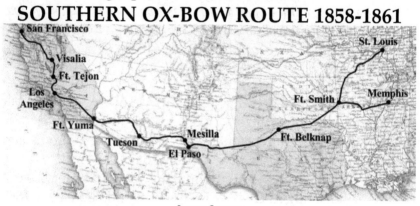

Image Source:
"Mails of the Westward Expansion, 1803 to 1861"
by Steven C. Walske and Richard C. Frajola, Western Cover Society, 2015, p. 161

After 130 weeks of operation on the southern route, at the dawn of the Civil War in March of 1861, the Southern Route was canceled. Butterfield's contract was amended to the Central Route, entirely avoiding the southern states.

CENTRAL ROUTE 1861-1864

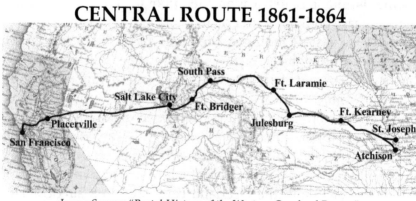

Image Source: "Postal History of the Western Overland Routes"
by Richard Frajola, L L C, Section 10

The 1859 California State Register contains an advertisement for a short lived competitor of Butterfield, the San Diego to San Antonio Route. This route is usually called the "Jack-Ass Route" since 180 miles of the route were on mule back.

OVERLAND TO TEXAS!

THE SAN ANTONIO AND SAN DIEGO MAIL LINE

Which has been in successful operation since July, 1856, are ticketing **PASSENGERS** through to San Antonio, Texas, and also to all intermediate Stations. Passengers and Express Matter forwarded in NEW COACHES, drawn by six mules over the entire length of our Line, excepting from San Diego to Fort Yuma, a distance of 180 miles, which we cross on mule back. Passengers GUARANTEED in their tickets to ride in Coaches, excepting the 180 miles, as above stated. Passengers are ticketed from San Diego to

FORT YUMA,	EL PASO,	MARICOPA WELLS,
FORT BLISS,	TUCSON,	FORT DAVIS,
LA MESILLA,	FORT LANCASTER	FORT FILLMORE,
FORT HUDSON	and	SAN ANTONIO.

The Coaches of our Line leave semi-monthly from each end, on the 9th and 20th of each month, at 6 o'clock, A. M.

An armed escort travels through the Indian country, with each Mail Train, for the protection of the Mails and Passengers.

Passengers are provided with Provisions during the trip, except where the Coach stops at Public Houses along the Line, at which each Passenger will pay for his own Meal. Each Passenger is allowed thirty pounds of Personal Baggage, exclusive of blankets and arms.

Passengers from San Francisco can take the C. S. N. Co.'s splendid

Steamer SENATOR, Capt. Tom Seeley,

which leaves San Francisco on the 3d and 18th of each Month, and connects with our Line.

Passengers going to San Antonio can take a Daily Line of Four-Horse Coaches to Indianola, from which place there is a Semi-Weekly Line of splendid Mail Steamers to New Orleans.

FARE on this Line as follows, including Rations:

San Diego to Fort Yuma...$40 | San Diego to El Paso.....$125
" " Tucson....... 80 | " " San Antonio. 200
Intermediate Stations beyond Fort Yuma, 15 cents per mile.

Passengers can obtain all necessary outfits in San Diego.

For further information, and for the purchase of Tickets, apply at the Office of the Company in this City, or to

H. VAN VALKENBURGH,

Corner Sacramento and Montgomery Sts.

(Freeman & Co.'s Express Office,).......... SAN FRANCISCO.

SAN DIEGO, Oct. 1, 1858.   R. E. DOYLE,
                            G. H. GIDDINGS. } PROPRIETORS.

The California State Register and year book of facts for 1859, page 425
Henry G. Langley & Co., Publishers
Image provided to the author from Gordon Nelson, Western Cover Society

Jackass Mail Route, Mails of Westward Expansion, Walske and Frajola, page 159

John Butterfield
November 18, 1801 – November 14, 1869

Bidding against eight others, John Butterfield was chosen September 16, 1857 by former Tennessee Governor, the Postmaster General Aaron Brown for a new Route #12578.

Concerning the selection of John Butterfield's bid over the competition, Gerald T. Ahnert, historian and authority on the Overland Mail Company, wrote: *"What was needed was someone with some of the most extensive experience in the United States."*
[Source: "Butterfield Makes the Southern Overland Trail His Own, Gerald T. Ahnert*, Overland Journal, Spring, 2020, pg. 13.]

Born in Berne, New York in 1801, Butterfield grew up on a farm located directly on a stagecoach route. By the age of 19, John was driving spring coaches for the Thorpe & Sprague Livery Stable in Albany. Moving to Utica he married Malinda Baker in 1822, eventually having eight children. To make ends meet he moonlighted at night driving a two-seat carriage. In 1825 John became manager of Parker and Co. Soon his enterprise grew into a boarding house, eastern stagecoach lines, packet boats and railroads.

"He had been a stagecoach driver when a young man, and had risen to be owner of nearly all the stage lines running in Western New York. In 1849 he was engaging in transporting freight across the Isthmus of Panama. He was also projector of the Morse Telegraph line between Buffalo and New York, and he not only built it, but also put it into successful operation. Enlisting others with him, he founded a line of Lake Ontario and St. Lawrence steamers, and in 1849 he formed the express company of Butterfield, Wasson and Co. We suppose he may claim to be founded of the American Express Company, for in 1850 he approached Henry Wells with the acceptable proposition that the three firms should be consolidated."
[Source: Harper's New Monthly Magazine, Aug., 1875, p.322]

In 1857, by the time John Butterfield was fifty-six he *"had accumulated a comfortable fortune, and it was widely known that no man in the country knew more about the ins and outs of horse-drawn transportation. He had an incredible memory and was a natural born leader, admired because of his basic generosity and genuine interest in public benefit. He was scrupulously fair... besides being deeply religious...*

A busy man in the field of stagecoach lines and transportation, Butterfield was able to attract and keep good workers. A successful businessman, he didn't seek glory and glamour but was much more interested in results. He had little formal education, but he made up for it with his natural organizational and managerial talents...

At a time when he should have retired to enjoy comfortable life with a comfortable fortune behind him, Butterfield instead chose to commit himself to the most outstanding achievement of his career: the Overland Mail Company..." [Source: "Butterfield Makes the Southern Overland Trail His Own, Gerald T. Ahnert, Overland Journal, Spring, 2020, pg. 13.]

Regarding Equipping
the St. Louis to San Francisco Route

On August 2, 1858, just six weeks before the planned start of the Overland Mail Route, Butterfield submitted a report to the board of his second trip to Fort Smith on company business equipping the route with needed materials.

The following excerpt is from a previously unpublished letter found in the files of the Wells Fargo Museum Historian, San Francisco.

In the words of John Butterfield himself: *"I left home on the 26th of May accompanied by Mr. Crocker. We met at St. Louis, Mr. Moore proprietor of the line from Jefferson City or more properly from the terminus of the Pacific Road to Springfield M. We purchased from him the entire property of the line with his mail contract to Warsaw MO and goodwill.*

The property consists of 100 horses with harness, Ten post coaches, Six wagons, Stable and lot at Warsaw MO, Stable and lot at Springfield MO. Price paid for contract etc $17,750.00 For the particulars of this purchase see the contract in the hands of the treasurer.

We made stations and arrangements at the different stations between California and Fort Smith for the teams at prices varying from $125 to $175 per quarter.

At Springfield Mo- Warsaw-Fayetteville-Fort Smith & California. We keep our own teams buying the necessary hay and grass as required. California MO the present terminus of the Pacific RR will probably be discontinued as a station and Round Hill or Tipton be made the point of departure from the Pacific R. Road. The details for the arrangements for stations are all known to Mr. Crocker the superintendent of that division and it is not deemed necessary to particularize them here.

In addition to the Horses and property purchased of Mr Moore we have purchased 182 horses at an average cost of $98.00 and 257 mules at an average cost of $102.54. Making in all 539 head. Every one of which we personally inspected and believe to be suited to our uses as serviceable animals. A detailed statement of these purchases is in the hands of the Treasurer.

Letters have been received from Mr Kinyon advising of the purchase by him of 220 horses further particulars of interest are contained in his letter to which is referred.

The aggregate of Kinyon's purchases and ours is 759 head. The balance of the stock necessary will be purchased and properly distributed previous to Sept 15th the date of our commencement of service.

The details of the arrangement for working the line are as follows.

Under the Supervision of Hugh Crocker, the line from the RR terminus to Colbert's Ferry about 200 miles beyond Fort Smith being say 500 miles in all.

Under supervision of Henry Bates the line from Colbert's Ferry to Fort Chadbourne 308 ¼ miles.

Under supervision of James Glover the line from Fort Chadbourne to El Paso 413 ¾ miles.

Under supervision of Gils Hawley the line from El Paso to Tucson 336 miles.

Under supervision of William Buckley the line from Tucson to Fort Yume 279 miles.

Under supervision of M. L. Kinyon and his apts the line from Fort Yuma to San Francisco 664 miles.

About 2500 miles in all.

The estimate of stock etc required to run the entire route is attached hereto in Schedule A at the end of this report.

The wagons for the western end of the route are all dispatched and by this time are, accidents excepted, undoubtedly properly distributed. More horses will be sent on to that portion of the route for which the parties mentioned below have started from the stock purchased by me-heretofore mentioned as in the hands of the Treasurer in detail.

From Fort Smith we have started the various superintendents westward for their divisions as follows.

James Glover with 21 horses and about 20 men
Henry Bates with 21 horses and about 20 men
William Buckley with 21 horses and about 20 men
Giles Hawley with 21 horses and about 20 men

The line will be sufficiently well provided and stocked with teams and men to commence the service on the day named in the contract.

.... In making this report I beg leave to state that the transaction of the Co. extending over so large a territory where there is no rail road or telegraph lines and mail connections by no means regular and at a slow pace where regular and the different superintendents moving on their separate divisions it cannot be expected to be as accurate and correct nor can estimates be made as correctly as to what will be needed for the service and what the expense will be as it can be after the men and teams shall have been stationed and an opportunity given to see where and what parts of the route will need double stock and men to run it with. As the Superintendents are at work on their respective divisions placing their teams and arranging their stations and feed it is confidently expected that all will be ready by the day stipulated in the contract. The wagons for the western division viz from El Paso to San Francisco that is as many as Mr Kinyon said he wanted have all been forwarded for his division.

In addition about one half of the wagons are ready for the Eastern Division and on the road to their destination and the balance will be forwarded without delay. As Mr. Abbott has assured Mr Holland that the balance shall all be ready and shipped by the 15th August that will give 30 days to get them on to the ground ready for service."

Regarding Equipping
the Bifurcation Route - Memphis to Fort Smith

While John Butterfield was a man committed to the stagecoach, on the route from Memphis to Fort Smith across the state of Arkansas, Butterfield had a different plan. Instead of stocking the route across central Arkansas with stations, stagecoaches, stock and employees, Butterfield reported to his Board of Directors on August 2, 1858:

"...With regard to the line from Memphis to Fort Smith I have deemed it prudent to wait and see what the condition of

the river and the country would be when the late great floods shall have subsided their effects somewhat removed. Should the water prove to be too low in the Arkansas River a purchase of boats might prove injudicious. I am of the opinion still (expressed in my former report) that the boats should be purchased at $7,500 each and run upon the Arkansas River. I think this will be the best method of doing our business and will be one of the best if not the very best paying portion of our entire route.

Negotiations are in progress for the purchase of boats and for the men to run them. Discretionary powers have been left with Mr. Crocker. Should these negotiations and arrangements fail to produce the necessary facilities on my return to Fort Smith I shall certainly see that portion of our contract fulfilled in proper shape."

"Fort Smith, Arkansas, American Civil War" (close up of portion of engraving)
from The Illustrated London News, vol. XXXVIII, May 25, 1861

On December 2nd, John Butterfield wrote another letter that was printed in the January 5, 1859 issue of the *Arkansas True Democrat*. John Butterfield wrote:

LETTER FROM COL. BUTTERFIELD

NEW YORK, DEC. 2, 1858

DEAR SIR – You are aware that it was my intention to put steamboat packets on the Arkansas River last summer, but was thwarted by the lowness of the water. You are also aware that the impossibility of using the river was apparent to me at too late a period to allow of my stocking the line between Memphis, Little Rock and Fort Smith in time to commence mail service on the 16th September, and was therefore compelled to make arrangements to have that service performed by others.

The service thus unintentionally confided to others has not been of a grade nor of a speed satisfactory to me, nor to the post office department, and is entirely below the just expectations of the people of Arkansas, Texas and of the Indian country, as well as of the traveling community generally...

Since writing the above, I have purchased a boat, the **Jennie Whipple**, with which I shall leave in the early part of the week to establish and start the route..."

Jennie Whipple's purchase was reported in the Thursday, December 16, 1858 issue of *The Louisville Daily Courier*:

"The steamer **Jenny Whipple**, a very excellent light-draught stern wheel boat, was yesterday sold to Messrs. Butterfield & Co., for the sum of $8,000. She is intended to run as a packet between Little Rock and Fort Smith, in the Arkansas River, for the accommodation of the Overland Mail."

Butterfield's purchase of the **Jennie Whipple** is also recorded in a newspaper clipping from December 21, 1858 provided by Shelley Blanton, Archivist of The Pebley Center, Boreham Library, University of Arkansas-Fort Smith:

> Messrs. Butterfield & Co. have purchased the steamer Jennie Whipple, to run as a packet between Little Rock and Fort Smith, in the Arkansas river, for the accommodation of the overland mail.

Source: Vicksburg Daily Whig, Tuesday, December 21, 1858

The **Jennie Whipple** arrived at the Little Rock port on December 20, 1858. *[Weekly Arkansas Gazette, Saturday, Dec. 25, 1858]*

In 1858 John Butterfield was misled to believe that the Arkansas River was navigable year round by boats with a draught under twelve inches. As a result, in September of

1858 the Arkansas River levels were so low that John Butterfield was forced to hastily sub-contract the Memphis to Fort Smith route to John T. Chidester's stagecoach line.

On only 8 occasions John Butterfield's steamboat, *Jennie Whipple,* was able to fulfill his original plan of carrying Overland passengers and mail between Memphis and Fort Smith.

On 73 additional occasions *Jennie Whipple* was able to complete the Little Rock to Memphis leg of the route.

On 4 additional occasions the *Jennie Whipple* made a run between Little Rock and Fort Smith, with stagecoaches completing the Little Rock to Memphis portion of the Overland Mail route. *[Butterfield's Overland Mail Co. Use of Steamboats, Crossman, page 401]*

Between April 1860 and Feb. 1861, the *Jennie Whipple* was stranded for more than a year in Indian Territory (Oklahoma) because of record low water levels in the Arkansas River.

In March of 1861, John Butterfield began moving employees and equipment north to the northern Central Route. Having no need for the *Jennie Whipple* steamboat on that route, on Friday, April 12, 1861 *The Courier-Journal* (Louisville), reported: *"The Memphis Bulletin says the steamer Jennie Whipple has quit the Arkansas River trade, very unexpectedly, leaving a number of bills unsettled. The Whipple was laid up in the Arkansas River for nearly twelve months, went to Memphis a few weeks since and loaded for Fort Smith, has returned, and gone no one knows where."*

On Sunday, June 2, 1861 Daily Missouri Republican (St. Louis) reported: *"The Jennie Whipple was yesterday sold by the U.S. Marshal at this port. She brought $1,760 and was purchased, we learned, for Captain White."*

NOTE:
For more information on John Butterfield's use of the steamboat *Jennie Whipple,* see the author's 2022 book (460 pages): ***"Butterfield's Overland Mail Co. use of STEAMBOATS to Deliver Mail and Passengers Across Arkansas 1858-1861"***

Before forming the Overland Mail Co., John Butterfield became aware that there was a need to ship parcels. This 1851 original waybill, mounted below, is from Wells, _Butterfield_ & Co.'s American Express Company.

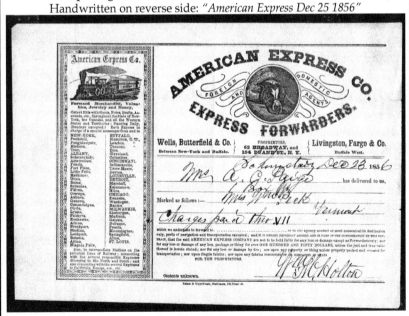

Purchased Oct., 2022 from
Wilkens, 1520 York Ave. 21D, New York, NY 10028-7011

Before forming the Overland Mail Co., John Butterfield founded Wells, _Butterfield_ & Co.'s American Express Co. This Dec. 23, 1856 is an original waybill, to transfer a package to Mrs. Wm. Peck in Vermont for Mrs. Alonzo Paige.
Handwritten on reverse side: *"American Express Dec 25 1856"*

Purchased on Ebay, February 2023 from
Russell Crow, 1117 Marney Ct., Henrico, VA 23229

What was the time schedule for the stages?

John Butterfield's son, Daniel, made out the time schedule. On a large sheet of paper, fifty or sixty feet long and about two feet wide, the different stations and points on the road were represented by horizontal lines. The days and hours were noted between the vertical lines. In this way the route was laid out and the time schedule distributed to the different employees. An abbreviated version of that schedule, shown below, was printed in every conductor's log book.

1]   [Sep. 16th, 1858.

OVERLAND MAIL COMPANY.

THROUGH TIME SCHEDULE BETWEEN

ST. LOUIS, MO., MEMPHIS, TENN. } **& SAN FRANCISCO, CAL.**

GOING WEST. / GOING EAST.

LEAVE.	DAYS.	Hour.	Distance to Place.	Time allowed.	Av'ge Miles per Hour.	LEAVE.	DAYS.	Hour.	Distance to Place.	Time allowed.	Av'ge Miles per Hour.
St. Louis, Mo. & Memphis, Tenn. P. R. R. Terminus, "	Every Monday & Thursday,	8.00 A.M	Miles	No.Hours		San Francisco, Cal. Firebaugh's Ferry, "	Every Monday & Thursday,	8.00 A.M	Miles	No.Hours	
	" Monday & Thursday,	6.00 P.M	160	10	16	Visalia, "	" Tuesday & Friday,	11.00 A.M	163	27	6
Springfield, "	" Wednesday & Saturday,	7.45 A.M	143	37½	3¾	Ft.Tejon, (Ft Los Angeles)	" Wednesday & Saturday,	5.00 A.M	82	18	4½
Fayetteville, "	" Thursday & Sunday,	10.15 A.M	100	26½	3¾	San Bernardino, "	" Thursday & Sunday,	9.00 A.M	127	28	4½
Fort Smith, Ark	" Friday & Monday,	3.30 A.M	65	17½	3½	Fort Yuma, "	" Friday & Monday,	5.30 P.M	150	32½	4½
Sherman, Texas	" Sunday & Wednesday,	12.30 A.M	205	45	4½	Gila River,* Arizona	" Sunday & Wednesday,	1.30 P.M	200	44	4½
Fort Belknap, "	" Monday & Thursday,	9.00 A.M	146½	32½	4½	Tucson, "	" Monday & Thursday,	7.30 P.M	135	30	4½
Fort Chadbourn, "	" Tuesday & Friday,	3.15 P.M	136	30½	4½	El Paso, "	" Wednesday & Saturday	3.00 A.M	141	31½	4½
Pecos River, (Em Crossing)	" Thursday & Sunday,	3.45 A.M	165	36½	4½	Soldier's Farewell, "	" Thursday & Sunday,	8.00 P.M	184½	41	4½
El Paso, "	" Saturday & Tuesday,	11.00 A.M	248½	55½	4½	Pecos River,(Em Crossing)	" Saturday & Tuesday,	5.30 A.M	150	33½	4½
Soldier's Farewell	" Sunday & Wednesday,	8.30 P.M	150	33½	4½	Fort Chadbourn, "	" Monday & Thursday	12.45 P.M	248½	55½	4½
Tucson, Arizona	" Tuesday & Friday,	1.30 P.M	184½	41	4½	Fort Belknap, "	" Wednesday & Saturday	1.15 A.M	165	36½	4½
Gila River,* "	" Wednesday & Saturday	9.00 P.M	141	31½	4½	Sherman, "	" Thursday & Sunday,	7.30 A.M	136	30½	4½
Fort Yuma, Cal.	" Friday & Monday,	3.00 A.M	135	30	4½	Fort Smith, Ark	" Friday & Monday,	4.00 P.M	146½	32½	4½
San Bernardino, "	" Saturday & Tuesday,	11.00 P.M	200	44	4½	Fayetteville, Mo.	" Sunday & Wednesday,	1.00 P.M	205	45	4½
Ft. Tejon, (Via Los Angeles)	" Monday & Thursday,	7.30 A.M	150	32½	4½	Springfield, "	" Monday & Thursday,	6.15 A.M	65	17½	3½
Visalia, "	" Tuesday & Friday,	11.30 A.M	127	28	4½	P. R. R. Terminus,* "	" Tuesday & Friday,	8.45 A.M	100	26½	3½
Firebaugh's Ferry, "	" Wednesday & Saturday	5.30 A.M	82	18	4½	(Arrive) St. Louis, Mo. &	" Wednesday & Saturday	10.30 P.M	143	37¾	3½
(Arrive) San Francisco, "	" Thursday & Sunday,	8.30 A.M	163	27	6	Memphis, Tenn. "	" Thursday & Sunday,	✳	160	10	16

This Schedule may not be exact—Superintendents, Agents, Station-men, Conductors, Drivers and all employees are particularly directed to use every possible exertion to get the Stages through in quick time, even though they may be ahead of this time.

If they are behind this time, it will be necessary to urge the animals on to the highest speed that they can be driven without injury.

Remember that no allowance is made in the time for ferries, changing teams, &c. It is therefore necessary that each driver increase his speed over the average per hour enough to gain the necessary time for meals, changing teams, crossing ferries, &c.

Every person in the Company's employ will always bear in mind that each minute of time is of importance. If each driver on the route loses fifteen (15) minutes, it would make a total loss of time, on the entire route of twenty-two (22) hours, or, more than one day. If each one loses ten (10) minutes it would make a total loss of sixteen and one half (16½) hours, or, the best part of a day.

On the contrary, if each driver gains that amount of time, it leaves a margin of time against accidents and extra delays.

All hands will see the great necessity of promptness and dispatch; every minute of time is valuable as the Company are under heavy forfeit if the mail is behind time.

Conductors must note the hour and date of departure from Stations, the causes of delay, if any, and all particulars. They must also report the same fully to their respective Superintendents.

* The Station referred to on Gila River, is 25 miles west of Maricopa Wells.

JOHN BUTTERFIELD,
Pres't.

*NOTE: The train from Tipton arrived in St. Louis at 8:40 am
[Columbia Herald-Statesman, Oct. 15, 1858, p.3]*

In the Butterfield's conductor log book it states, *"This schedule is provided for the use and benefit of the Employees of the Overland Mail Company. The Company do not (sic.) intend, by it, to bind themselves in any manner to the public, to run at any stated time or hour. They will endeavor to conform as nearly as possible to the Schedule. The length of the Route, the state of the roads and streams, will, of necessity, cause variations during certain seasons of the year."* Image source: *"Butterfield Overland Mail Record Book" Smithsonian National Postal Museum*

*See content of this handbook
in Appendix H*

Schedule Change Advertisement, 1859

OVERLAND MAIL COMPANY,
VIA LOS ANGELES.

TIME OF DEPARTURE CHANGED

On and after the first day of December, 1858, the Coaches of THE OVER-LAND MAIL COMPANY will leave the Office,

CORNER of WASHINGTON and KEARNY STS.

(PLAZA,) as follows :

THROUGH MAIL,

MONDAY AND FRIDAY, at 12 o'clock, M.

Fort Yuma and Intermediate Stations,

MONDAY, WEDNESDAY AND FRIDAY,

At 12 o'clock, MERIDIAN, instead of 12 o'clock, Midnight, as heretofore.

FARE—FROM SAN FRANCISCO TO FORT SMITH, ARKAN-SAS, OR TO TERMINUS OF THE PACIFIC RAILROAD,

☞ ONE HUNDRED DOLLARS ! ☜

LOUIS McLANE, Agent Overland Mail Co.

The California State Register and year book of facts for 1859, page 426
Henry G. Langley & Co., Publishers
Image provided to the author from Gordon Nelson, Western Cover Society

The image above is from the California Register for 1859. It contains an advertisement for the Overland Mail Company that lists departure days and times for eastbound mail. The Overland Mail Company Employer book list gives departure as *"Every Monday and Thursday, 8:00 A.M."* This advertisement states *"Time of departure changed...after the first day of December, 1858..."* from San Francisco on *"Monday and Friday, at 12 o'clock, M."*

It also advertises that the eastbound fare for passengers is only $100. Initially, passenger fare was $100 ($3,680 in 2023 adjusted for inflation) for eastbound and $200 ($7,360 in 2023) for westbound, and ten cents per mile for way fare ($3.68 in 2023), either direction. The passenger fare was later raised to $200 in either direction.

Harper's Weekly: A Journal of Civilization, New York, December 11, 1858
Complete original Dec. 11th issue from the collection of Bob Crossman.
This sketch of a Butterfield Stagecoach is based on a photograph taken at the time.

The December 11, 1858 issue of New York's *Harper's Weekly* featured Butterfield's Overland Mail Company on the front page. The lengthy front page article reads, in part:

"The people of California have been accustomed to receive with grateful joy, for years, the semi-monthly mails of the steamers; and when they found that, instead of twice a month, their new mails were to come twice a week - that the great Overland Mail which has for years been talked about was not a myth, but a decided reality - they evinced an enthusiastic joy which it would hardly have been reasonable to expect of us in New York...

But the great Overland Mail is a fixed fact; and as such, we propose to enlighten some of our readers concerning it. This is necessary, because, in spite of the many scientific publications which have been made with regard to it, many people have no idea whether is goes by the South Pass or not; when the fact is, its most southern point is full six hundred miles below the South Pass. This popular desire for information can only be met - and met properly - by a brief but comprehensive description of the whole route, showing at a glance its advantages and disadvantages, what it is doing, which way it goes, and all about it, in a very few words.

The 'Butterfield Overland Mail' was authorized, at a late hour of the session, by the Congress of 1857, which provided for a compensation of six hundred thousand dollars per annum for a term of six years. The route was expressly set forth in the Act to be such 'as the contractors may select;' and as Congress could not agree over the matter, it was passed in this shape to the hands of Postmaster General Aaron V. Brown to award the contract. Messrs, John Butterfield, William B. Dinsmore, William G. Fargo, J. V. P. Garner, M. L. Kinyon, Alexander Hollard, and Hamilton Spencer - most of them well known in New York - were the successful bidders; but, strange to say, instead of being allow to select their own route, they were compelled to adopt one which made their road a semicircle, and took them nearly four degrees further south than they wished to go, and than there was any need of going - and thereby hangs a tale. The contract was signed on the 16th of September, 1857, and on the 16th of September, 1858, stages started simultaneously from St, Louis to San Francisco... The route, starting from St. Louis to... Fort Smith, where it meets the mail from Memphis, Tennessee; and both mails proceed thence on a common line to San Francisco...." [Source: Harper's Weekly: A Journal of Civilization, New York, December 11, 1858, page 1-2]

The Alternate "Via Panama" Mail Route

Concerning the Isthmus crossing - starting in 1855 mail and passengers were carried across the 48 mile Isthmus by the newly constructed Panama Railroad under a contract with the Postmaster General. Previously the crossing was by wagon.

Below are two advertisements for Isthmus routes. The first crossed at Tehuantepec, Mexico and the second at Panama.

FOR NEW ORLEANS,

—VIA—

THE ISTHMUS OF TEHUANTEPEC.

THROUGH IN FIFTEEN DAYS!

CARRYING THE UNITED STATES MAILS.

Arrangements having been made with the **PACIFIC MAIL STEAM-SHIP COMPANY**, for the transportation of Freight and Passengers from SAN FRANCISCO to VENTOSA, conveyance will hereafter **LEAVE VENTOSA** regularly on the arrival of said Company's vessels, on or about the 15th and 30th of each Month, **FOR SUCHIL**, connecting there with the Company's new and beautiful light-draught Iron Steamer "SUCHIL," down the Coatzacoalcos River to Minititlan, and the fast and favorite side-wheel Steamship "QUAKER CITY," R. W. Shufeldt, Commander, will **LEAVE MINITITLAN FOR NEW ORLEANS**, with the California Mails and Passengers, on or about the 2d and 17th of each Month.

THE PACIFIC MAIL STEAMSHIP COMPANY

Will sell Tickets from San Francisco to the anchorage at Ventosa, and

THE LOUISIANA TEHUANTEPEC COMPANY

Will sell Ttckets from the anchorage at Ventosa to New Orleans.

PRICES OF THROUGH TICKETS:

First Cabin, $250···· Second Cabin, $175·····Steerage, $100

☞ For Freight or Passage from Ventosa to New Orleans, apply at the **AGENCY OF THE LOUISIANA TEHUANTEPEC COMPANY,** Southeast corner of Montgomery and Jackson Sts.
LUCIEN HERMANN, AGENT.

The California State Register and year book of facts for 1859, page 424
Henry G. Langley & Co., Publishers
Image provided to the author from Gordon Nelson, Western Cover Society

The California State Register and year book of facts for 1859, page ii
Henry G. Langley & Co., Publishers
Image provided to the author from Gordon Nelson, Western Cover Society

The 1859 California Register lists three different steamship companies available for passengers and mail to be carried from California to to the Central American Coast, to then catch a second ship to complete the journey.

Ocean Steamers.

NEW YORK AND NEW ORLEANS, *via* **PANAMA.** — Pacific Mail Steamship Co.: 5th and 20th of each month. When either of these dates fall on a Sunday, the departure takes place on the following day. Steamers, Golden Gate, Golden Age, J. L. Stephens and Sonora. Forbes & Babcock, Agents, office cor Sacramento and Leidesdorff.

NEW YORK AND NEW ORLEANS, *via* **PANAMA.** — The New York and California Steamship Co.: 5th and 20th of each month. Steamers, Orizaba, Uncle Sam, Sierra Nevada and Cortez. C. K. Garrison & Co., Agents, SE cor Sacramento and Leidesdorff.

NEW ORLEANS, LA.—Louisiana-Tehuantepec Company, *via* Ventosa: 5th and 20th of each month. Passengers by this route are conveyed to Ventosa by the steamers of the Pacific Mail Steamship Co., and from Manatitlan on the Atlantic by the Company's steamer Coatzacoalcos. Lucien Hermann, Agent, SE cor Montgomery and Jackson.

The California State Register and year book of facts for 1859, page 402
Henry G. Langley & Co., Publishers
Image provided to the author from Gordon Nelson, Western Cover Society

In 1859 Three Overland Routes Were Available

The California Register of 1859 lists three different overland routes for eastbound mail, and a fourth route that was not yet in operation.

XIV.—OVERLAND MAILS.

1. GREAT OVERLAND MAIL.

The Great Overland Mail, from Memphis and St. Louis to San Francisco, *via* Fort Smith near the head of navigation on the Arkansas River; thence in the direction of Preston on the Rio Grande; thence to Fort Fillmore above El Paso on the Rio Grande; thence to Fort Yuma on the Colorado, to Los Angeles, and thence by the Tejon Pass to San Francisco. Semi-weekly; schedule time, twenty-five days. Butterfield & Co., Contractors.

---

2. CENTRAL OVERLAND MAIL.

The Central Overland, or Salt Lake City Mail, from St. Josephs, Missouri, to Salt Lake; thence through Carson Valley to Placerville. Weekly; leaves St. Josephs and Placerville every Saturday. Schedule time from St. Josephs to Salt Lake, twenty-two days; from Salt Lake to Placerville, sixteen days. Hockaday & Chorpenning, Contractors.

---

158   STATE REGISTER.   [1859.

3. SAN ANTONIO AND SAN DIEGO MAIL.

The San Antonio and San Diego Mail, from New Orleans, by Indianoloa, to San Antonio; thence by El Paso and Fort Yuma to San Diego. Semi-monthly. R. T. Doyle & Co., Contractors.

---

4. INDEPENDENCE AND SANTA FE MAIL.

The Independence and Santa Fe Mail, from Independence to Santa Fe by Albuquerque, to Stockton. (Not yet in operation.)

The California State Register and year book of facts for 1859, pages 157, 158
Henry G. Langley & Co., Publishers
Image provided to the author from Gordon Nelson, Western Cover Society

---

Appearing here in print for the first time:

The Travel Diary of passenger Rev. Thomas M. Johnston on the Butterfield Stage from Missouri to San Francisco

In 1859, Rev. Thomas M. Johnston headed for California from Missouri on the Butterfield stage. He became one of the first Cumberland Presbyterian ministers in California, founded a church at Alamo, Contra County, California and he printed *"The Pacific Cumberland Presbyterian,"* a weekly newspaper.

Transcribed verbatim by his great-granddaughter, Janet J. Johnston retaining original spelling and grammar.

MARCH 1859

Thursday, 10 Morning cloudy & likely for rain. Stage from Cal. Passed this morning for St. Louis. Faired off in the evening & turned cool. Feel better today than I have since I left home. Very anxious to be traveling. Stage for the west, not yet arrived. Hope the Lord will protect me, & be glorified by me whether it be by my life or by my death. My heart is sad.

Friday, 11 Morning cloudy & cool but soon faired off. Stage arrived at 9 last night but had to wait for the Memphis stage *[at Fort Smith]*. Left at 10 A.M. Made a fine days travel over a good country through Chocktaw Nation. Stage crowded. A dreary day to me. I may be buried on the plains. Thy will be done O God.

Saturday, 12 Morning fair & frosty. Made a good nights travel, but I did not sleep much. Wind S.E. & very chilly. Feel badly. Met Eastern bound stage. Felt a little like turning back. Country not so good today. A good deal of Pine timber. No one any company to me.

Sunday, 13 Day cloudy & very chilly. Wind S. Crossed Red River last night. Reached Sherman at 4 A.M. Took breakfast at Gainsville a vilage in the prairie. Quite unwell. Feel like giving out. Country level Praire country not much timber. Range good. Saw fields planted with corn.

Monday, 14 Sick all night. Too sick all day to notice the country much. Took pills. Traveled through Jacksville & Ft. Bellknap during the night. Range giving out. Though very sick, I feel calm & clear, & do not regret having started. God be praised for his mercy unto me.

Tuesday, 15 Day fair & quite windy. Making good speed. Passed Ft. Chadburn last night. Entered the Staked plains this morning. Feel much better today. Country level but poor. Green grass give out. No timber. Some Muskeet brush. Cannot think of home, but tears flow from my eyes.

Wednesday, 16 A very pleasant day. Feel calm & serene. Healthe stil better. Traveling on finely. Reached the Pecos River. Scenery dull & monotonous. Saw large herds of Antelope today. Traveled over a barren sandy plain. My mind constantly wandering to my poor distressed wife & children. Oh God take care of them & bless them.

Thursday, 17 Day unpleasant. Wind from the North. Traveled up the Pecos all last night & all day today. Not very well today. Did not sleep much last night, the road was so rough. Pecos is an ugly stream. Narrow deep channel runs swiftly & is muddy.

Friday, 18 Day fine. Crossed the Pecos last night. Took breakfast at a station where there are some fine springs & some pine timber, where we met a Surveying party. Crossed the Guadalupe Mountains. Feel tolerably well today. Wonder how my poor family are.

Saturday, 19 Day pleasant except high winds. I feel like I was recruiting some. Reached El Paso on the Rio Grande at 2 P.M. Stoped to spend the Sabbath. A Mexican town built of Adobies on both side of the River. Crossed the River into Mexico. Some find land in the Valley & fine vineyards.

Sunday, 20 A beautiful clear morning. The birds singing like Spring. Met with Claud Jones here. Had preaching here today. The first Protestant preaching every done. Preaching at 11 & at night. Had an interesting meeting & was very kindly treated. O God water the seed sown.

Monday, 21 Morning clear & beautiful. Day windy. Feel that I am recruiting some. Spent the day in writing. Wrote home & to St. Louis Observer. Left at 8 P.M. Had some flattering offers to remain at El Paso. A fine field for Missionary labors.

Tuesday, 22 Morning Clear & calm, but day windy. Passed Ft. Fillmore last night. Crossed the Rio Grande, & passed the town of Mesilla in the valley of the same name. A very pretty & rich valley of land mostly settled by Spaniards. Made a good days travel over a poor rough country.

Wednesday, 23 Day pleasant. Made a good days travel, mostly over a level somewhat sandy plain. Passed in sight of snow caped mountains. Writing every chance to Letitia. Health improving. Wish my family was along.

Thursday, 24 Morning fine. Day warm. Crossed San Pedro last night. In sight of snowy mountains this morning. Passed Tucson about 5 o'clock P.M. Situated in the valley of the Santa Cruz. Some good land & fine prospects of wheat crops.

Friday, 25 Day very fine, rather too warm. Traveling down the Gila River. Passed the Peg More vilages *[Pimo Indian Villages]* this morning. Some good land. Indians farming in their rude way. A good deal of Alkali. Wonder how all are at home.

Saturday, 26 Morning fair & pleasant. Feel tolerably well only. Day very warm. Suffered with heat & Alkali dust. Not much country today. Met the Eastern bound Stage. Feel very lonesome. Wish I was home.

Sunday, 27 Morning fair but windy. Passed Gila City last night & arrived a Ft. Yuma this morning. Not very well. Could get no breakfast. Had an awful time with dust. Caught in sand storm. Poor days travel. Lay be nearly all night.

Monday, 28 Sand storm stil raging furiously. Dared not leave camp. Wind abated about 11. Left camp but had a pretty hard gale all day. Very unpleasant. Traveled slowly over a sandy plain. Not very well, & quite gloomy in mind. Dont know whats to become of me.

Tuesday, 29 Day fair but cool. Traveling in the Coast, or rather Gulf Mountains where there are some cove with fine Springs & some Spanish Rancharies, & herds of Goats, Sheep, & Cattle, & plenty green grass, the first for a long time. Made a good days travel.

Wednesday, 30 Morning fair & frosty. Traveling in a beautiful valley covered with rich green sward. Some fine buildings & farms. Appearance of wealth & civilization. Large herds of beautiful stock grazing. Scenery romantic & delightful. Passed Los Angeles at 10 A.M.

Thursday, 31 Last night rather cold. Passed Ft. Tejon at 2 last night. Morning cloudy & spitting snow. Sun broke out occasionally through the day. Traveled all day in sight of snowstorm on Mountains. Another month gone, & such a one I never spent before. Feel that my health has improved. God be praised.

APRIL 1859

Friday, 1 Day clear with cool chilly wind from N.W. Passed Visalia last night, & crossed Kings River. Traveling in the beautiful Valley of San Joaquin. Crossed Coast Mountains at Pacheco pass. Entered upon another month, but what will be the result. God only knows but he will do right.

Saturday, 2 Day fair, with frost this morning. In sight of San Francisco Bay at day light. Arrived at the City at 9 & stoped at the What Cheer House. Feel that God has been very kind to me. Feel a little sore & tired. Gained 7 lb. Since I left home.

**In early 1860, Rev. Johnston sent for his family.
His daughter's account of that trip is on the following pages.**

Printed with permission of his great-granddaughter, Janet J. Johnston

Personal Account of a Butterfield Passenger

In 1934, the daughter of Rev. Thomas M. Johnston, Rebecca Johnston Yoakum of Merced, California, told her story of being a passenger on Butterfield's Overland Mail Co. stagecoach.

Eleanor Steele Johnston, known as the first woman to journey to California on the Butterfield stagecoach, traveled with her children Finis age 17, Rebecca age 15, John age 7 and William age 3. They were passengers on the westbound Butterfield stage in 1860 which departed from near Hurley, Stone County, Missouri to reach San Francisco.

[Source: "Adventure of the Butterfield State" by Ralph L. Mulliken, The Los Banos Enterprise, Thursday, June 30, 1966, Section A-1]

Mrs. Rebecca Yokum, a delightful old lady who lived long, long ago in Merced, came to California in 1860 on the Overland stage. If you will listen to her story you will have a deeper feeling for this little bit of the Overland road that passes through Los Banos.

Mrs. Yokum told me in January 1934, of her trip seventy-four years before over this very piece of road. By the way it was through the San Joaquin Valley that the Butterfield Overland stages made their fastest time.

Here is Mrs. Rebecca Yokum herself to tell you her story in her own words:

"... Father was a Cumberland Presbyterian minister. He went by stage to California in 1859. At first he wrote us that we were to come to California by water by way of the Isthmus of Panama. '*Don't come by stage under any circumstances,*' he wrote us. Later he sent word that he was coming back to Missouri.

Mother had made up her mind that she was coming to California. She was a very determined woman and without waiting for father to get back she prepared to set out without delay for California on the Butterfield Overland Stages...

It was April, 1860 Mother wrote that we were coming. Our tickets were bought several days in advance and called for our trip to begin at Springfield, Missouri and end at Santa Clara, California. Grandfather Steel lived five miles this side of Springfield, and as the Overland stages passed right beside his plantation, where we were staying at the time, it was arranged that the stage should stop at the plantation and take us on board.

On the appointed day the stage coach drawn by six horses came to a sudden stop at my grandfather's gate. All of us children were filled with glee at the prospect of our great adventure. With mother and the older ones it was different. Their eyes were filled with tears now that the time for parting had arrived. Our trunk was hastily stowed away in the boot at the end of the stage. The top of the stage was covered with men sitting back to back. Inside the coach were still more men. There were three wide seats and one of these had been reserved for my mother and us children. On a high seat in front sat the Conductor and the driver.

We were five that set out that Friday morning, my mother, my three brothers and myself. My oldest brother was seventeen. He had a belt buckled around his waste and a pistol stuck in it. Wasn't he going out West where the Indians were and wouldn't he need a gun!

I was fifteen and had a very beautiful hat, of which I was very proud. It had a wide brim and lots of flowers on it.

My youngest brother was three and was all decked out with the cutest pair of little red topped boots. The stage was so crowded that mother had to hold him on her lap. Between mother and I sat my younger brother, John, who was seven. Everything on the stage was so shiny and new that we felt we were in a palace. The driver kicked off the brake and we were off for California with the horses on the run.

We had a large lunch basket filled with provisions to last us until we got well along on our way. In our trunk we had enough clothing to last us for the entire trip. The only person we knew on the stage was a neighbor man.

He was about to set out for California by water, but had decided to come by stage instead and be of assistance to mother with us children.

We soon found that the stage made no stops whatever except to change horses. It ran continuously day and night. About every fourteen miles there was a stage station. At these stations there was generally only men. The moment we rolled into the station the tired horses were dragged away and fresh ones put in their places.

Speed seemed to be the one and only thing the stage people desired. As soon as the horses were securely fastened to the stage away we would go on the run. Usually the two horses in the lead were unbroken mustangs and the faster they ran the better satisfied the driver seemed to be.

Of course we didn't sleep any the first night. But the second night out I was that tired that I just had to sleep. When I awoke I found that I had fallen over in my sleep and had been lying with my head in a young man's lap. He was the meanest man in the world, I thought, to let me sleep that way. He tried to be nice to me but I was so mortified that I wouldn't even look at him.

I think it was at Fort Smith that we lost our lunch basket. There were large steps on the side of the coach for the passengers to enter the stage. It was about ten o'clock at night and we happened to set out basket on the step for a minute. Some dog or something must have grabbed it in the darkness, for when we looked for it, our lunch was gone.

Sunday morning we passed through an Indian reservation and saw our first

Indians. These were the only good Indians we saw on the whole trip. As we galloped along that morning I remember in particular seeing a cabin where an old Indian was sitting outside and playing away to himself on his fiddle. He was serenely happy.

After the loss of our lunch basket we had to buy our meals at the stage stations. But I would just like to see you eat what they served. Beans! Black bread! Often mother would pay a dollar for bread only to find it was spoiled. At the stage stations there were generally only men. Usually they would bring it right to to the stage and hand it to us. There were only a very few times that we got to eat at a table.

When we had been about a week on our journey the stage company took off the Concord coach we had been riding in and put us on board a two seated mud wagon. There wasn't near room enough for all the passengers and some of the men were forced to wait behind for the next stage.

The Indians were simply terrible. When we got into the real Indian country we would see them at every stage station. They would come swarming around us as soon as the stage drove up.

They were regular thieves and would have stolen the clothes right off of our backs if they could. Somewhere at one of these stops my beautiful hat disappeared and mother had to fish out a sunbonnet out of our trunk for me to wear the rest of the way to California.

That older brother of mine who really meant to be so brave was sitting in the stage at one stop watching the Indians. They were surging all around us. No doubt some clever Indian brave saw the pistol he was wearing and schemed how he could get it. In all probability he slipped up behind my brother with a sharp knife and so skillfully did he slit the belt that my brother never once missed his gun until the station was miles behind.

The little red topped boots my baby brother was wearing were the envy of every Indian squaw and the Conductor told mother emphatically that on no occasion whatever was she to leave the little boy alone for a single minute or the Indians would steal boots, little boy and all.

The same conductor and driver went with us for a day or so at a time. We never changed conductors and drivers at the same station. One of the men was always fresh. They were very stoical about things. It was just a part of their business to take risks. When we arrived at a station one of them always stayed on the stage with the passengers. The other tended to the stage business. Fresh horses were always ready for us the minute we drove up. The horses were given no rest on the road between stations but were rested for days at the stations. The horses always went on the run. We would never have gotten through it they hadn't.

We came to a stage station where the Indians a day or two before had massacred not only the stage station keepers but the passengers on the incoming stage as well. The only persons to escape were a white woman and child and two men, one of them a negro.

The man himself was wounded and the party remained at the station until he died. Then the woman and child and the negro man set out on foot to go the fourteen miles or so to the next station.

The refugees reached the station in safety but when we arrived the Indians were swarming around this station and apparently getting ready for another massacre. Besides this woman and her little girl there was also another woman and two children at the station. Although our stage was filled to over flowing the station keepers piled these five people right in with us.

They wanted to get them away before the Indian attack on the station could commence. We were piled two and three deep in the seats. They road with us until sometime the next day when we came to a fort and the stage people put them off.

While the horses were being changed I said to the negro who was being left behind:

"Aren't you afraid the Indians will kill you?"

"No mam," he replied. "Not while there are any white men around. The Indians never take a black man if there are any white men."

Oatman Flat is where an emigrant train was massacred. There is a high mountain on one side. On the other side there is a flat and beyond that another mountain. Here the Oatman people were massacred. A while flag was flying when we went by. We saw what was left of the wagons and the place on the mountain where the people are buried.

The wreckage was all heaped up in a pile. The canvas was gone off the wagons and the bows were all bare. The Oatman children that got away were Olive and Lorenzo. We saw them afterwards in California. Olive was a pretty little girl but the Indians had tattooed her face something terrible and cut lines in her cheeks.

Three or four times on the way we changed stages. One time was at the river. The water was high and the stage couldn't get across. The stage drove up to the river bank and we all got out. A great mass of drift wood had been washed down by the flood. We had to walk across the stream on this drift wood. On the opposite bank another stage was waiting for us. Two men were helping me keep my footing on the drift wood.

I got smart and jumped ahead. As I did so I slipped and fell into the water up to my waist. As they pulled me out they said sternly: "Now you stay where we put you after this!' To add to my discomfort our trunk with all our extra clothes had been left behind several days before by the stage company. They had put it off in order to lighten the stage one place where the Indians were so bad.

One dark night we were traveling without lights. We were not even allowed to talk out loud for fear of an Indian attack. We had to cross a stream and as we plunged down the bank the two horses in the lead broke away in the darkness. There was great excitement. Everyone had to get out as the stage was unable to haul the passengers through the stream.

The stage men were endeavoring to recover the horses and we could hear them calling out, *"Catch the leaders!"* Mother and the boys had to wade through the water. But someone, I don't know who, grabbed me in the darkness and carried me across the stream in his arms.

Of course at first we didn't sleep much at night, but we soon got so we could sleep sitting up in the seat while the stage rocked back and forth over the road. I can still go sound asleep sitting bolt upright in a chair. I learned to do so the three weeks we traveled in those overland stages.

Several times we saw Indians dancing around their camp fires at night. Mother would wake me up to look. The naked warriors would dance around in a circle in the firelight, imitating with their leaping and prancing the darting and shooting of the flames.

One time we saw the Indians dancing as we passed down by the bank of a river. Another time we saw a wild band dancing in the woods right near our road. We could see them perfectly plain as we went past. They were leaping and yelling like fiends. Our conductor and driver were very worried that night. The Indians were having a war dance and the stage men felt sure that the Indians were getting ready for a massacre.

Oh, the Indians were terrible. They made us stay right in the stage while they changed horses at the stations. I felt so bad I began to cry. Mother heard me. *"Brace up, Rebecca,"* whispered my mother bravely, *"you're going to California."*

One day we thought the Indians were chasing us. We could see a large band of horsemen gradually gaining on us in the distance. The stage men were very uneasy. When finally the band overtook us, it turned out to be a lot of Mexicans who were running down some Indians that had been on a raid.

We had only alkali water to drink much of the way and when we would come to a place where it had rained the stage driver would stop and stage and let us scoop the water off the rocks to drink.

I never knew there were so many buffaloes in the world. We saw thousands and thousands of them. in going through one herd they were so thick in front of us that the stage horses had to slow down and go on the walk. Two of the men on the stage jumped out and caught one of the little baby buffaloes. They wanted to take it right along with us and were going to put it in the boot with the baggage. But the Conductor wouldn't let them.

Somewhere after we got into California we were all, one forenoon, going through mountains. The road was very narrow and every few minutes the conductor would play a little tune on a bugle to warn any other travelers that the stage was coming. The long notes of his bugle, echoing through the mountains, sounded very romantic. Before we got out of the mountains we met another stage coming up the grade.

There had been a mistake in the signals and the two stages met in a narrow part of the road where it was impossible for the two to pass. The stage men took off four horses from the up coming stage and tied them to a tree while the men on both stages got out and piled up rocks beside the grade. Then with the two horses they pulled the stage over on the rocks and let us get past.

Father had no way of knowing whether we were on our way to California or not and he was at the point of starting back to Missouri. There was a telegraph line that followed the stage road over the Pacheco Pass and ran part way down into the San Joaquin Valley. He telegraphed ahead as far as he could to see if we were on the stage that was coming from the East. The report came back that the stage had gone by on the run but that they could see a woman and some children on board. Father felt sure that it

was us and proceeded at once to get a house in readiness for us.

I was so tired I don't remember how many days it was, but sometime after we got into California we reached a town called San Jose. I know it was half past seven in the evening on the third of May, 1860. It was dark and cold. The lamp inside the coach was lit and the curtains all fastened down to make it as warm as possible. We were again in a Concord coach and were sitting four in a seat. The coach was crowded.

My little brother was sitting in my mother's lap. She had held him the entire twenty-one days of our trip. The only sleep we had had was what we could catch while the stage coaches traveled along with the horses on the run. For three weeks we had no change of clothing. We were little short of dead!

There seemed to be some sort of difficulty. The stage people came over to the stage and inquired if there wasn't a woman and some children to get off at San Jose. Mother replied: *"No. Our tickets call for Santa Clara."*

While the stage was still waiting, a tall strange looking man with whiskers all over his face stepped out of the darkness. He poked his head through the curtains and peered into the coach. He looked us over carefully in the dim light and then said firmly: *"I guess you will get off right here!"* Then he smiled. It was father!!

Arising from her easy chair, Mrs. Yokum, the little girl of long ago, made her way over to the mantle where an old fashioned clock was ticking boisterously.

"This is the same clock that was sitting on the mantle piece when father took us that night to our new home in California. It has been running ever since."

She placed her hand on the sturdy wooden case and peered carefully into its face - a face stained like her own with the tears and joys of a long life-time.

"I can't hear you tick any more," she said to the clock, "but I can see your hands go round and so I know that you are still running."

Then turning to me:

"Stage coach days weren't so awfully long ago, after all. They tell me that I have been seventy-four years here in California. But our journey across the plains" - she paused and I knew she was gazing far back into the past - "it seems like only yesterday."

Source: Los Banos Enterprise,
June 30, 1966, page A-1 to A-7

This article was provided by Janet J. Johnston, the great-granddaughter of the passenger.

The parents and a brother of the above passenger.
Rev. Thomas McConnell Johnston, Eleanor Steele Johnston
and one of their sons, James Richard Johnston. ca. 1865
Photo courtesy of Janet J. Johnston

Did Indians Ever Attack a Butterfield Stage?

No passengers of Butterfield's Overland Mail Company stages were ever killed by outlaws or Indians. However, on several occasions employees were killed or livestock was stolen during Indian raids on swing stations. Also, some employees and passengers did die in accidents caused by unbroken mustangs or mules running wild. (*New York Herald, Sunday, July 22, 1860*)

INDIANS ATTACKING AN OVERLAND EXPRESS COACH.

Harper's New Monthly Magazine, Aug. 1875, p. 323, from the collection of Bob Crossman.

On February 5, 1861, *"about two miles west of the Apache Pass station, the passengers of a westbound Butterfield stage were horrified by the sight of a wagon train recently attacked by Apaches. All members of the party were killed and some of their mutilated bodies stall lay in the smoldering embers. Eight of the unfortunate victims were chained to the wagon wheels, where they were burned alive."* ("Historic Guide to the Mormon Battalion and Butterfield Trail," by Dan Talbot, page 78)

The *Arizonian* reported that near midnight, Wednesday, February 6, 1861 the Butterfield Overland stage with eight passengers was attacked. Passengers included Butterfield agent Mr. Buckley, Lieut. Cook of 8th Infantry, and W. S. Grant of Tucson. Arriving at Apache Pass they *"were fired upon some two miles this side of the Station, by what appeared to be a large body of Indians."* Some fifteen rounds were fired, and a ball hit driver King Lyon in the leg breaking his leg. One mule was killed, and another badly wounded. Lieut. Bascom had arrived on Monday, taking the Chief and six Indians prisoners. The next day, James F. Wallace a Butterfield driver, was captured by the Indians, tying his arms behind his back, and placing a rope about his neck. *[Source: Cincinnati Daily Press, March 2, 1861, page 1]*

In March of 1859, one stage was surrounded by 60 Indians for an hour, frightening the passengers. *"At Horsehead Crossing, on the Pecos River, the stage was surrounded by some sixty Indians, who, however, done no harm, they remained about an hour, frightened the passengers very much, and retired."* (Washington Telegraph, Washington, Arkansas, March 30, 1859, page 2)

Was the Overland Mail Co. Profitable?

We do not have a complete record of expenses, salaries or profitability of Butterfield's Overland Mail Company when it operated on the Southern Ox-Bow Route. However, we do have a few scattered primary source financial references.

John Butterfield, in his August 2, 1858 letter to the Directors of the Overland Mail Company made reference to the financial arrangements he initially established with swing and home stations. He writes, *"We made stations and arrangements at the different stations between California and Fort Smith for the teams at prices varying from $125 to $175 per quarter."*

In the same letter, Butterfield refers to the cost of stock placed along the route when he writes, *"...we have purchased 182 horses at an average cost of $98.00 and 257 mules at an average cost of $102.54. Making in all 539 head."*

Also in the same letter, John Butterfield refers to his projection of the profitability of using Steamboats to transport the Overland Mail on the Fort Smith to Memphis portion of the route when he writes, *"I am of the opinion still (expressed in my former report) that the boats should be purchased at $7,500 each and run upon the Arkansas River. I think this will be the best method of doing our business and will be one of the best if not the very best paying portion of our entire route."*

We do not have a record of salaries paid on the Southern Route, however, when The Overland Mail Company route was relocated north to the Central Route to avoid the southern successions states, we have a mention of salaries during that 1861-1864 period. Frank Root, in his 1901 book *"The Over-*

land Stage to California", records his personal reminiscences as an employee of the Overland Mail Co. He writes on page 72, *"Drivers in the employ of the stage company received from $40 to $75 a month and board; stock tenders, $40 to $50; carpenters, $75; harness-makers and blacksmiths $100 to $125; and division agents, $100 to $125."* On page 74 he writes, *"The harness used by the stage company was of the very best Concord make, and cost in staging days, during the '60's, in the neighborhood of $150 for a complete set of four..."* Concerning the cost of feed he writes on page 74, *"Feed for the stock was one of the important items of expense in running the great stage line. At each station there was annually consumed from forty to eighty tons of hay. The cost of hay in staging days was all the way from fifteen to forty dollars a ton. At the various stations it required about 20,000 tons annually to supply them, costing an average of about twenty-five dollars per ton, or say, $500,000 per annum. In grain, each animal was apportioned an average of twelve quarts of corn daily, which then cost two to ten cents a pound."*

Also in the same source, Frank Roots mentions the cost of the stagecoaches themselves when he writes on page 76, *"There were also on the main line, most of them in constant use, about 100 Concord coaches, which delivered, cost, in the early '60's, during war times, about $1,000 each, or say, an aggregate of $95,000. The company owned about one-half of the stations, besides thousands of dollars worth of other miscellaneous property at different places along the route. It cost an enormous sum of money to equip and operate the 'Overland.'*

The post office was slow to make the quarterly $150,000 contract payments to the Overland Mail Co. As reported in the March 30, 1859 issue of the Washington Telegraph (page 2), it states: *"It is said that there are a large number of contractors in Washington endeavoring to settle with the Government. They have been carrying the mails since October 1st at their own expense, and cannot collect a dollar of the Government. Butterfield & Co., the Overland Mail Contractors, are among this class. On April 1st, the Government will owe them $300,000. Those now in Washington say they cannot go on longer on credit."*

We also know that in early 1860 the Overland Mail Co. was having difficulty repaying a loan of $162,400 to the bank of Wells Fargo & Co. and this resulted in John Butterfield losing his position as President of the Overland Mail Company Board of Directors on March 20, 1860.

For more financial details, see Appendix O

Postmaster Brown Died Unexpectedly

Postmaster Brown died unexpectedly on March 8, 1859.

Aaron Brown
Postmaster General

The new postmaster, Joseph Holt of Kentucky, believed the Post Office Department should pay its own way. He was critical of the "enormous sums" paid to stagecoach companies to transport mails. Holt believed, the light volume on all of the mail routes to California never paid more than half their expense in postage collected. Holt reduced the contractors' pay on many routes, and Congress delayed paying them.

Delays such as this made it impossible for Butterfield to make timely payments on the OMC's debt to the banks, and led to the end of John Butterfield's Presidency of the Overland Mail Company.

Postmaster General Hale was concerned that the cost of the route at $600,000 per year, far exceeded the revenue of $119,766. He suggested that the $600,000 should come from the general budget of the U.S. treasury and not from his postal budget: *[Report of the Postmaster General, Dec. 1, 1860, p. 435]*

"In view of this extremely limited revenue, as compared with the outlay, and of the fact that these route were established and are maintained mainly for the advancement of certain national objects and not at all postal in their character, I respectfully but earnestly renew the recommendation contained in my last annual report, that they shall be at once put upon the public treasury."

The following year, the *Report of the Postmaster General* dated December 2, 1861, repeated this request on pages 576-577:

> *"I have in a previous part of this report alluded to the refusal at the treasury to pay the appropriation for the overland mail service to California. It seems to me so evidently to have been the purpose of Congress to require the payment of the amount stipulated from the treasury, under the 9th and 11th sections of the act, that I again call the attention of Congress to the subject for further legislation as may be required. It certainly cannot be supposed that a contract of that magnitude could be required by postal interest alone. The general interest of the country required it, and the compensation should therefore be made by a general appropriation from the treasury, as this department presumes to have been the intention of the law."*

John Butterfield's Term as President Ends

On March 16, 1860 the Board of Directors of the Overland Mail Company met in New York. It was a tense meeting. At this meeting Vice President William Dinsmore was not present. The meeting was so tense in fact, John Butterfield abruptly stood up and left the room. Without a President or Vice-President present, the meeting adjourned, with plans to reconvene on the following day.

The original handwritten minutes of the Overland Mail Company, page 131, record what happened:

Wm Fargo offered the following Resolution.

> *"Whereas the Overland Mail Company are indebted to Wells Fargo & Co in the sum of $162,400, One Hundred Sixty two thousand four hundred 00/dollars, for advances heretofore made by them to said Overland Mail Co. and whereas it may hereafter become necessary to enable said last mentioned Co. to carry out its business, the said Wells Fargo & Co. should make still further advances, Now Therefore, for the purpose of securing said Wells Fargo & Co. the payment of the money as advanced, and that may hereafter be advanced,*

Resolved, that the Overland Mail Co., do hereby assign to said Wells Fargo & Co., all its horses, Mules, harness, stage Coaches, Wagons, and other property and effects now owned by, and being on its several mail lines as well Overland, as [two illegible words] *above, And the officers of this Company are hereby authorized and directed to cause to be made and presented as aforesaid and assign such in accordance with the resolution."*

Seconded by E. P. Williams. A vote will be called for when
[secretary stops writing mid sentence]

Mr. Butterfield left the chair, protesting against this step. The Motion adjourned to meet tomorrow...

In fact, the Board of Directors did not meet until three days had passed. On March 20, 1860 the Board reconvened to consider the above resolution. With John Butterfield in attendance, a compromise was made. The Overland Mail Company would retain its structure and name, but John Butterfield would be replaced as president. William B. Dinsmore was elected president, and John Butterfield would remain as a voting stockholder.

Turmoil Inside the Overland Mail Company With Wm Dinsmore as President

Under this new leadership, the company's services and morale suffered greatly. Six months into the leadership of this new president of the company, Assistant Treasurer of the Overland Mail Company, Hiram S. Rumfield, expressed his discontent with decisions of the new leadership in a personal letter to his wife on September 25, 1860. He wrote:

"I am comparatively indifferent as to whether I retain my position here or not; and certainly will have no desire to remain in the service of the Mail Company in any position whatever, unless the controlling parties in New York concede to Robinson the several reforms in management and the enlarged authority he demands. The matter will doubtless be determined on at an early day — perhaps in time to advise you of the result by the next mail but one. For the sake of our friend Mr. R. I fondly hope that he may succeed in the

object of his mission east. *Among the numerous officials in the service of the Company with whom I have been brought in contact since my arrival here there is none so eminently qualified for a high and responsible position as himself. And yet under the present system of* **mismanagement,** *this man has been obliged to be subordinate to a set of* **ignorant** *and* **brutish road-agents,** *—who, years ago graduated from the stables of the Ohio Stage Company, and are now, in morals, better fitted for the* **depraved associations** *of Mott and Mulbury Streets* than for the companionship of men of moderate decency. Should the Directory in New York so far ignore the true interests of the Company as to compel Robinson to give way to these* **insolent and bombastic interlopers,** *they will discover, at no very remote day, that they have committed an error fraught with incalculable damage to the prospects of this "great enterprise."*

[*"*Mott and Mulbury Streets*" refers to lower Manhattan's notorious slum neighborhood in the 1800's called 'Chinatown.']

Source of Letter: American Antiquarian Society, 1928, p. 245-246

Apparently, Mr. Robinson's trip to New York to meet with the Overland Mail Company Board of Directors went well. In an unpublished letter in the files of the Huntington Library in San Marino, California, there is a letter written in New York by Mr. Robinson on September 21, 1860 addressed to H. S. Rumfield. He writes:

Office of United States Express Company

72 BROADWAY

New York, Sept. 21st, 1860

H. S. Rumfield

Dear Sir,

I leave for Ohio to day - Have received your letters to the 7th, and telegraphed you for news from Fuller but can get no answer.

Have heard nothing from him since I left Fort Smith – As [illegible word] *the Supt. has gone to California I presume Fuller has gone with him.* **I have** ~~made~~ **found matters in good shape for the future.** *I hope Fuller has sent all the papers – as they are much out of him as for the delay. Beckleys* papers were here 6 weeks ago. **I think these matters will be ordered differently in future.**

I shall go direct to Mansfield and remain there 3 days and then for Fort Smith – and will get there about the 1st of October.   *Yours truly,*

J. R. Robinson

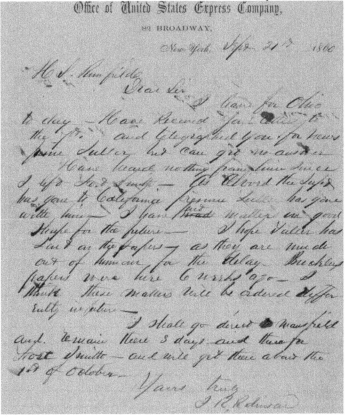

Unpublished letter from J. R. Robinson to Hiram Rumfield, September 21, 1860
Source: Rumfield Collection at the Huntington Library, San Marino, California

It appears that J. R. Robinson's trip to New York resulted in his promotion to Division Superintendent. Among the 75 items in the Rumfield collection at the Huntington Library in San Marino, California, there is an unpublished three page letter that J. R. Robinson wrote to Hiram Rumfield on Oct. 20, 1860:

Friend Rumfield,   *Fort Smith Oct. 20th 1860*
... [on page 2] *Fuller was anxious to learn of me what*

was said in N.Y. when I was there. He said they were so cross they would scarcely speak to him. Barney would have nothing to say or do with him, and Camp was very cool. He thought they were not satisfied with the treatment I had received here. I said to him they were cross at the way the Business was done and they would no doubt insist on the Return of ____ on a more thorough Systematic Method of doing this business. I further told him my desire was to go west in Buckleys place - if any change was made - and had to written Barney.

To this he replied that there would undoubtedly be a change. And he would do all he could to have me go there. That if I would consider he would give me Hawleys Division immediately as he had it in his power to do that. I fact, I found him ready to promise & do anything he could. =What a change = ...

[on page 3] I shall leave on the next stage for Fort Chadbourne to get a list of the property from that point here. ... I sincerely hope you will find Mrs. Rumfield much better in health. I miss you very much ... as Ruddy can do nothing but receipt fare until your return....

When I return here my papers must be ready for Mr. Jones [or James] to take to N.Y. The understanding is when Ward & Fuller return that we all go to N.Y. and there arrange the changes & so may be necessary for us to move west this winter if practicable. ...

Your Friend,
J. R. Robinson

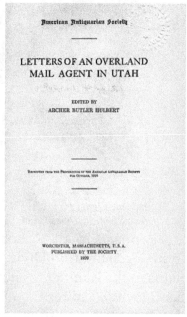

The book above reprints many of Hiram Rumfield's letters. There is additional unpublished correspondence in the Rumfield collection at the Huntington Library in San Marino, California

Minute Book of the Overland Mail Company

In 1970, the actual *"Minute Book of the Overland Mail Company"* was in the "History Room of the Wells Fargo Bank." This is based on note 26 of the journal article, *"Wells Fargo Staging over the Sierra"* by W. Turrentine Jackson in *California Historical Society Quarterly*, Vol. 49, No. 2 (June 1970), pp. 99-133 (35 pages)

There is every indication the minute book is still in the possession of Wells Fargo's Historian, and this author continues to attempt to gain access to this resource.

These minutes may well reveal the answer to countless questions, including:

- Exactly what was the contract with the J. T. Chidester stage line from 1858 to 1861 to carry the Overland Mail from Memphis to Fort Smith? Was that relationship profitable?
- What were the passenger counts, eastbound and westbound each year of the Overland Mail contract, 1858-1864?
- What is the record of expenses, passenger counts, and profitability of the steamboat Jennie Whipple that the Overland Mail Company purchased in hopes of using it on the Arkansas River and Mississippi between Fort Smith and Memphis?
- Copies of the semi-annual reports that were required to be open to shareholders.

Article VIII in the 1858 Articles of Association of the Overland Mail Company required that:

"They shall cause semi-annual reports to be made and filed with the Treasurer or Secretary, containing a clear and simple statement of the business and affairs of said Company, showing its capital, earnings and expenses, profits and losses, cash in hand, property, debts and indebtedness. Which said report, together with all books of account and other records, shall, at all reasonable times, be open to the inspection of any of the Shareholders."

I can only dream what history would be revealed in these semi-annual reports, and the book of minutes.

I trust that soon Wells Fargo will allow the full content of the *"Minute Book of the Overland Mail Company"* to be made available.

Butterfield Overland Mail Route
Memphis to Fort Smith Route

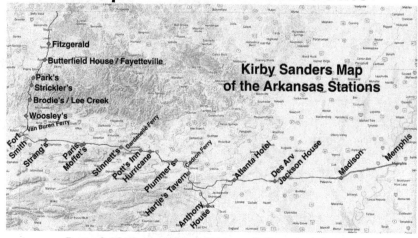

Fitzgerald
Butterfield House / Fayetteville
Park's
Strickler's
Brodie's / Lee Creek
Woosley's
Van Buren Ferry

Kirby Sanders Map
of the Arkansas Stations

Butterfield Overland Mail Stagecoach Stops in Arkansas
Map by Kirby Sanders
To learn about the STAGECOACH LAND ROUTE across Arkansas,
see Bob Crossman's 2021 book: "Butterfield's Overland Mail STAGECOACH Route
Across Arkansas: 1858-1861"

On the map above, Kirby Sanders has attempted to mark the home stations and swing stations set up by sub-contractor John T. Chidester and John Butterfield between Fort Smith and Memphis.

These are the stations that were used when water levels did not permit the use of the *Jennie Whipple* to carry the Overland Mail and passengers on the Arkansas River.

Simultaneously, at 8am every Monday and Thursday, the Overland Mail left St. Louis and Memphis. From Memphis, the mail crossed the Mississippi River by ferry to Hopefield to board the train for a short 24 miles over the "Great Swamp." At tracks end 12 miles east of Madison, the mail transfered to a light wagon to Des Arc. From Des Arc, a Concord Mail stagecoach carried the Overland Mail and passengers west to Fort Smith. There, merging with the St. Louis stage, a Celerity stage headed west to San Francisco.

1858 map of Memphis, Tennessee by E. W. Rucker
The bold print and red arrows were added by the author of this book.

Above is the 1858 map of Memphis, Tennessee by E. W. Rucker showing location of the Commercial Hotel where the Butterfield Overland Mail Co. office was located, and the location of the railroad depot in Hopefield, Arkansas.

The location of the ferry shown here is from a map of Memphis printed in the May 14, 1862 issue of the New York Times.

Today, an historical marker on northeast corner of Jefferson and 3rd marks the post office's 1862 location.

Butterfield Mail on the St. Louis to Fort Smith Route

"The first Butterfield Overland Mail Run in 1858 -
St. Louis to Tipton to Transfer to Stagecoach bound for Fort Smith"
Painted by Frank Nuderscher (1880-1959) for the Missouri Pacific Museum.

"Butterfield Overland and National Historic Trail"
— *Memphis to Fort Smith* —
— *St. Louis to Fort Smith* —
— *Fort Smith to Texas* —
Image Source: Kirby Sanders

Memphis & St Louis to Texas Border
Map by Kirby Sanders

In 1858 the Pacific Railroad from St. Louis arrived at Tipton, Missouri and John Butterfield personally carried the first mail bag, boarding the Overland Stagecoach headed to Fort Smith. Butterfield deboarded at Fort Smith and the stage went on to San Francisco.

In late 1858 the Missouri Pacific Railroad had laid track farther west to Syracuse, Missouri. At that time the Shackleford Station in Syracuse became the eastern terminus of Butterfield's stage line from 1859 into 1861.

NOTE:
For more information on the background and operation of the Overland Mail Co. and the STAGECOACH ROUTE across Arkansas, see:
"Butterfield's Overland Mail Co. STAGECOACH Trail Across Arkansas 1858-1861" by Bob Crossman

End of Butterfield's Southern Ox Bow Route

When Abraham Lincoln was elected President in November of 1860, the southern states began to move toward secession.

On February 1, 1861 the Texas Convention passed a secession ordinance. Shortly after this, sympathizers of the Confederacy began to confiscate equipment and stock from Butterfield's stations in Texas.

Writing from Tucson, Arizona on April 1, 1861 a newspaper correspondent reporting on the Overland Mail route in Texas, wrote that:

"The Texas Rangers had taken the stock at five stations near Fort Belknap... We are filled with consternation at learning the probability of an almost immediate withdrawal of our mail communication with the States. When the Overland route ceases, we will only be able to receive and forward letters via Santa Fe, thence to Mesilla, and must send private expresses over the remainder of the route. The postmaster at St, Louis, should send all Arizona letters in that way." [Source: *Daily Missouri Republican, April 25, 1861.*]

As secession tensions increased, on March 9, 1861 *The Weekly Commonwealth* reprinted an article from *The Missouri Democrat*: *"...we learn from the telegraph operator at Fort Smith that... mail... has been:*

been stopped at Fort Chadbourne by Texan Rangers, and whether the mail bags are to be forwarded or not, the Company's property, consisting of coaches, horses, stables, harness and feed, is reported to be in the hands of the same parties, and the employees of the Company under arrest also. What possible motive the Texans can have for this act is almost beyond conjecture. The Overland Mail Company has been a perfect godsend to that region. Besides affording means of easy and safe communication between different parts of the country, which is a dense wilderness at best, the Company has expended tens of thousands of dollars for stock and supplies, improved roads, built stations—giving occupation to men who, before its advent, were living on what they could pick up.

Seizure of private property, in this instance is specially outrageous. As well might the

The Weekly Commonwealth, Topeka, Kansas, March 9, 1861

When word of this reached Washington, the Congress passed the Post Office Appropriation Bill on March 2, 1861 which ordered that route #12578 along the Southern Route by Butterfield be converted to a daily route #10773 along the Central Route as of July 1, 1861. [see **Appendix M**]

The last Southern Ox Bow Route Butterfield Overland mailbag left St. Louis by train on March 21, 1861. Transferring to a stagecoach at Syracuse, Missouri, and collecting several additional bags at Tucson, Arizona and arrived at San Francisco on April 13, 1861. The final eastbound mail left San Francisco on April 1 and arrived in St. Louis on May 1.

The April 5, 1861 San Francisco Bulletin reported that:

"The Overland Mail by the Butterfield route did not leave this city today for St. Louis, as usual and will be discontinued ... from this day until the 1st of June next, that being the time fixed for the commencement of the new service via the Central route." [Source: "Mails of the Westward Expansion, 1803 to 1861" by Steven C. Walske and Richard C. Frajola, Western Cover Society, 2015 pages 170-171]

The Van Buren Press, March 8, 1861, Van Buren, Arkansas

STOPPAGE OF THE OVERLAND MAIL TO CALIFORNIA. – *We learn, by telegraph, that the contract for the transportation of the Overland Mail on the Butterfield route, is to be abrogated. We are sorry to learn this, for no mail over so lengthy a route has ever before been transported with such celerity and certainty as this had, and we are sure that on a more northern route when it is hereafter ordered to be carried, that failure must and necessarily will be of common occurrence, especially in the winter season, when snows are certain to be an obstruction.*

The California mail through this section of country had become to be considered as a fixed fact, and was an regularly looked for on time as any of the local mails, and we cannot see any good grounds for its abrogation.

The mail has been carried to California by Butterfield & Co., under the present contract, and over the present route with more efficiency than it is possible to make over any more northern route, except it be the 35th parallel, and its abolish-

ment seems to us, must be taken as a sectional movement on the part of the Black Republicans in Congress. The mail on this route, we are informed, will stop on the 25th inst.

The Overland Mail.

The last coach on the Butterfield route, through Texas and Arizona, left ten days ago, and the stock, coaches, &c., are now being removed. The Pike's Peak Express Company and the Butterfield Company have united in this enterprise, and the best energies of both will be put forth, which insures success. The former Company will perform all the service between the Missouri river and Salt Lake, and the latter Company from that city to Placerville, California. The route of the mail will be that of the Pony Express, which has run so successfully during the past year between this city and California. The new service on this route will commence on the 1st of July.

The Elwood Free Press, Elwood, Kansas, April 6, 1861

The Overland Mail Company Moves To The Central Route

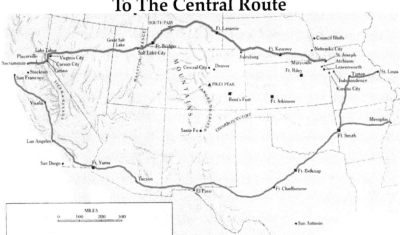

Map 6 – Central Contract Route and Southern (Butterfield) Contract Route

Source: Richard Frajola

The Central Route

"This northern route was initially scouted in 1855 by Howard Egan, and used by him to drive livestock between Salt Lake City and California. The trail Egan used led straight through the high mountain ranges that most earlier explorers had worked so hard to avoid.

Egan had discovered a series of mountain passes and mountain springs that aligned to allow an almost straight path across the middle of Utah and Nevada.

In 1858, hearing of Egan's Trail, the U.S. Army sent an expedition led by Captain James H. Simpson to survey it for a military road to get supplies to the Army's Camp Floyd in Utah. Simpson came back with a surveyed route that was also about 280 miles (450 km) shorter than the "standard" California Trail route along the Humboldt River.

The Army then improved the trail and springs for use by wagons and stagecoaches in 1859 and 1860. When the approaching American Civil War closed the heavily subsidized Butterfield Overland Mail southwestern route to California along the Gila River, George Chorpenning immediately realized the value of this more direct route, and shifted his existing mail and passenger line from the "Northern Humboldt Route" along the Humboldt River. [Source: Wikipedia "Central Overland Route"]

Details of the New Central Route Contract

The *"Report of The Postmaster General Respecting the Operations and Condition of the Post Office Department During the Fiscal Year Ending June 30, 1861"* summarizes the change in the six year contract, and a temporary rerouting to avoid the "threatening disturbances in Missouri":

Postmaster Montgomery Blair
March 5, 1861 - Sept. 23, 1864

[Editor's Note: In the PMG report below, I broke the large original singe paragraph into smaller paragraphs to make it easier for the reader. Also, I placed a few words in bold to highlight important topics.]

*"...an order was made on the 12th of March, 1861, to modify the present contract, so as to discontinue service on the **southern route**, and to provide for the transportation of the entire letter mail six times a week on the **central route**, to be carried through in* [the summer] *twenty days eight months in the year, and in* [the winter] *twenty-three days four months in the year, from St. Joseph, Missouri, (or Atchison, Kansas,) to Placerville* [California], *and also to convey the entire mail three times a week to Denver City and Salt Lake;*

the entire mail to California to be carried, whatever may be its weight, and in case it should not amount to 600 pounds, then sufficient of other mail to be carried each trip to make up that weight, the residue of all mail matter to be conveyed in thirty-five days, with the privilege of sending it from New York to San Francisco in twenty-five days by sea, and the public documents in thirty-five days;

*a **pony express** to be run twice a week until the completion of the overland telegraph, through in ten days eight months* [summer], *and twelve days four months* [winter], *in the year conveying for the government free of charge, five pounds of mail matter;*

*the **compensation** for the whole service to be one million of dollars per annum, payable from the general treasury, as provided by the act; the service to commence July 1, 1861, and terminate July 1, 1864* [on the Central Route].

*The **transfer of stock** from the southern to the central route was commenced about the 1st of April, and was completed so that the first mail was started from St. Joseph on the day prescribed by the order, July 1, 1861.*

*While the carriages have, it is believed, departed regularly since that time, the mail service has **not been entirely satisfactory** to the department. The causes of complaint, however, it is hoped, will be removed by the measures now in progress.*

*The **route** selected is that by Salt Lake City, so that that* [sic] *office has now the advantage of a daily mail, and Denver City is* *supplied three times a week.*

*The overland **telegraph** having been completed, the running of the **pony express** was discontinued October 26, 1861.*

*By the terms of the law the contractors were required to **convey only the California letter mail** each trip by the short schedule, and this they were to do whatever might be its weight; but by voluntary agreement they stipulated that in case it should fall short of 600 pounds on any occasion they would take other mails [newspapers & express packages] so as to make that weight. As the letter mails are seldom or never equal to 600 pounds in weight, some papers are conveyed in connection with the letter mails each trip by the short schedule, while others are necessarily delayed.*

*This has occasioned **complaint;** and complaints have also been made of other delays, and that bags of printed matter have been thrown off 'en route' for the admission of passengers and express matter. These charges are denied by the contractors; but while the conditions of the contract, fixed by law, allow a longer time for the transit of some mails than others, complaint and disappointment must be of necessity occur.*

*At the commencement of **threatening disturbances in Missouri,** in order to secure this great daily route from interruption, I ordered... an alternative and certain route between the east and California was obtained through Iowa, by which the overland mails have been transported when they became unsafe on the railroad route in Missouri. In sending them from Davenport, through the State of Iowa, joining the main route at Fort Kearney, in Kansas, the only inconvenience experienced was a slight delay, no mails being lost so far as known. ("Report of The Postmaster General Respecting the Operations and Condition of the Post Office Department During the Fiscal Year Ending June 30, 1861")*

Wm Dinsmore's [Butterfield's] Overland Mail Co. Contract Continued on Central Route 1861-1864

The March 2, 1861 Post Office Appropriation Bill ended the Southern Route #12518, and provided that the original six-year contract be continued for the balance of the term and increase from $600,000 to $1,000,000 per year on the Central Route #10773 beginning July 1, 1861. The new route would have daily mail stagecoaches Tuesday to Sunday, and a Pony Express semiweekly of ten days for eight months and twelve days for the four winter months. It also provided that the Pony Express would discontinue upon completion of the transcontinental telegraph. **[see Appendix L & M]**

On March 16, 1861 the Overland Mail Co. sub-contracted the Pony Express route from St. Joseph to Sacramento to the C.O.C. & P.P.Ex.Co. (who had already been operating the Pony Express since April 3, 1860); and the stagecoach route from Atchison, Kansas to Salt Lake City to the C.O.C. & P.P.Ex. Co. (Central Overland California & Pikes Peak Express Company) to receive the sum of $475,000 per year. The Overland Mail Co. would operate the section of the Central Route from Salt Lake City to Placerville as the new western terminus for the $525,000 balance of the $1,000,000 annual sum.

[see Appendix N]

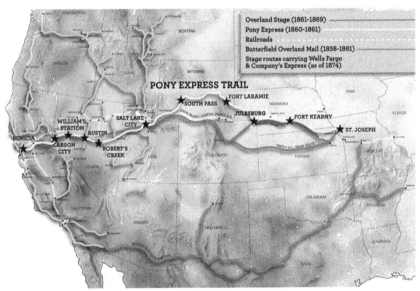

Source: WellsFargoHistory.com

The Pioneer Stage Company already had the Postal contract to carry the mails from west from Placerville to Sacramento, California.

PIONEER STAGE COMPANY
FROM SACRAMENTO TO VIRGINIA, CARRYING THE GREAT OVERLAND MAIL & WELLS FARGO & Cos EXPRESS.

Pioneer Stage Company: from Sacramento to Virginia
by George Holbrook Baker, American, lithographer

The 1861-1864 Central Route postal contract covered the distance from St. Joseph, Missouri to Placerville, California. The Pioneer Stage Company had the postal contract to carry the mails west from Placerville. It is interesting to note that the Pioneer Stage Company used river steamboats to carry the mail between Sacramento and San Francisco for 19 months from April 3, 1860 to November 20, 1861. The horse and rider were on the boat and would gallop off at the dock. The steamers saved 5½ hours off using a stagecoach over that 100 mile distance.

Interim Between April 1 and July 1, 1861

In the interim between April 1 and July 1, when the Butterfield's Overland Mail Company was not in operation, the Overland Mail Company was busy transferring what equipment and staff they could move north to the Central Route for completion of their six year contract.

Gerald T. Ahnert, Butterfield Historian, gives a summary of this transfer of equipment in his "Butterfield Overland Mail" article in Wikipedia:

At the closing of Butterfield's operations on the Southern Overland Trail in March 1861, because of the start of the Civil War, many of the stages were confiscated and used by the Confederate Army as military vehicles. [Tri Weekly Commonwealth, Frankfort, Kentucky, "Letter from Texas, Fort Smith, Feb. 20," February 22, 1861]

As much of the equipment as possible was transferred to the central trail to continue the Overland Mail Company con-

tract. **Only enough of the stages made it to the central route to operate the line from Salt Lake City, Utah, to western Nevada.**

The biography of Edwin R. Purple tells of transferring the stages to the central route. He was employed by the Overland Mail Company as a financial agent at Fort Yuma, California, in May 1860. At the closing of the line, on the Southern Overland Trail, in March 1861, he was ordered to transfer the stock and stages from Tucson, Arizona, to Los Angeles, California, to supply the central route line, which was to commence operations on July 1, 1861. On May 8, 1861, with 30 men, he left Los Angeles and successfully arrived at Salt Lake City on June 16 with 18 stage wagons and 130 horses.[Edwin R. Purple, The New York State Genealogical and Biographical Record, New York, July, 1879]

In a discussion by Gerald T. Ahnert with members of the True West Historical Society, it was suggested that many of these original stagecoaches and stage wagons were bought by movie companies in the 1930s through 1950s and used in their movie productions. Many were destroyed in scenes of the stages being attacked. [Gerald T. Ahnert, Butterfield's Overland Mail Company Stagecoaches and (Celerity) Wagons on the Southern Overland Trail, 1858–1861.]

However, during these 90 days, there were still alternate carriers available for passengers and mail. Starting on April 1, 1861 transcontinental mail could be directed toward steamships headed to the Isthmus of Panama, or mail could be redirected north, avoiding the southern states, to the Central Overland Mail Route.

The *Daily Alta California*, May 16, 1861 printed a letter from their St. Louis correspondent: *"We have had no Overland Mail [in St. Louis] since that of March 26th arrived, and the agents inform me today that the remaining ones due in this city have probably been sent to San Antonio, to be brought hence by steamer to Galveston, and so on to New Orleans. By this irregular route, there is no knowing when the letters which left your city between March 25th and April 2nd, by Overland Mail, will arrive here."*

During these months, the Central Overland Mail Route was operating by contractors Central Overland California &

Pikes Peak Express Company (C.O.C. & P.P.Ex.Co.). This was similar to the route and stations that were currently in use by the Pony Express. This is also similar to the route that Wm Dinsmore's Overland Mail Co. would soon inherit from the postal service when their six year contract was shifted from the Southern Ox-Bow Route to the Central Route effective July 1, 1861 to avoid all of the southern states due to a growing secession movement.

Comparing the Pony Express & the Central Stage Routes

Map of the PONY EXPRESS Route in April 1860
The Pony Express, A Postal History, by Richard Frajola, page 16

CENTRAL STAGECOACH ROUTE used by the Overland Mail Co. 1861-64
The Pony Express, A Postal History, by Richard Frajola, page 6

The clipping below, from the 1859 California Register, lists the Central Overland Mail Route along with it's major stops and frequency of operation.

> 2. CENTRAL OVERLAND MAIL.
> The Central Overland, or Salt Lake City Mail, from St. Josephs, Missouri, to Salt Lake; thence through Carson Valley to Placerville. Weekly; leaves St. Josephs and Placerville every Saturday. Schedule time from St. Josephs to Salt Lake, twenty-two days; from Salt Lake to Placerville, sixteen days. Hockaday & Chorpenning, Contractors.

The California State Register and year book of facts for 1859, pages 157
Henry G. Langley & Co., Publishers
Image provided to the author from Gordon Nelson, Western Cover Society

According to Frank Root, eye witness and participant in the stirring events on the Central Route,

"There were from eight to twelve animals kept at each station. At some of the stations it was necessary to keep a few head of extra stock, as occasionally an animal would be liable to get lame, sick, or be crippled, and at times unable to work; hence the necessity of a few extra head where they could be got without delay." [Source: The Overland Stage to California, Frank Albert Root, page 74]

FRANK A. ROOT

The two-sided Central Route Schedule below lists the various stations between Salt Lake City and Sacramento. Note that the home stations are printed in *italics*.

Wm Dinsmore's Overland Mail Company carried the mail between Salt Lake City and Virginia City.

OVERLAND MAIL CO.
KE CITY TO VIRGINIA, NEV.—Stations and Distances.

Station	MILES.		Station	MILES.
*SALT LAKE CITY	0	0	*Ruby Valley	9	278
Union Inn	11	11	Jacob's Well	13	291
Rockwell's	9	20	*Diamond Springs*	12	303
Jordan	10	30	Sulphur Springs	12	315
Fort Crittenden	10	40	Robert's Creek	13	328
Center	10	50	*Grubb's Well*	13	341
Rush Valley	10	60	Dry Creek	17	358
Point Lookout	9	69	Cape Horn	13	371
Simpson's Springs	17	86	*AUSTIN	16	387
River Bed	8	94	Reese River	9	396
Dug-Way	12	106	Mount Airy	11	407
Black Rock	14	120	New Pass	11	418
Fish Springs	10	130	Edward's Creek	12	430
Boyd's	10	140	*Cold Spring*	13	443
Willow Springs	10	150	*West Gate	15	458
Cañon	11	161	Fairview	11	469
Deep Creek	15	176	*Mountain Wells*	14	483
Eight-Mile	8	184	Stillwater	15	498
Antelope Spring	18	202	Old River	15	513
Spring Valley	13	215	Cottonwood	15	528
*SCHELL CREEK	11	226	Nevada	15	543
Egan Cañon	14	240	Desert Wells	15	558
Butte	15	255	*VIRGINIA	14	572
Mountain Springs	14	269	*Telegraph Stations, Italics, Home Stations.		
			Capitals, Terminus of Division. [OVER.		

The Overland Mail Co. From Salt Lake City to Virginia, Nevada - Stations and Distances
H. S. Rumfield, Agent O. M. Co., 1866, 2 ¾ x 4 ¼ inches
Courtesy of The Newberry Collection - Everett D. Graff Collection of Western Americana

The Pioneer Stage Company carried the mail between Virginia City to Sacramento.

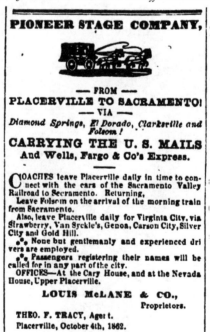

PIONEER STAGE COMPANY.

FROM VIRGINIA, NEV., TO SACRAMENTO, CAL.—Stations and Distances.
(Connecting with Overland Mail Co.)

PLACERVILLE OR LAKE TAHOE ROUTE.		Miles.		DONNER LAKE AND DUTCH FLAT ROUTE.		Miles.	
*Virginia	to Gold Hill.........	2	2	Virginia	to Brown's..........	13	13
*Gold Hill	" Silver City......	3	5	Brown's	" Truckee Meadows..	3	16
*Silver City	" Empire City......	7	12	Truckee M'dows	" Hunter's.......	9	25
Empire City	" Carson............	4	16	Hunter's	" Crystal Peak.....	8	33
*Carson	" Genoa.............	13	29	*Crystal Peak	" Ingram's........	7	40
*Genoa	" Friday's.........	12	41	Ingram's	" Little Truckee.....	4	44
*Friday's	" Yank's..........	10	51	Little Truckee	" Prosser Creek.....	8	52
*Yank's	" Strawberry........	12	63	Prosser Creek	" Donner Lake.......	10	62
*Strawberry	" Webster's........	11	74	*Donner Lake	" Jones'..........	10	72
*Webster's	" Pioneer Station....	10	84	Jones'	" Woodward's......	7	79
*Pioneer Station	" Sportman's Hall..	10	94	Woodward's	" Polly's or Crystal L.	3	82
*Sportman's Hall	" Placerville........	12	106	*Crystal Lake	" Zerr's..........	10	92
*Placerville	" Shingle Springs....	10	116	Zerr's	" Dutch Flat........	10	102
*Shingle Springs	" SACRAM'TO.(R.R.)	46	162	*Dutch Flat	" Gold Run.........	4	106
				*Gold Run	" Colfax..........	10	116
				*Colfax	" SACRAM'TO (R.R.)	55	171

Sacramento to San Francisco (via Sacramento River)..............................120 Miles.
Total distance, Salt Lake City to Sacramento (via Placerville)...........734 Miles.
"   "   Salt Lake City to San Francisco,   "   ....854 "

SALT LAKE CITY, January 1st, 1866.   THE NEWBERRY LIBRARY   H. S. RUMFIELD, Agent O. M. Co.

*Pioneer Stage Company, From Virginia, Nevada to Sacramento - Stations and Distances
Connecting with Overland Mail Co.*
H. S. Rumfield, Agent O. M. Co., 1866, 2 ¾ x 4 ¼ inches
Courtesy of The Newberry Collection - Everett D. Graff Collection of Western Americana

PIONEER STAGE COMPANY,

— FROM —
PLACERVILLE TO SACRAMENTO!
— VIA —
Diamond Springs, El Dorado, Clarksville and Folsom!

CARRYING THE U. S. MAILS
And Wells, Fargo & Co's Express.

COACHES leave Placerville daily in time to connect with the cars of the Sacramento Valley Railroad to Sacramento. Returning,
Leave Folsom on the arrival of the morning train from Sacramento.
Also, leave Placerville daily for Virginia City, via Strawberry, Van Syckle's, Genoa, Carson City, Silver City and Gold Hill.
* None but gentlemanly and experienced drivers are employed.
* Passengers registering their names will be called for in any part of the city.
OFFICES—At the Cary House, and at the Nevada House, Upper Placerville.

LOUIS McLANE & CO.,
Proprietors.

THEO. F. TRACY, Agent.
Placerville, October 4th, 1862.

The Mountain Democrat, Placerville, California, March 19, 1864

Marysville Home Station on the Central Route, Marysville Kansas
Marysville, Kansas is 100 miles due west of St. Joseph, Missouri
The Marysville station is the only remaining original home station from the Central Route.
This station was used by The Overland Mail Company and the Pony Express.
The original station, as shown in the painting above, has been remodeled and added on to
multiple times in the past hundred years. It now houses the Pony Express Museum.

Wm Dinsmore's Overland Mail on the Central Route 1861 to 1864

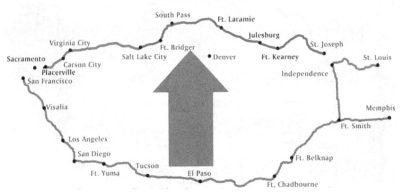

Butterfield's Overland Mail on the Southern 'Oxbow' Bifurcated Route 1858 to 1861

Butterfield's Mail Route Moves Northward out of Confederate States

In March of 1861, primarily due to increasing conflict along the route due to southern secessionists, the Post Master General closed the southern 'Oxbow' Overland Mail Co. route. Transcontinental mail was redirected north, avoiding the southern states, to the Central Overland Mail Route. On behalf of the Overland Mail Company, the order was signed by president W. B. Dinsmore. William B. Dinsmore became president after John Butterfield was voted out of office on March 20, 1860. Butterfield still remained a major stockholder and active participant in the company board meetings, however with Dinsmore as president, the other directors had a larger voice in financial matters.

First Day on the Central Route, July 1861

The newspapers reported that the departure of the first stagecoach was celebrated by an *"immense"* group of citizens.

> SAN FRANCISCO, July 4.—The first daily Overland Mail Coach started from Placerville, on the 1st inst., escorted out of town by an immense concourse of citizens, with bands of music, and cannon firing. The coach and horses were decorated with American Flags.
>
> There were six bags of letter mail and 29 bags of newspapers, in all weighing 1776 pounds.

Weekly News-Democrat, Emporia, Kansas, July 20, 1861

> OVERLAND MAIL.—The first Daily Overland Mail from California, arrived here on Thursday, making the trip in about seventeen days. It brought thirty bags of mail matter, and three passengers. The coaches going West were met 190 miles this of Salt Lake City.

The Elwood Free Press, Elwood, Kansas, July 20, 1861

The newspapers reported that the volume of mail accumulating at St. Joseph waiting for the westbound mail stages was *"immense."*

> THE OVERLAND MAIL.—The amount of mail matter destined for the Pacific Coast proves to be immense. On Monday evening two hundred sacks of "through mail" were received at the office in this city. The coach departs regularly every morning, carrying from twelve to fifteen hundred pounds of letters and papers. Although by the provisions of their contract the company are not bound to carry over six hundred pounds daily, they are exhibiting most commendable spirit in hurrying it forward regardless of the amount specified.—*St. Jo. Journal.*

Weekly Commonwealth, Topeka, Kansas, Juy 20, 1861

The success of the Overland Mail Company on the Central Route was even celebrated in the Boston newspapers. The *Boston Traveler* article below was reprinted in *The Daily Missouri Republican* on August 1, 1861.

Success of the Daily Overland Mail.

In the war excitement our people have quite overlooked one of the most substantial triumphs of peace which has marked our recent history. We refer to the entire success of the Daily Overland Mail, which went into operation on the 1st inst. The first coach of the new line, which left Placerville on the morning of the 1st July, arrived at St. Joseph on the 18th inst., in only *seventeen days and one hour* from one terminus to the other. The schedule time during the summer season is twenty days. The agents write that their drivers had not the slightest difficulty in making their time; on the contrary, they came in ahead of time, without any effort, to that end. Four passengers came with the first coach, and some two hundred additional passengers from California were booked for the coaches to come as soon as they could be brought.

The public should not forget that the steamers no longer carry the mail. Notwithstanding this fact has been widely published, a large number of correspondents still accumulate their letters and newspapers at the principal postoffices on the steamer days and each day preceding the sailing of a California steamer. Let it be remembered that the California mail now leaves St. Joseph every day in the week, and letters may be mailed on each and every day at any postoffice in the loyal States. Postage ten cents, always pre-paid.—[Boston Traveler.

The Daily Missouri Republican, St. Louis, August 1, 1861, page 3

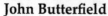

John Butterfield

John Butterfield was the president of the Overland Mail Co. Fellow contractors of the company included William B. Dinsmore of New York City; William G. Fargo of Pompey, New York; James V. P. Gardner of Utica, New York; Marquis L. Kenyon of Rome, New York; Alexander Holland of New York City; and Hamilton Spencer of Bloomington, Illinois. The financial sureties on the contract were Danford N. Barney, Johnston Livingston, David Moulton, and Elijah P. Williams.

William B. Dinsmore

William B. Dinsmore became president after John Butterfield was voted out as president on March 20, 1860. John Butterfield continued to serve on the board and to purchase additional shares. When the '58-'64 contract ended, Dinsmore organized a new Overland Mail Co. with himself and only Danford N. Barney and A. H. Barney as directors.

Even on the Central Route, it was often still called "the Butterfield"

Sacramento Daily Union, California, June 11, 1861
"Letter from Salt Lake, From our Special Correspondent."

"Great Salt Lake City, June 5, 1861. ... William Buckley, formerly the Superintendent of the Butterfield route from San Francisco to El Paso, F. Cluggage, an Agent in that route and Bolivar Roberts, the Superintendent of the western division on this route, came in a week ago yesterday from Carson, which I noticed in my last letter, and on Friday Edward Fisher, and four other employees in some department, came in from St. Joseph. ...They have, whatever else besides, at least made all the necessary arrangements for a vigorous start to the daily mail, and everything will be ready by the first week in July [July 1 was when the line was ordered to start by the

new contract] *to fulfill the of obligations of the million dollar contract... Last evening, profiting by a conversation with Mr. Buckley, I obtained from him a copy of his measurement of the road from Carson to this city* [Salt Lake City]. *... Placerville* [California] *being the terminus, another 100 miles should be added between that and Carson, as the entire distance of the* **Butterfield new route.** *These are the stations now in use and to be continued, from the facilities they afford of proximity to wood, water and feed; but I am informed the* **Butterfield Company** *propose erecting intermediate stations every twelve miles, on account of the greater amount of horses required for the accomplishment of the journey within the specified time of sixteen days from St. Joseph to Placerville."*

In March of 1861, as plans were being made to move the Overland Mail Company's route from the Southern Ox Bow Route to the Central Route, an announcement was made in the newspapers about the postage rate on the Central Route. The postage rate for newspapers, unsealed circulars, periodicals or printed matter under three ounces would be charged 1¢ for every ounce and fraction of an ounce. The rate for letters crossing the Rocky Mountains would be 10¢ per half ounce. [Source: Kansas State Journal, Lawrence, Kansas, March 28, 1861.]

Newspapers reported that within the first ninety days of operation, the western terminus of the Central Route was moved from St. Joseph, Missouri to Atchison, Kansas.

☞ We learn by reliable authority, that the Overland California Mail Depot has been transferred from St. Joseph to Atchison. We are glad to hear it.

The Weekly Commonwealth, Topeka, Kansas, September 21, 1861

SAN FRANCISCO DIRECTORY.   lxvii

DAILY
OVERLAND MAIL.
THROUGH IN TWENTY DAYS.

SACRAMENTO CAL., TO ATCHINSON, KANSAS,
VIA
PLACERVILLE,
VIRGINIA CITY, and
SALT LAKE CITY.

TARIFF OF FARES:
FROM SACRAMENTO

TO VIRGINIA CITY	$28	TO JULESBURGH-Crossing of South	
" REESE RIVER	68	Platte	$205
" FORT CRITTENDEN	100	" FORT KEARNY	205
" SALT LAKE CITY	110	" OMAHA	205
" FORT BRIDGER	125	" ATCHINSON	205

The Mails & Passengers will lay over one night at Salt Lake City.

Passengers will be permitted to lay over at any point on the road, and resume their seat when there is one vacant. To secure this privilege, they must register their names with the Stage Agent at the place they lay over. Passengers allowed 25 pounds of Baggage; all over that weight will be charged extra.

The Company will not be responsible for loss of Baggage exceeding in value Twenty-Five Dollars.

FOR PASSAGE, APPLY AT THE
STAGE OFFICE Second St., between J and K, to
H. MONTFORT, Agent,
SACRAMENTO.

San Francisco Directory, 1863, Henry G. Langley

The Overland Mail Co.
Performed Admirably on the Central Route

The Postmaster General was pleased with the level of service provided by the Overland Mail Co. In the Postmaster General's Report of 1863, he wrote: *"The service on this route has been performed during the past year with commendable regularity and efficiency, and no accident, Indian hostility, or other casualty has occurred to prevent or retard the safe and prompt transmission of mails and passengers, the trips being, with rare exception, accomplished within the scheduled time."*

In 1864 The Original Overland Mail Co. Closed
A newly organized Overland Mail Co. Started

The Overland Mail Company that John Butterfield founded closed on June 30, 1864, when the original six year postal contract expired. Mail still needed to be delivered, so the Postmaster General advertised for bids for this new postal contract.

A bid for this contract was made by William Dinsmore

who had just reorganized a new Overland Mail Company with himself as President and only two board members— Danford N. Barney and A. H. Barney.

The *"Annual Report of the Postmaster General of the United States for the fiscal year 1864,"* gives the details: *"The contract for services on the route from the Mississippi River via Salt Lake, to Placerville, California, under act of March 2, 1861, expiring on the 30th of June last, an arrangement was made with the same parties for continuing the service on the same terms to September 30, 1864.*

Under an advertisement dated March 22, 1864, inviting proposals for service from Atchison, Kansas, or St. Joseph, Missouri, to Folsom City, California.

John H. Heistand, of Lancaster, Pennsylvania, was the lowest bidder, at $750,000 per annum; but his bid having been subsequently withdrawn, contracts have been made with Ben Holladay, of New York, for the service between Atchison, or St. Joseph, and Salt Lake City, at $365,000.

Wm. B. Dinsmore, president of the Overland Mail Company, also of New York, from Salt Lake City to Folsom City, at $385,000 making as aggregate of $750,000, per annum.

These parties are believed to be able to fulfill their obligations. The contracts are from October 1, 1864, to September 30, 1868; the trips are to be made in sixteen days eight months in the year, and in twenty days the remaining four months; to convey through letter mails only, mail matter prepaid at letter rates, and all local or way mails. (Annual Report of the Postmaster General for the fiscal year 1864, page 12)

Under the new contract, the Overland stagecoaches would not have to carry the bulky newspapers. The Postmaster General explains:

"Paper and document mails for the Pacific coast are to be carried by sea, via New York and Panama, temporary arrangements having been made for their conveyance, within the sum named in the law of March 25, 1864, viz: $160,000 per annum, making the whole expense of territorial and Pacific mails not over $910,000 per annum, or $90,000 less than under the former contract." (Annual Report of the Postmaster General for the fiscal year 1864, page 12)

The contractors could operate at this reduced price because of the revenue that increasing passenger and express traffic was bringing in. It was even suggested that the route would be profitable to the contractors even without the mail contract. It is also reported that the stagecoaches generally ran full, and that extra coaches were frequently required to carry additional passenger demand. *(The Overland Mail: 1849-1869 - Promoter of Settlement - Precursor of Railroads, by LeRoy Hafen, 1969, Ams Press, page 277)*

Gerald T. Ahnert describes this **"Great Consolidation"** of stage lines by Ben Holladay and then a few weeks later, selling to Wells Fargo & Co:

"In September 1864, Butterfield's six-year mail contract expired on the Central Overland Trail. A new mail contract was needed to continue mail service. While on the Central Overland Trail, William B. Dinsmore had been the president of the Overland Mail Company. In August 1864, when a new mail contract was issued it was signed by William B. Dinsmore, as president, and only two other directors—Danford N. Barney and A. H. Barney.

In 1866, there were three separate stage lines that came under the Overland Mail Company contract. The remnant of the old Butterfield line, which was only enough equipment transferred from the Southern Overland Trail to supply the line from Salt Lake City, Utah, to Virginia City, Nevada. From Virginia City west was the Pioneer Stage Line. From Salt Lake City east was a line run by (The Stagecoach King) Ben Holladay.

In December 1866, Holladay bought out the other lines and achieved the "Great Consolidation." He sold out to Wells Fargo & Co. for $1.5 million in cash and $300,000 in Wells Fargo & Co. stock. He retired shortly after.

In 1867, for the first time the company now had their name "Wells, Fargo & Company" on the transom rail of a stagecoach when they scraped off the name of the Pioneer Stage Line and added their own.

In 1867, for the line, Wells Fargo & Co. ordered 40 mail stagecoaches from Abbot-Downing Co., Concord, New Hampshire. [see painting below]

In 1869, with the completion of the Transcontinental Railroad, stage lines were no longer needed on the Central Overland

Trail, they sold out completely and distributed the proceeds to the stockholders. Shortly after a new company was started with the new name of "Wells, Fargo and Company." The "and" was used instead of "&" for legal purposes with its new charter now in Colorado." [Gerald T. Anhert, email to Bob Crossman, of May 3, 2023]

"A trainload of thirty brand-new Concord Coaches en-route to Wells Fargo's depot at Omaha, Nebraska, in April 1868" John Burgum
According to the Burgum Family History Society, in 1850 John Burgum began working for Abbot-Downing at Concord', having been recruited by George Main, foreman of the paint shops at the Abbot-Downing Coach factory. This paint was based on a photograph taken on April 15th, 1868. The shipment was worth $45,000 including coaches and harnesses. The landscape scenes painted on the door of each stagecoach was by John Burgum, while the scroll work was completed by another ornamentor, Charles Knowlton. [Source: www.burgum-family.co.uk/article_3.php]

The Great Express Consolidation

As Gerald T. Ahnert reported above, this merging of stage companies in 1866 was called "The Great Consolidation." *The New York Times* issue of November 5, 1866 (page 8) reported:

Great Express Consolidation - Another important consolidation of business interests centering in New York has just been effected. The well-known house of WELLS, FARGO & CO., the Overland Mail Company, the Holladay Mail and Express Company, and the Pioneer Stage Company of California have been concreted into one concern. The new Company also becomes a proprietor of all the rights, interests, &c. of the American and United States Express Companies West of the Missouri River, and is, accordingly, sole and exclusive owner of all the express business done between that river and the Pacific Ocean, or between the Atlantic States and the States of the Pacific. Under this consolidation over four thousand miles of stage lines come under control of the new management, an addition to the general express business by sea and land.

The capital of the new Company is $10,000,000. It adopts the old name of WELLS, FARGO & CO. - the late house of that style going into liquidation upon the 1st of the current month. MR. LOUIS McLANE, for many years the Superintendent and manager of WELLS, FARGO & Co.'s business on the Pacific coast, has removed to this city, and as President of the new organization will assume its management. His associate Directors are D. N. BARNEY, A. H. BARNEY, EUGENE KELLY and BEN HOLLADAY. The principal managers of all the old companies retain their respective interests in the present one, and take part in the conduct of its affairs.

All the gold-bearing Territories of the United States, except Arizona, will now be reached and served by the stage lines of WELLS, FARGO & CO., their express and their banking offices. Arrangements are also in progress to extend the fullest benefits of mail and express facilities to China and the East Indies, via the new line of steamships of the Pacific Mail Company." [The New York Times, New York, November 5, 1866, page 8]

Ben Holladay's Overland Stage Company at Idaho's Boise City Post Office
Source: Idaho State Historical Society.

Wells Fargo and Co.
Soon Regretted the Great Consolidation

Waddell F. Smith, great grandson of Pony Express founder William B. Waddell reports:

"With this merger Wells Fargo ceased to be a New York corporation, and the board of directors of the Holladay Overland Mail Company changed the name to 'Wells Fargo and Company,' which corporation is still in existence, and has been in existence without interruption as a Colorado corporation to this day.

This newly merged company inherited the mail contract held by Ben Holladay and, beginning November 1, 1866, operated stage lines in the Middle West between the converging ends of the transcontinental railroad.

Wells Fargo's directors soon realized their mistake and recognized that staging was at sunset. On May 16, 1868, the board directed the president to sell all of the company's stage lines. This short period of stage line operation nearly ruined the company. [Source: The Boom Days of Staging" by Waddell F. Smith, True West magazine, July-August, 1966, page 52]

Localized staging did, however, continue for some time as a service to transport passengers from railroad terminals to more remote areas. ["Boom Days of Staging," page 22]

During the stagecoach era, Wells Fargo's principal business was in the express business in California. When Lloyd Tevis assumed the presidency of Wells Fargo in 1872, he moved the operating headquarters from New York to San Francisco where it remained until 1905 after which it was moved back to New York City. Wells Fargo & Co has, however, been continuously a Colorado corporation from 1866 to date, and was never incorporated in California." ["The Boom Days of Staging," page 53]

In late 1866, after the remnants of Dinsmore's Overland Mail Co. along with other routes were bought out by Holladay, and then Holladay sold out to Wells Fargo - the western terminus of the Central Route was changed from Atchison, Kansas to have two points of departure - one from Junction City, Kansas and a second at Fort Kearney, Nebraska.(see below)

By a recent order of the department, the overland mail route to California, of which Atchison, Kansas, had been the initial point, has been changed so as to have two points of departure—one from Junction City, Kansas, on the Union Pacific railroad route, (eastern division,) running from Wyandotte, Kansas; and the other from Fort Kearney, Nebraska, on the Union Pacific railroad route, running from Omaha City, Nebraska. The lines from these two points meet at Denver City, in Colorado Territory.

The Junction City road connects at Wyandotte with the Pacific railway from St. Louis, Mo., making a continuous railway connection with the eastern cities. By this route the stage travel is diminished one hundred and sixty-eight miles, and the time occupied in the transit should be proportionally reduced. The mails to and from California, which before were sent via Chicago and St. Joseph, were consequently ordered, on the 15th of August last, to be sent via St. Louis, Wyandotte, and Junction City. The reports so far received of the actual running of the mails since the change took effect do not show the average diminution of time in the performance of the through trip which the department was led to expect. ... (Report of The Postmaster General, November 26, 1866, p. 4)

The 1866 advertisement shown below is not from the Wm Dinsmore's reorganized Overland Mail Co. Rather, by 1866 Ben Holladay continued to expand his stagecoach empire and began to use the name Overland Mail Company. This advertisement is for Holladay's various routes under that name before the "Great Consolidation."

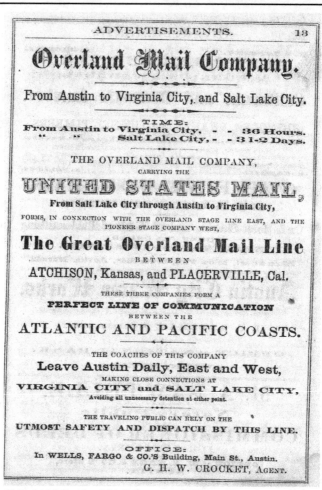

1866 [Ben Holladay's] Overland Mail Company full page advertisement, as it appeared in Harrington's Directory of the City of Austin (Nevada) for the Year 1866 with a Historical and Statistical Review of Austin, and the Reese River Mining Region, by Myron Angel.

The Postmaster General Reported: *"The contracts with Holladay and Dinsmore... expired on"* Sept. 30, 1868. The new contract for the replacement routes were not awarded to Dinsmore or Wells Fargo. *(Report of the Postmaster General for the Fiscal Year 1868, page 6-7.)*

This postcard was postmarked in 1966 with a circular red ink hand stamp: "Pony Express, April 3, St. Joseph." This 1966 postcard was purchased from RKA Covers.

Overland Mail Company's Pony Express

The Pony Express stamps displayed are from the author's personal collection.

John Butterfield is most widely known as the major stockholder of the Overland Mail Co. and its southern ox bow route from San Francisco to Memphis and St. Louis between 1858 and 1861. However, the story of John Butterfield's Overland Mail Company did not end in 1861. Soon, the phrase *"Overland Mail Company's Pony Express"* would be found in the newspapers.

The aim of this chapter is to tell the story of how the Overland Mail Company became responsible for the Pony Express contract.

In 1875, the Harper's New Monthly Magazine reported:

*"The new service consisted of a **pony express**, with stations sixty miles apart, across the continent. A large capital was necessary, and the risks assumed were sufficient to frighten away all but the daring Western speculators. The rate fixed was five dollars **in gold** per quarter ounce, which of course, limited the matter carried to business letters. The eastern terminus of the route was St. Joseph, Missouri, and the western terminus Sacramento. From the latter town to San Francisco the messengers traveled by steamboat, and from St. Joseph to New York by railroad. The time occupied between*

– 95 –

ocean and ocean was fourteen days, and between St. Joseph and San Francisco ten days...

The express was dispatched weekly from each side with not more than ten pounds of matter. The riders chosen were selected from plains-men, trappers, and scouts, familiar with the Indians, and capable of great bodily endurance. In consideration of the danger to which they were exposed, their salary was fixed at the enviable amount of $1200 a month each. [sic. $1200 per year]. The ponies were swift and strong, a cross in breed between the American horse and the Indian pony. Messengers and steeds were run sixty miles, and then awaited the arrival of the express from the opposite direction.

Such was the plan of the Central Overland California and Pike's Peak Express Company; and a memorable day, the 3rd of April, 1860, the first messenger was to start from St. Joseph. The Daily Express of that town issued a 'Pony Express Extra' in honor of the occasion. It was a small single sheet, printed on one side only...

In a cloud of dust, and amidst the loud cheers of the population, the messenger galloped through the straggling streets on to the broad prairies reaching beyond the horizon. The route chosen was somewhat north of the present track of the Pacific Railroad. It lay, as the time-table shows, from St. Joseph to Laramie, thence up the Sweet Water to Salt Lake, and down the Humbolt to Sacramento.

Night and day the express went forward at the greatest speed attainable with ordinary horseflesh. As soon as the station was reached, one messenger, without waiting to dismount, tossed his bag to another already mounted, who in a few minutes was out of sight in the direction of the next relay. So for eight days, with fresh horses and messengers

Genuine Pony Express Stamp
Scott # 143L 1, 1861
APS Certificate #68156

Purchased from Byran J. Sandfield
Parks City Stamps, Dallas

every sixty miles, the ride was continued through the awful canyons of the mother range, up the boulder-strewn foot hills, between forests of hemlock, pine and fir, through hot little mining towns, until Sacramento was reached, scarcely a minute behind the prescribed time.... (Source: Harper's New Monthly Magazine, Aug. 1875, pp. 323-4)

Who Started the Pony Express?

Initially the Pony Express was a completely private enterprise started by Russell, Majors and Waddell.

William H. Russell, Alexander Majors, and William Bradford Waddell
These men were primarily overland freighters. They were also the founders, owners and operators of the Pony Express.

In *"Wells, Fargo & Company 1861 Pony Express Issues"* by Scott R. Trepel, on page 1 it states:

> *"The original owners and operators of the Pony Express were three experienced expressmen, William H. Russell, Alexander Majors and William Waddell, who controlled The Central Overland California & Pikes Peak Express Company (Central Overland). The company needed to win a lucrative government subsidy and launched the Pony Express in April 1860 to promote the efficacy of the Central Route to members of the 36th Congress while they were deliberating the Overland Mail contract.*

Genuine Pony Express Stamp
Scott # 143L 2, 1861
PF Certificate # 93-824

Purchased from Byran J. Sandfield
Parks City Stamps, Dallas

The advertised Pony Express trip was ten days, although in reality many trips took 12 to 13 days, and sometimes longer during the winter months. By linking with telegraph lines at the terminus stations, the Pony Express could convey a message between coasts in as few as ten days. Compared with normal 21-23 day travel time by other routes, this great leap forward in communication speed had practical benefits, but it was also part of Central Overland's public relations and lobbying strategy for winning the mail contract."

Efforts to convince Congress were unsuccessful and pushed Russell to creative financing. On Dec. 24th 1860 Russell was arrested in New York on charges of receiving stolen property ($870,000 worth of bonds) and conspiring to defraud the government. In January - February 1861 he appeared four times before a House Select Committee investigating the scandal. Russell's case was dismissed, but during March 1861 the Butterfield Overland Mail was being moved to the central route, with Russell, Major and Waddell's Central Overland California and Pike's Peak Express Company (C.O.C.&P.P.)getting only the Salt Lake City to St. Joseph part of the route.

At the C.O.C.&P.P. board meeting on April 26th Russell was forced to resign, with attorney Bela M. Hughes becoming President. In 1861 Ben Holladay kept supplying money. By November 1861 Holladay had not been paid, so he filed foreclosure on his claims. An auction was held in March 1862 where Ben Holladay acquired the C.O.C.&P.P. as the only bidder for $100,000.

Richard Frajola writes in *"The Pony Express: A Postal History"* (page 43):

"Ben Holladay assumed effective control of the Central Overland California & Pikes Peak Express after the collapse of Russell, Majors & Waddell in January 1861. After the negotiation of the March 16, 1861 contract between Central Overland California & Pikes Peak Express and Overland Mail Company by Russell, Holladay took complete control by removing Russell and installing his cousin, Bela Hughes, as President on April 26, 1861."

Below is a newspaper announcement, ten days in advance, of the upcoming sale of the Central Overland California and Pike's Peak Express to the highest bidder for cash in hand.

TRUSTEES SALE.

WHEREAS, on the 22d of November. A. D., 1861, the Central Overland California and Pike's Peak Express Company, made, executed, and delivered to the undersigned as Trustees, a deed conveying to said Trustees all the horses, mules, cattle. coach: s. wagons, buggies. setts of harness, hay. grain, provisions, lumber, tools, materials and furniture. held and used by said Company in carrying the overland mail from Atchison in Kansas. to Salt Lake City in Utah, and from Overland City to Denver, and from Denver to Central City and to Tarryall, in Colorado Territory. together with all the stations on said several roads, which said deed is made to secure the payment of a penal bond to Benjamin Holladay, of even date with said deed, for the sum of Four Hundred Thousand Dollars and for the performance of the conditions of said bond and the covenants of said deed. And whereas the conditions of said bond and the covenants of said deed have been broken and said penalty is unpaid ; in pursuance of said deed the undersigned as such Trustees will on Tuesday, he 31st day of December, A. D. 1861. at the Massasoit House. in the city of Atchison, in the State of Kansas, proceed to sell all the above conveyed property in one body to the highest bidder for cash in hand to satisfy the conditions of said deed.

T. F. WARNER, } Trustees.
ROS. L PEASE

Atchison. Dec. 6, 1861.   n43.3w,

Weekly Atchison Champion, Atchison, Kansas, December 21, 1861

"Pursuit of Express Mail-Carriers"
Harper's New Monthly Magazine, Aug. 1875, page 321

THE PONY OVERLAND EXPRESS. — The Central Overland Express Company will start their letter express between San Francisco and New York on Tuesday the third of April next, and it will leave weekly thereafter. Letters will be received in Sacramento until 12 o'clock of each Tuesday night, at the Alta Telegraph office in this city; and telegraphic dispatches will be received at Carson City until 6 P. M. of each Wednesday. The time from San Francisco to New York is for telegraphic dispatches *nine* days, for letters *thirteen* days. Letters will be charged, between San Francisco and Salt Lake City, $3 per half ounce and under, and at that rate according to weight. To all points beyond Salt Lake City, $5 per half ounce and under, and at that rate according to weight. Telegrapic dispatches will be subject to the same charges as letters. All letters must be inclosed in stamped envelopes.

The Sacramento Bee, Tuesday Evening, March 20, 1860, page 1

From the Memoir of Alexander Majors

Alexander Majors, one of the founders of the Pony Express, recorded his life story in the 1893 book, *"Seventy Years on the Frontier: Alexander Majors' Memoirs of a Lifetime on the Border."*

[NOTE: Scott Alumbaugh, author of *On the Pony Express Trail*, points out that Majors's memoir was funded by Buffalo Bill who (1) made sure his publisher would publish the book, and (2) hired Prentiss Ingram, a dime store novelist, to edit and possibly ghostwrite the book for Majors. This resulted in exaggerations about the quality of the horses, the role of Buffalo Bill Cody, just to name two. The closest Buffalo Bill Cody came to being a Pony Express rider was his employment as a messenger for Russell, Majors & Waddell for two months in 1857, at the age of 11 and 12.]

Alexander Majors

Alexander Majors
"Seventy Years on the Frontier:
Alexander Major's Memoirs" 1893

In chapter nineteen and twenty-one, he tells the story of Russell, Majors & Waddell. In 1859 they obtained a daily stage line from Atchison to Denver that had been started by W. H. Russell and John S. Jones. A few months later Russell and Jones bought out the semi-monthly line of Hockaday & Liggett, running from St. Joseph to Salt Lake City, thinking that blending the two lines might bring in enough business to cover expenses.

Majors writes: *"This we failed in, for the lines, even after being blended, did not nearly meet expenses."*

Majors continues his story: *"As soon as we bought them out we built good stations and stables every ten to fifteen miles all the way from Missouri to Salt Lake, and supplied them with hay and grain for the horses and provisions for the men, so they would only have to drive a team from one station to the next, changing at every station."* (page 166)

"Instead of our schedule time being twenty-two days, as it was with Hockaday & Liggett, and running two per month, we ran a stage each way every day and make the schedule time ten days, a distance of 1,200 miles. We continued this line from the summer of

1859 until March, 1862, when it fell into the hands of Ben Holladay. From the summer of 1859 to 1862 the line was run from Atchison to Fort Kearney and from Fort Kearney to Fort Laramie, up the Sweet Water route and South Pass, and on to Salt Lake City." (page 166)

"We had on this line about one thousand Kentucky mules and 300 smaller-sized mules to run on through the mountain portion of the line, and large number of Concord coaches." (page 166)

"This is the route also run by the **Pony Express**, each pony starting from St. Joseph instead of Atchison, Kansas from which the stages started." (page 166) "Mr. Russell proposed to cover this distance with a mail line between St. Joseph, Mo., and San Francisco, that would deliver letters at either end of the route within ten days. Five hundred of the fleetest horses to be procured were immediately purchased, and the services of over two hundred competent men were secured. Eighty of these men were selected for express riders. Light-weights were deemed the most eligible for the purpose; the lighter the man the better for the horse, as some portions of the route had to be traversed at a speed of twenty miles an hour. Relays were established at stations, the distance between which was, in each instance, determined by the character of the country." (page 173-174)

"... At each station a sufficient number of horses were kept, and at every third station the thin, wiry and hardy pony-riders held themselves in readiness to press forward with the mails... The men were faithful, daring fellows, and their service was full of novelty and adventure." (page 174) ...Not only were they remarkable for lightness of weight and energy, but their service required continued vigilance, bravery, and agility. (page 175)

Among the most noted and daring riders of the Pony Express was Honorable **William F. Cody,**

Wm Cody "Buffalo Bill"
"Seventy Years on the Frontier: Alexander Major's Memoirs" 1893

better known as Buffalo Bill, *whose reputation is now established the world over."* (page 176)

"*Only two minutes were allowed at stations for changing the mails and horses. Everybody was on the qui vive." "... The riders received from $120 to $125 per month for their arduous services."* (page 175)

**Genuine Pony Express Stamp
Scott # 143L 3, 1861**

Purchased from Byran J. Sandfield Parks City Stamps, Dallas

"*The Pony Express enterprise continued for about two years, at the end of which time telegraph services between the Atlantic and Pacific oceans was established."* (page 175) "*It so transpired that the firm of Russell, Majors & Waddell had to pay the fiddler, or the entire expenses of organizing both the stage line and the Pony Express, at a loss, as it turned out, of hundreds of thousands of dollars.* (page 167)

After the United States mail was given this line it became a paying institution, but it went into the hands of Holliday (sic) *just before the first quarterly payment of $100,000 was made. The Government paid $800,000 a year for carrying the mails from San Francisco to Missouri, made in quarterly payments."* (page 167)

"*The part of the line that Russell, Majors & Waddell handled received $400,000 and Butterfield and Co received $400,000 for carrying the mails from Salt Lake to California."* (page 167)

Majors includes a statement by former employee J. G. Kelley:

"*I want to say one good word for our bosses, Messrs. Russell, Majors & Waddell. The boys had the greatest veneration for them because of their general good treatment at their hands... Russell, Majors & Waddell were God-fearing, religious, and temperate themselves, and were careful to engage none in their employ who did not come up to their standard of morality. Calf-bound Bibles were distributed by them to every employee. The one given to me was kept till 1881 when I presented it to Masonic Lodge #35 of Leadville, Colorado."*
["Seventy Years on the Frontier: Alexander Major's Memoirs" 1893, by Alexander Major page 192]

Did Wells Fargo Own
Butterfield's Overland Mail & the Pony Express?

Wells Fargo & Co. **never** owned The Pony Express or John Butterfield's Overland Mail Company. However, three years after the end of Butterfield's Overland Mail Co., in 1867 after buying almost all the western stage line companies from Ben Holladay, Wells Fargo did operate the world's largest passenger stagecoach line from April 1867 to 1869.

In 1861 Wells Fargo & Co. did have an arrangement with the Overland Mail Company to collect mail from across California, and carry transcontinental letters to the Placerville, California terminus to meet Overland Mail Company stages and the Pony Express horses.

Genuine Pony Express Stamp
Scott # 143L 4, 1861

Purchased from Byran J. Sandfield
Parks City Stamps, Dallas

The Overland Mail Company and Wells Fargo & Co., American Express, Adams Express, and others shared several directors and stockholders. In spite of these several ways the companies were interconnected, they remained separate entities.

How Did the Overland Mail Company Get Involved With the Pony Express?

John Butterfield was impressed with the Pony Express. As early as March of 1860, the newspapers were reporting plans of the Overland Mail Co. to offer a competing Horse Express to California.

> OVERLAND ROUTE. —Butterfield & Co., have for some time been maturing a plan for running a horse express from Syracuse, the terminus of the Pacific Railroad, to San Francisco; and there is reason to believe that it will soon be in operation.

The Mountain Democrat, Placerville, California, March 24, 1860

Anthony Godfrey, in the *Historic Research Study Pony Express National Historic Trail* (page 68) writes:

> "*So successful did the Pony Express appear during the first few weeks of operation, that it was rumored as early as April 14, 1860, that the Butterfield Overland Mail Company planned on starting their own horse express to compete with Russell, Majors, and Waddell.*
>
> *Reportedly, the Butterfield express proposed covering the 1,500 miles between Fort Smith, Arkansas, and Los Angeles in five or six days, and transmitting telegraph messages between these two points.*
>
> *Not to be outdone, C.O.C. & P.P. Express Co. agents confidently promised they would compete by establishing a similar enterprise reaching California in four and a half days, whether or not the telegraph was extended further westward from St. Joseph, Missouri.*"

On April 14, 1860, *The Sacramento Bee*, Sacramento, California reported that Butterfield's Overland Mail Co. started a Horse Express on the same day as the Pony Express, and that it was soundly beaten by the Pony Express. No additional primary sources mention such a competition, and this may have been a false rumor that spread in the press.

"Arrival of the Pony Express at Sacramento City, and Enthusiastic Reception"
The New-York Illustrated News, May 19, 1860, page 21

NOT HEARD FROM YET.—The other Pony Express—that by the Southern or Butterfield route—has not yet been heard from. Our readers are perhaps aware that two Pony Expresses started from St. Louis, on April 2d, both for San Francisco, one by the Central and one by the Southern route, on a trial of speed, or test of routes. The news of the former was published all over the State yesterday morning, and the pony itself reached San Francisco last night, and the latter was not yet *The*

Sacramento Bee, Sacramento, California, April 14, 1860, page 2

In fact, one month later a Superintendent of the Butterfield revealed that the idea of a horse express was waiting for the telegraph to reach Fort Smith and Los Angeles. *"A correspondent of the S. F. Alta, writing from St. Louis May 5th says: ...*

"There is scarcely a doubt, that when this is done [telegraph to reach Fort Smith], *that the Butterfield Company will put on a **horse express**, between the two points, that will beat anything ever heard of, in the way of fast riding. One of the Superintendents, who was in the city recently, stated that a careful calculation had been made, by request of the managers of the Co., in New York, and that five days was the extreme limit given for the enterprise. There are portions of the route, now, where coaches are dragged along at the rate of twelve miles an hour, and the Superintendent says horses can*

Genuine Pony Express Stamp
Scott # 143L 5, 1861

Purchased from Byran J. Sandfield Parks City Stamps, Dallas

be put through over the places, by one change, at twenty miles an hour. The distance between Fort Smith and Los Angeles is 1,500 miles, and the calculation is to make 300 miles per day, which is only 13½ miles per hour, an undertaking that seems insignificant, when the energy and ability of the Company are considered."
[Daily Alta California, San Francisco]

Forgery A, pg. 1147 Lyons Vol 3
Scott # 143L 6, 1861

Purchased from Bob Miller, Lyn Co. Stamps, Lincoln, NE

This plan never got off the ground. While the above May 5th report was positive, by May 9, 1860, *The Red Bluff Beacon* (Red Bluff, California, page 1) was reporting that John Butterfield had been *"deposed from the Presidency and superseded by Wm. B. Dinsmore."*

The paper goes on to speculate, an unsubstantiated rumor, stating:

> Probably one cause of difference between the retiring President and his co-laborers, was the Pony Express. It has been understood for a long time that Mr. Butterfield wished to start a horse express for the conveyance of valuable packages, but was opposed by others in the Company.

The Red Bluff Beacon, Red Bluff, California, May 9, 1860, page 1

The Nov. 11, 1860 issue of *The Marysville Appeal*, (Marysville, California, page 3) reported that the Pony Express was planning a special trip to carry the anticipated results of the Presidential election. Also, concerning the possibility of a 'competing' horse express on this occasion over the Butterfield route, the company is *"exceedingly mum on the subject."*

> Mail coach. We have as yet received no positive information regarding the transmission of any Presidential election news by horse express on the Butterfield route, and if the company proposes to try it, they are exceedingly mum on the subject

The Marysville Appeal, Marysville, California, Nov. 11, 1860, page 3

Although John Butterfield's plans for a Horse Express over the Southern Route never materialized, Overland Mail Company would soon have a contract to oversee and continue the Pony Express over the Central Route until the continental telegraph was completed.

Anthony Godfrey, *Historic Research Study Pony Express National Historic Trail*, p. 86-87, states:

"On March 2nd [after Confederate troops had destroyed Butterfield's line in Missouri and Texas], to solve the contracting predicament with the C.O.C. & P.P. Express Co. and Overland Mail Company, and to protect communication lines with California, both houses of Congress, with President Buchanan's approval, modified the Overland Mail Company mail service contract by discontinuing the transportation of mail along the southern route and transferring it to a new central overland route.

This new service would originate in St. Joseph, (or Atchison) Kansas and provide mail service to Placerville, California, six times a week. **In addition to this new route, the contract required that the company 'run a pony express semi-weekly at a schedule time of ten days . . . charging the public for transportation of letters by said express not exceeding $1 per half ounce' until the completion of the transcontinental telegraph line.**

Essentially the federal government turned over the western half of the central route mail contract (Salt Lake City to Placerville, California) that the C.O.C. & P.P. Express Co. previously operated, over to the Overland Mail Company. In exchange for giving this segment of the passenger/mail route to the Overland Mail Company, the government promised to indirectly support the Pony Express until the completion of the telegraph."

What Did Pony Express Mail Cost?

In the very beginning, Russell, Majors & Co. charged $5 per half ounce. $5 in 1860 is equivalent in purchasing power to about $181 in 2023.

In August 1860 the rate was changed to $2.50 per quarter ounce. And in April 1861 to $2 per half ounce.

Once the Pony Express was receiving a Government subsidy, starting July 1, 1861 during the Overland Mail Co. contract, a Pony Express letter cost $1 per half ounce, 10¢ for US mail. An additional 10¢ fee if Wells Fargo carried the letter to Placerville, and later the fee was 25¢ or only 20¢ if the letter was enclosed in a preprinted Wells Fargo envelope. If the postal system carried the letter to Placerville, no additional fee was charged since the required 10¢ US stamp covered delivery to and from the Pony Express.

When did Butterfield subcontract the operation of the Pony Express?

As Anthony Godfrey mentioned in the above passage, the Act of Congress of March 2, 1861 (the Post Office Appropriation Bill) ended the Southern Overland Mail Route. On March 16, 1861, with California Senator Milton Latham acting as moderator, the Overland Mail Co. sub-contracted the Pony Express route from St. Joseph to Sacramento (the Central Overland California and Pike's Peak Express Co. had already been operating the Pony Express since April 3, 1860); and the stagecoach route from Atchison, Kansas to Salt Lake City to the C.O.C. & P.P. Express Co. to receive the sum of $475,000 per year. The Overland Mail Co. would operate from Salt Lake City to Placerville as the new western terminus for the $525,000 balance of the $1 million annual sum.

The Pioneer Stage Co. already had a contract to carry the mail from Sacramento over the Sierra mountains to Carson City/Virginia City, Nevada.

The Sacramento Valley Railroad had been carrying mail to Folsom part of the way from Sacramento to Placerville. It is interesting to note that Pioneer Stage Company used river steamboats to carry the mail between Sacramento and San Francisco for 19 months from April 3, 1860 to Nov. 20, 1861. According to Joe Nardone, former Executive Director of the Pony Express Trail Association, the Pony Express made twenty trips on land between Sacramento and San Francisco because the rider arrived too late to catch the steamboat.

[See Butterfield Contract March 3, 1857 in Appendix B & S]
[See Central Route March 2, 1861, March 12, 1861 and March 16, 1861 documents in Appendix L, M & N]

DAILY OVERLAND MAIL.—The daily Overland Mail service commences from Pla cerville on Monday. The Pony Express as heretofore, will run semi-weekly. The charg- es for half ounce letters per Pony will be one dollar.

The Placer Herald, Auburn, Placer County, California, June 29, 1861

MISCELLANEOUS.—W. H. Russell, the founder of the Pony Express has conclu- ded a contract with the Overland Mail Company—transferred by the last Con- gress to the Central Route—to run the mail and Pony from the Missouri river, connecting with the Overland company at Salt Lake city.

Marysville Daily Appeal, Marysville, CA, April 6, 1861, Saturday, Page 2

New Route Occasionally Still Called "Butterfield's"

By this time, board member John Butterfield had been replaced as board president by William Dinsmore. However, the Overland Mail Co. was still frequently referred to as *"The Butterfield:'* An example of this is found in the June 11, 1861, *Sacramento Daily Union*, which refers to "the Butterfield new route" and "the Butterfield Company."

Why is "Wells Fargo" on the Pony Express Stamps?

Soon the Pony Express would be known as *"The Overland Mail Company's Pony Express."* The postage stamps used by the Pony Express, however, have the words *"Wells Fargo & Co"* on the bottom of each stamp, and this has resulted in a great deal of confusion. As Richard Frajola writes in *"The Pony*

Express: A Postal History" (page v), there were *"complex and evolving relationships between the operators, owners and managers of the Pony Express."*

The Pony Express ran between Atchison (or St. Joseph), Kansas and Placerville, California. This left a void between San Francisco and Placerville. About April, 1861 Wells, Fargo & Company was appointed as agent to operate a private express horse service between San Francisco and Placerville to connect with the Pony Express. In this arrangement, Wells Fargo assumed the responsibility for collecting and delivering the mail to and from Placerville.

As part of this arrangement, Well, Fargo & Company began issuing special Pony Express adhesive stamps and franked envelopes. Very few of the printed franked envelopes have survived. The May 8, 1861, San Francisco Daily Alta California describes the envelopes:

WELLS, FARGO & Co.'s PONY EXPRESS ENVELOPES – The new style of Pony Express Envelopes with Wells, Fargo & Co.'s express mark upon the margin, bears a very elegant and tasteful design – a combination of red letters reading each way: "W. F. & Co., ½ ounce, paid from St. Joseph to Placerville, per Pony Express." Wells, Fargo & Co. have charge of the Pony Express henceforth until the first of July, when it becomes a portion of the great Daily Overland Mail arrangement, of which they are the managers on this side."

WF&Co. envelope image from
Richard Frajola's Pony Census

After April 15, 1861, mail intended for the Pony Express was collected throughout California at Wells Fargo offices and forwarded to the San Francisco and Sacramento Wells Fargo offices. Twice a week these envelopes were carried to Placerville from San Francisco and Sacramento by Wells Fargo. These envelopes received an adhesive Pony Express stamp. They also received a blue oval "Paid" hand stamp to indicate that the sender also paid the additional route charges for Wells Fargo to carry the letter to the Pony Express Terminus at Placerville.

– 111 –

Pony Express Stamps Are Not Really Stamps

"Stamps" are officially issued by the US Postal Service to cover the cost of postage.
For the Pony Express, "Franks" are privately issued to indicate payment of the fee.

Waddell F. Smith, historian and collector, was the great grandson of William B. Waddell, member of freighting firm of Russell, Majors and Waddell, founders of Pony Express.

In his article,"*The Boom Days of Staging,*" (True West, July-August, 1966) Waddell tells the story: "*About six months before the close of the Pony Express, Mr. Russell appointed Wells Fargo and Company as local agent at Sacramento and San Francisco. Wells Fargo soon had the Pony Express 'stamps' printed for the use of their customers.*

Actually, they were not stamps but 'franks,' *and their use only indicated that the Pony Express fee had been paid to the agent. Wells Fargo then paid the fee to the Pony Express. In addition, the Post Office Department required that each letter should carry a 10¢ postage stamp.*

These so-called Pony Express franks only came into use at the very last, but after the close of the Pony Express, Wells Fargo officials gave them away freely, and since that time they have turned up in quantities in the philatelic sales.

In recent years what might seem to be an abnormal number of Pony Express covers have turned up, with Wells Fargo adhesive franks thereon, some of them with apparently falsified handstamp cancellations.

The prevalence of these has been such as to cast doubt on any and all Pony Express covers bearing these franks. When the regular fee was paid direct to the Pony Express, only the rubber handstamps were applied.

No Wells Fargo franks were ever used on letters from east to west. Some were used at the very last on eastbound letters by Wells Fargo as agent, but only for its own customers. There are those who doubt if any were ever used.

It is certain, however, that these "stamps," actually franks, were printed. And it is also certain that they were counterfeited in Germany and that they were reprinted in 1897 in San Francisco. Claim

– 112 –

has been made that these franks were issued by Wells Fargo to meet the requirements of the Postmaster General but they were actually receipts for advance express charges paid to the agent.

The use of these franks and the agency connection of Wells Fargo Express have given the impression that Wells Fargo operated the Pony Express. Nothing could be farther from the truth..."[Source: The Boom Days of Staging" by Waddell F. Smith, True West magazine, July-August, 1966, pages 22-24, 50, 52-53]

Five Examples of Forgery 'Franks'

Forgery of $2 Frank
The official were in red ink
Scott # 143L 1, 1861

Purchased from Paul Williams,
Rochford, Essex, England

Forgery of $2 Frank
The official were in red ink
Scott # 143L 1, 1861

Purchased from Paul Williams,
Rochford, Essex, England

Forgery of $4 Frank
The official are green ink
Scott # 143L 2, 1861

Purchased from
Paul Williams,
Rochford, Essex, England

Forgery of $4 Frank
Forgery B2, according to
Larry Lyons p.1133
Scott # 143L 2, 1861

Purchased from
S & P Stamps, Salina, KS

Forgery of $1 Frank
Forgery B, according to
Larry Lyons p.1147
Scott # 143L 6, 1883

Purchased from
Bob Miller, LynCo Stamps
Lincoln, Nebraska

The Overland Mail Company's Pony Express?

In *"The Pony Express History"* by Richard C. Frajola, George J. Kramer, and Steven C. Walske, on page 51, it states: *"The advertisement at right, from the June 26, 1861 San Francisco Evening Bulletin, includes some very interesting information. The top segment of the advertisement states that the Pony Express is* **"The Overland Mail Company's Pony Express"** *and is signed by William Buckley, Superintendent, Overland Mail Co.*

San Francisco Evening Bulletin, June 26, 1861

This June 26, 1861 advertisement further states that:

"Messrs. Wells Fargo & Co. have been appointed agents and letters will be received and delivered at their offices."

This advertisement describes the relationship between the two companies as one of Wells Fargo acting as agent for the Overland Mail Company. The lower segment of the advertisement includes:

"Connecting with the Overland Mail Company's Pony Express at Placerville. Letters must been closed in our twenty cent government franked envelopes and charges from Placerville prepaid at the rate of one dollar for each half ounce, or any fraction thereof. All letters not enclosed as above will be charged at the rate of 25 cents each."

Use of Wells Fargo to reach the Pony Express in Placerville was optional. For the extra ten cents, Wells Fargo may have carried the senders mail to Placerville faster, but the post office system was still available for no additional fee. On July 6, 1861 *The Sacramento Bee* explained that senders had a choice of using Wells Fargo or the post office to meet the Pony Express.

The Pony and Wells, Fargo & Co.

It was stated in yesterday's BEE that a party in San Francisco complained that Wells, Fargo & Co., who are agents in this State for the Pony Express, charge—in addition to the dollar Pony postage and the Government ten cent stamp—twelve and a half cents for one of their own envelopes, which he contended was contrary to the contemplation of the law, etc. The Pony runs from St. Joseph to Placerville only, and it is for conveying the letter by fast express to Placerville and from St. Joseph that Wells, Fargo & Co. make this extra charge, which is but their ordinary tariff on letters conveyed by them within this State.

_____ ___ ___ the dollar Pony postage, put

ua charge, which is ~~~ ~~~~~

on letters conveyed by them within this State. A man may pay the dollar Pony postage, put on the Government stamp, and deposit his letter in any post office. This will carry it by regular mail to Placerville, where it will be transferred to the Pony and conveyed by it to St. Joseph, where it will again take the course of the regular mail: but if he purchase a Wells, Fargo & Co's envelope, they will take charge of it on both ends to the extent of their routes, and put it through in the quickest time possible. Besides, they will run a Sunday express between San Francisco and Placerville, which will be much expense—for there is no Sunday mail—and the entire funds received by them on these letters will not begin to meet the outlays necessary for this new enterprise. In justice to them we make this explanation. The public will see that they do not attempt any imposition. It is their regular charge for like services, and if any one don't want to employ them, the post office is open.

The Sacramento Bee, Sacramento California, July 6, 1861 page 2

Production of the Stamps

Starting July 1, 1861 the Pony Express was no longer a private enterprise, and the Postal System set the rates. This change in rate required Wells Fargo & Co. to order new stamps: $1 in red, $2 in green, and $4 in black. These stamps were used almost exclusively on eastbound Pony Express mail when Wells Fargo had served as the agent to carry the letter across California to meet up with the Pony Express at Placerville, California.

All of the Pony Express stamps were lithographed from stones. The original copper engraving was done by Jacques J.

Rey of Britton & Co., San Francisco. From this copper die, an impression was made on the lithographic transfer paper, then transferred to the printing stone to yield the forty stamps on each printed sheet. [Source: *The Pony Express*, Collectors Club Handbook No. 15, by M. C. Nathan and W. S. Boggs, 1962, page 45, 68]

This sheet of forty $1 stamps was printed in 1861. This sheet is one of only four known to survive. The $2 and $4 stamps were printed twenty to a sheet. The sheet shown above was sold in the Siegel Auctions on February 25, 2020 for $4,500.
Sadly, this sheet is not in the author's collection.

Brief Central Route Time Line

1860 **Jan.-March, 1860:** The private firm "Russell, Majors and Waddell" sets out to add a new service to their stagecoach and mail enterprise within the Central Overland California & Pikes Peak Express Company. That new service, a completely private enterprise, was to be called The Pony Express.

April 3, 1860: The first Pony Express rider left St. Joseph, Missouri at 5:00 pm. The mail pouch *(mochila)* arrived in Sacramento, California ten days later on April 14th. During the first few months, additional stations were added as needed, so eventually riders stopped at swing stations which on average were 10 to 15 miles apart. The National Pony Express Association website records that there may have been as many as 190 different stations used at various times along the route.

April 3, 1860: Initial rate $5.00 per ½ ounce.*

July 31 1860: Additional rate introduced of $2.50 per ¼ ounce.**

Dec. 24, 1860: Russell was arrested in New York on charges of receiving stolen property ($870,000 worth of bonds) and conspiring to defraud the government.

1861   **Jan.-Feb. 1861:** Russell appears four times before a House Select Committee investigating the funding scandal. Russell's criminal case dismissed.

March 2, 1861 Congress agrees to financially support the Pony Express, under a contract with the Overland Mail Company who is also to run a stagecoach with mail six days a week over the same route to start July 1, 1861.

March 16, 1861: The Overland Mail Co. subcontracts the eastern portion of the route and the Pony Express back to the Central Overland California & Pikes Peak Express Company.

April 1, 1861: For three months, April 1 to June 30, 1861, the Pony Express continues as a joint operation of the Overland Mail Company and the Central Overland California & Pikes Peak Express Company, with Wells Fargo acting as agent.*

April 1, 1861: Rate reduced to $2.00 per ½ ounce.*

April 26, 1861: Central Overland Co. Board met and Russell resigned, with attorney Bela M. Hughes becoming President.

July 1 to Oct. 31, 1861: Pony Express becomes a government mandated postal service operating in conjunction with Wells Fargo's private service between San Francisco and Placerville.*

July 1, 1861: Rate reduced to $1.00 per ½ ounce.*

Sept. 23, 1861: Atchison replaced St. Joe as eastern terminus.

Oct. 24, 1861: The Pony Express is discontinued, because as of this date, both the east and west coast are finally linked up by the trans-continental telegraph line.

Oct. 26, 1861: Last eastbound Pony Express trip.*

Oct. 31, 1861: Last westbound Pony Express trip.* Between July 1, 1861 and October 31, 1861 during Butterfield's time of oversight, *"there were thirty five westbound trips from St. Joseph orf Atchison, including two trips that were likely carried by stage. An average of 141 letters were carried per trip."***

1862   **1862:** The Overland Mail Co. stagecoaches continue to run between St. Joseph, Missouri and Placerville, California under Postal contract #10773.

March 1862: Ben Holladay had provided the Central Overland Co. with significant funding. In Nov. he foreclosed on his unpaid claims and in March an auction is held where Ben Holladay acquired the Central Overland Co. for $100,000.

1863   **1863:** The Overland Mail Co. stagecoaches continue to run between St. Joseph, Missouri and Placerville, California under Postal contract #10773.

1864   **July 1, 1864:** Butterfield's Overland Mail Co.'s postal contract #10773 to carry the mails over the Central Route expires.

Source: The Pony Express: A Postal History by Richard C. Frajola,
    George J. Kramer, and Steven C. Walske, page 3.
**Source: San Francisco's *Daily Alta California*, August 13, 1860; and a note
    signed by Wm Russell reproduced in *The Pony Express: A Postal
    History* by Richard C. Frajola, George J. Kramer, and Steven C.
    Walske, page 25.
***Source: *The Pony Express: A Postal History* by Richard C. Frajola,
    George J. Kramer, and Steven C. Walske, page 59.

Genuine Pony Express Stamp
Scott # 143L 7, 1861

Purchased from Byran J. Sandfield
Parks City Stamps, Dallas

Genuine Pony Express Stamp
Scott # 143L 8, 1862-1864
APS Certificate # 68234

Purchased from Byran J. Sandfield
Parks City Stamps, Dallas

Genuine Pony Express Stamp
Scott # 143L 9, 1862-1864

Purchased from John A. Hunter
The Stamp Professor, St. Augustine

The 10¢ and two 25¢ Pony Express stamps shown above were never used on the Central Route. Rather, they were used exclusively for the Virginia City Pony Express, which offered 24 hour service between San Francisco and Virginia City. It was in operation from August 11, 1862 to March 2, 1865, with a July 29 to December 29, 1864 hiatus.

PONY EXPRESS.

NINE DAYS FROM SAN FRANCISCO TO NEW YORK.

THE CENTRAL OVER-LAND PONY EXPRESS COMPANY will start their LETTER EXPRESS from San Francisco to New York and intermediate points

ON TUESDAY..............**APRIL 3, 1860,**

And upon EVERY TUESDAY thereafter, at four o'clock P. M.

Letters will be received at SACRAMENTO until twelve o'clock every Tuesday night.

OFFICE—Alta Telegraph Office, Second st.

Telegraph Dispatches will be received at Carson City until six o'clock P. M. every Wednesday.

SCHEDULE TIME FROM SAN FRANCISCO TO NEW YORK.

For Telegraph Dispatches........Nine Days
For Letters....................Thirteen Days

Letters will be charged, between San Francisco and Salt Lake City, $3 per half ounce and under, and at that rate according to weight.

To all points beyond Salt Lake City, $5 per half ounce and under, and at that rate according to weight.

Telegraphic Dispatches will be subject to the same charges as letters.

All letters must be inclosed in stamped envelopes.

WM. W. FINNEY,
m21-1m   Agent C. O. P. E. Company.

The Sacramento Bee, Sacramento, California, March 23, 1860

PONY EXPRESS.

CHANGE OF SCHEDULE!

ON AND AFTER THE FIRST DAY OF DECEMBER NEXT, the Schedule time of the EXPRESS will be changed, and run as follows :

Fifteen Days between St. Joseph and San Francisco.

Eleven Days between Fort Kearny and outer Telegraph Stations in Utah.

This Schedule will be continued (running as now semi-weekly trips) during the winter, or until Congress shall provide for a tri weekly mail service, which alone will enable the Company to return to the present or a shorter Schedule. the present mail service between Julesburg and Placerville, being only semi-monthly, which is not sufficient to keep the route open during winter.

W. C. MARLEY,
General Agent for the Pacific.

Sacramento, Nov. 30, 1860.   d8 3w

The Mountain Democrat, Placerville, California, December 12, 1860

PONY EXPRESS.

EIGHT DAYS FROM SAN FRANCIS- CO TO NEW YORK.

THE PONY EXPRESS OF THE CENTRAL OVER-LAND CALIFORNIA & PIKE'S PEAK EXPRESS COMPANY, will leave San Francisco for New York and intermediate points

ON FRIDAY.................APRIL 20, 1860,

And upon EVERY FRIDAY thereafter, at four o'clock P. M.

Letters will be received at SAN FRANCISCO until four o'clock P. M., each day of departure.

OFFICE—Alta Telegraph Office,

153 Montgomery street, corner of Merchant:

AT SACRAMENTO, until twelve o'clock the same night.

OFFICE—Alta Telegraph Office, Second st.

AT PLACERVILLE, until six A. M., every Saturday.
Office—Alta Telegraph Office.

AT GENOA, until seven o'clock, P. M., every Saturday.
Office—Placerville and St. Joseph Telegraph Office.

AT CARSON CITY, until eight o'clock P. M., every Saturday.
Office Placerville and St. Joseph Telegraph Office.

Telegraph Dispatches will be received at Carson City until 7½ o'clock P. M. every Saturday.

SCHEDULE TIME FROM SAN FRANCISCO.

For Telegraph Dispatches.......Eight Days
For Letters.....................Twelve Days

Letters will be charged to any point on this side of Salt Lake $3 per half ounce and under, and at that rate according to weight.

To all points beyond Salt Lake City, $5 per half ounce and under, and at that rate according to weight.

☞ All letters must be enclosed in Government envelops.

The Pony Express charges on each Telegraphic Dispatch (of any number of words) intended to be transmitted by Telegraph from St. Joseph, will be $2 45—the tariff due the Telegraph Companies on either end will of course be added.

WM. W. FINNEY, General Agent
J. W. COLEMAN, Agent for Sacramento.

N. B.—The public will understand that by telegraphing to Carson City, twenty-seven and one-half hours' later intelligence can be sent to St. Joseph, Mo., than by letter from San Francisco. A dispatch to Carson City may be forwarded to St. Joseph to be sent on from that point by telegraph, or to be committed the United States Mail as a letter, in which latter case it will be charged as a letter over the Pony Express Route. [a17] W. W. F.

The Sacramento Bee, Sacramento, California, April 23, 1860

PONY EXPRESS.

CHANGE OF TAR- IFF.—We will hereafter forward LETTERS at **$2 50** per QUARTER OUNCE, charging the same for each additional ¼ ounce and fraction of ¼ ounce.

WM. W. FINNEY,
J. W. COLEMAN, General Agent.
Agent at Sacramento. a14-1w

The Sacramento Bee, Sacramento, California, August 15, 1860

Pony Express Ended October 24, 1861
With Completion of the Telegraph

"The Overland Pony Express" Harper's Weekly, Nov. 2, 1867
Photographed by Savage, Salt Lake City, From a Painting by George M. Ottinger.

FIRST HAND REPORT
OF TELEGRAPH'S CONSTRUCTION:
"Wiring A Continent:
The making of the U.S. transcontinental telegraph line"
by James Gamble
(Originally published in *The Californian* magazine, 1881)

"...the work of construction was to be commenced without delay. The material was ordered, and preparations were made to complete the entire line before the close of 1861. The work on the eastern end was under the superintendence and general direction of Edward Creighton, while the construction from this end was directed by the writer. The lines of the California State Telegraph Company had already been extended as far as Virginia City after the consolidation of the lines, and it was decided that the work of extending the overland telegraph was to commence at Carson City. Part of the wire and insulators had in the meantime been ordered from the East, and were shipped round by Cape Horn. The next most important item of material was the poles. These had to be hauled on wagons and distributed along the route from Carson City to Salt Lake, a distance of six hundred miles. As there was not a stick of timber in sight throughout the entire distance, it seemed at first a mystery how they were to be procured, and the work finished within the time named.

...Early in the spring of 1861 I was authorized by the company to fit out an expedition and commence the work of construction. It was estimated that it would take twenty-six wagons to carry the material and supplies across the Sierra Nevada Mountains, and these I was instructed to purchase, together with the necessary animals to move them. This was accomplished and the expedition was ready to move on the 27th of May, 1861. It

comprised 228 oxen, 26 wagons, 50 men, and several riding-horses. ... In the meantime, the poles were being distributed from both ends of the line of route, and, as the wire and insulators for the eastern end had been ordered shipped from the Missouri river to Salt Lake, the work began energetically from both ends. ...

Deserts had to be crossed, which in many cases taxed the efforts and strength of the expedition to its very utmost. In one instance sixteen miles of line were built in one day, in order to reach a point where water could be obtained. As the weather was extremely hot, teams with barrels of water had to he kept with the different parties when crossing these deserts. ... the opening of the great trans-continental telegraph line which took place on the evening of October 24th, 1861."

Within days of the Telegraph's completion, the Overland Mail Co.'s Pony Express ceased operations, but Overland Mail Co. daily stagecoaches continued to run along the same Central Route's stations until the contract ended July 1, 1864.

Linemen stringing telegraph wire beside the transcontinental railroad on the Great Plains, 1860s. Hand-colored woodcut of a 19th-century illustration

Pony Express Ended October 24, 1861
But Wells Fargo Express
Continued to Operate

Wells Fargo Express Co. Deadwood S.D. Treasure Wagon with $250,000 in gold, 1890

Wells Fargo & Co. never owned The Pony Express or John Butterfield's (or Wm Dinsmore's) Overland Mail Company.

However, *Wells Fargo & Co.* did have an arrangement with the *Overland Mail Co.* to collect mail from across California, and carry transcontinental letters to the Placerville, California terminus to meet the Overland Mail Company stages or Pony Express horses.

Wells Fargo & Co. also designed special stamps to be used when they carried newspaper.

Scott # 143 LP5, 1861
*Purchased from Stan Iceland,
Seal Beach, California*

Scott # 143 LP7, 1883
*Purchased from Stan Iceland,
Seal Beach, California*

**Genuine, Type I, page 1161 in Lyons
Scott # 143 LP9, 1883**
*Purchased from F. A. Stamps
Shalimar, Florida*

**Genuine, page 1152 in Lyons
Scott # 143 LP10, 1876**
*Purchased from Stan Iceland,
Seal Beach, California*

Brief History of Wells Fargo

The website, Legends of America.com writes, *"Wells Fargo began when prosperous New York businessmen, Henry Wells, and William Fargo saw a great opportunity in the west after gold was discovered. The pair, who had joined with John Butterfield to start the American Express Co. in 1850, officially created Wells Fargo & Co. on March 18, 1852, with two primary objectives – transportation and banking.*

In California, where no railroads yet existed, the Wells, Fargo & Co Express, planned to provide "express" services to the many gold miners, as well as freight services to businesses. Its banking division, Wells, Fargo & Co Bank advertised both financial services and general forwarding businesses for mail, valuable deliveries, and freight.

Within the year Wells Fargo & Co. established its first office in San Francisco, soon followed by offices in Sacramento, Monterey, and San Diego, and within a short time, in almost every mining camp in California."

Wells Fargo & Co. also designed special stamps to be used when they carried Freight as seen in this 1908 example in brown ink.

**Genuine Wells Fargo Stamp
Mosher #WFCX-F8**

*Purchased from Jamie Schwartz
Lawrence, Kansas*

"... In 1866, Wells Fargo & Co. expanded its operations again, buying, what was then, Ben Holladay's Overland Mail Express, and consolidating all the other independent companies on what was known as the "Central Route," to create the largest stagecoach company in the world. They controlled virtually all the stage lines from Mississippi to California. It was 1867 when Wells Fargo & Co. finally achieved the total running of a stage line with its logo actually on the side of a stagecoach. They placed their first order for 30 Concord stagecoaches with Abbot-Downing & Company on April 20, 1867."

The advertisement below was run in 1866 before Wells Fargo & Co. bought out Ben Holladay's stagecoach businesses in the Great Consolidation.

12 ADVERTISEMENTS.

WELLS, FARGO & CO.

Express and Exchange Company.

CAPITAL, - - $2,000,000.

PRINCIPAL OFFICES:

No. 84 Broadway, ... NEW YORK.
N. W. cor. of Montgomery and California Streets, ... SAN FRANCISCO.

EXPRESS.

DAILY—To all parts of California, Nevada and Utah.
WEEKLY—To Crescent City, Oregon, Washington and Idaho Territories, British Columbia and Southern Coast of California.
TRI-MONTHLY—To New York, the Atlantic States and Europe, via Panama.
MONTHLY—To Cape St. Lucas, La Paz, Guaymas, Mazatlan, and other Mexican Pacific Ports.

FAST FREIGHT.

DAILY-Via Sacramento, over Central Pacific and Placerville Railroads, connecting with Pioneer Stage Co. and Freight Wagons, for Virginia City, Carson, and other principal points in Nevada and Utah.

Bills of Exchange and Telegraphic Transfers

On New York, Boston, and Philadelphia, Payable in the principal cities of the United States and Canada.

BILLS ON LONDON, DUBLIN, AND PARIS,
FOR SALE AT CURRENT RATES.

LETTERS OF CREDIT,

NEGOTIABLE THROUGHOUT CALIFORNIA, NEVADA, OREGON, WASHINGTON, IDAHO, AND UTAH.

CIRCULAR LETTERS.

We issue Credits on our New York House, exchangeable for CIRCULAR LETTERS, payable in all parts of Europe, affording to those going abroad, the safest and most convenient mode of providing themselves with funds.

COLLECTIONS AND COMMISSIONS

Of all kinds executed, and General Express Business promptly attended to throughout the United States, Canada and Europe.

SHIPPING BULLION AND COIN.

We ship BULLION, COIN, and other articles of special value, on the most favorable terms, which can be insured if desired, under our open policies with English Underwriters.

PASSAGE ORDERS.

Orders for Passage from Queenstown, London, Liverpool, Hamburg and Havre to New York; also, from New York to San Francisco.

LETTERS, FREIGHT and **SMALL PARCELS** forwarded to the Atlantic States and Europe.

Wells Fargo & Co. *full page advertisement, as it appeared in*
"Harrington's Directory of the City of Austin (Nevada) for the Year 1866
with a Historical and Statistical Review of Austin,
and the Reese River Mining Region" by Myron Angel.
Image provided to the author from Gordon Nelson, Western Cover Society

Purchased May 5, 2022 from F. G. Kappelmann of Jamaica Plain, Maine

The San Francisco to Oregon northbound cover shown above, was marked *"Overland"* by the sender. However, in this case the letter was directed toward a due north destination. So, it did not meet up with the Overland Mail Co. stage at Placerville. Instead, this piece was carried on the California and Coast Route of Wells Fargo due north from San Francisco to its destination in Roseburg, Douglas County, Oregon.

This three cent envelope (Scott #U10) shown above was postmarked on April 16 at San Francisco, marked *"Overland"* and addressed to S. Marks Esq. of Roseburg, Douglas County, Oregon.

The 1874 *S. Marks & Co.* building still stands in downtown Roseburg, Oregon.

On this map, the overland road from San Francisco to Roseburg, Oregon has been added in red to the 1874 *"Railroad and County Map of Oregon, California and Nevada"* by Frank A. Gray.

Butterfield's Overland Mail Co. did not carry freight. Wells Fargo carried freight, however they had lots of competition in California and across the country.

For example...

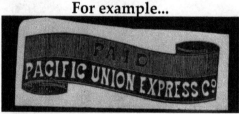

Purchased July 2014, from Lin-Co Stamps, Lincoln, Nebraska

Pacific Union Express, 1868-1869

A direct competitor of Wells Fargo & Co. was Pacific Union Express, whose primary business was to carry of treasure, letters, packages, and heavy freight. They were actually a $3 million stock company that *"started actual operations in June, 1868, with biweekly steamer express service from San Francisco to New York, and with a physical route south of San Francisco to San Jose, Santa Cruz, and to Monterey, Routes expanded quickly to approximately 180 stations in California, Nevada, and Oregon."*

The Weaverville, California, *Weekly Trinity Journal* reported on December 11, 1869: *"No More Pacific Union Express – The Pacific Union Express ceased operations December 1st, turning over its stock to Wells, Fargo & Co. The President of the Pacific Union says the company sunk $128,000, and had been running behind, for some time, at the rate of fifteen to twenty thousand dollars per month. It is stated that the amount paid by Wells, Fargo & Co. was $800,000."* [Source: Pacific Union Express, by Gordon L. Nelson, Western Express, June 2021.]

Langton's Pioneer Express, 1855-1865

When Adams Express collapsed February 23, 1855, Samuel W. Langton formed *Langton's Pioneer Express.* Langton had already been in the express business on his with partners since 1850. When he started extensive routes from the mining areas, he included steamboat service from Marysville and Sacramento to San

Francisco. He began connecting with Wells Fargo & Co. at Marysville in 1856. There was even a Humbolt Express stamp for service from the Humbolt (northeast of the Comstock) to California.

In the late 1850s and early 1860s Langton served the rapidly growing Nevada mining regions from Northeastern California. He did so with distinction until his untimely death on August 24, 1864 when he was run over by a heavy team of oxen the week before.

In Nov. of 1865, the firm was sold to *Lamping & Co's Express*.

[Source: Langton's Humbolt Express, by Gordon L. Nelson, Western Express, March, 2020.]

Purchased July 2014, from Lin-Co Stamps, Lincoln, Nebraska

United States Express, 1854-

The *United States Express Company* was organized in 1854, with the view of doing a western business over the *N.Y. & Erie Railroad.* It also provided service in and to Colorado. Its capital stock was $500,000 with D. N. Barney, president; H. Kip, superintendent, and Theo. B. Marsh, treasurer. This express had about 200 agencies, and many employees. Source: History of the Express Companies, by Alexander Lovett Stimson, page 78

Both of the stamps purchased July 2014, from Lin-Co Stamps, Lincoln, Nebraska

For more information, see History of the Express Companies, 1858 by Alexander Lovett Stimson, page 78

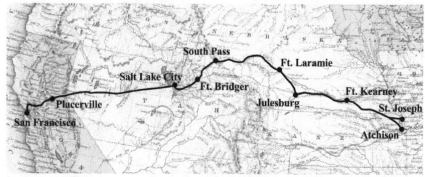

Image Source: "Postal History of the Western Overland Routes"
by Richard Frajola, LLC, Section 10

The Central Overland Mail Route
AFTER THE JULY 1, 1864 END OF
The Overland Mail Company's contract

Beginning in 1860 William Russell's Pony Express used this Central Route for part of their fast 10-day mail delivery from St. Joseph, Missouri to Sacramento, California.

Beginning July 1, 1861, The Overland Mail Co. began using this route when their use of the Southern Ox-Bow route ended and the Postal System rerouted the Overland north to avoid the southern states.

As construction progressed on the transcontinental railroad, the Overland Mail Co. continued to fill in the gaps until the eastward and westward construction crews met in Utah.

> The Overland Mail Company are now carrying the mails between the ends of the Union and Central Pacific Roads, a distance of 110 miles. All delayed mails are carried across the Steplos Swamp, and soon reach their destination.
>
> The Central Pacific Road to-day commened transporting the mails to the 615 mile post. Only 52 miles of track remains to be laid to complete the Pacific Railroad.

The Evansville Daily Journal, April 12, 1869, page 1

As the transcontinental railroad neared completion, the article above reports that the Overland Mail Company filled the gap between the ends of the Union and Central Pacific Railroad tracks. As of April 12, 1869 there was a 110 mile gap in the tracks that relied on the Overland Mail.

The transcontinental railroad was constructed along the Humboldt River and followed some of the Central Route. The completed railroad was faster and cheaper than the stage and freight lines using the old Central Route, and therefore absorbed much of their business.

The photograph below captured the moment when a golden spike was driven by Leland Stanford to join the rails of the first transcontinental railroad across the United States connecting the Central Pacific Railroad from Sacramento and the Union Pacific Railroad from Omaha on May 10, 1869, at Promontory Summit, Utah Territory.

"East and West Shaking Hands at Laying of Last Rail" by Andrew J. Russell

_____ ***End of Chapter One*** _____

Unsolicited stamp design submitted in 1957 by the California Overland Mail Centennial Committee submitted to the USPS commemorative stamp program to honor the Centennial of the Overland Mail.

CHAPTER TWO
Postal History

Postal Rates on Letters Carried by Butterfield's Overland Mail

The Postal Act of March 3, 1855, required that all domestic letters be prepaid. This ended the practice of sending letters without postage requiring the recipient to pay when picking up the letter at the Post Office.

During Butterfield's Overland Mail Co. time, the Postal Act of March 3, 1855, established the rate for ½ ounce letter of 10¢ if the distance was over 3,000 miles, and the rate of 3¢ if the distance was less than 3,000 miles.

 The 1851 3¢ stamp was issued without perforations as shown on the image to the left. In 1857, the 3¢ stamp was issued perforated along the edges as shown on the image to  the right.

The first 10¢ green postage stamp was issued in April 1855 for this new transcontinental rate. A 10¢ embossed pre-stamped envelope was also issued.

The Scott Specialized Catalog lists eleven numbers for the various 10¢ green stamps. Four of the numbers (13, 14, 15, and 16) are for stamps issued in 1855 without perforations as shown on the image to the right.

 The Scott Specialized Catalog also lists five numbers (31, 32, 33, 34, 35) for the 10¢ green stamps issued in 1857 - all of which were perforated along the edges as shown on the image to the left. **These green 10¢ stamps were the most common stamp used on Butterfield's Overland Mail Company southern ox bow route.**

During the last month of Butterfield's ox bow southern route operation, starting February 27, 1861 the rates changed to require 10¢ prepaid postal rate on ½ ounce letters which crossed the Rocky Mountains.

All U. S. postage stamps, including both denominations of the above illustrated stamps, were demonetized (declared useless for postage) in September of 1861 to keep the Confederacy from selling these stamps to finance their war efforts.

The new 1861 issued 10¢ green replaced the halo of stars above Washington's head with the words, "U.S. POSTAGE" as shown on the image to the right.

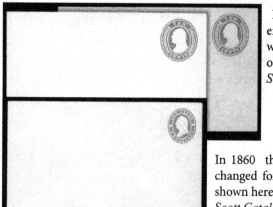

In 1861 a new 3¢ stamp, for distances under 3,000 miles was issued in pink changing the frame around Washington to a lace pattern, as shown in the image to the left.

The Postal Act of March 3, 1863 eliminated the 10¢ transcontinental rate, so that effective July 1, 1863, all mail was charged 3¢ per ½ ounce regardless of distance.

Apr 1, 1855	to 3,000 miles	3 cents	prepayment compulsory
	over 3,000 miles	10 cents	
Feb 27, 1861	over the Rockies	10 cents	1855 Act modified to require 10 cent prepaid postal rate on letters from any point east of the Rocky Mountains to any point on the Pacific side and vice versa **Ship rate:** 2 cent fee added to inland postage if transmitted by mail; 5 cents due if delivered at port of entry (any weight)

Image source: Mails of the Westward Expansion, 1803 - 1861
by Steve Walske and Richard Frajola, Appendix G: Postal Rates

In 1855 these 10¢ stamped envelopes were issued on white and buff paper for use on transcontinental mail. *Scott Catalog #U15-16*

In 1860 the 10¢ envelope design was changed for transcontinental mail as shown here. *Scott Catalog #U32*

In 1861 the 10¢ envelope design was changed again as shown here.
Scott Catalog #U41

In 1861 pre-printed envelopes, like the one shown here, indicated that the franking fee to Wells Fargo had been paid to carry the letter up to Placerville, to meet the Overland Mail.

This 1861 pre-printed envelope, indicated that the franking fee to Wells Fargo had been paid to carry the letter up to Placerville, to meet the Overland Mail. Also, a Pony Express stamp has been added in the upper left, paying the cost of transportation by the Pony Express from Placerville to St. Joseph.

**Post Office,
San Francisco, Cal.
(ca. 1850)
Engraving by William
Endicott (1816–1851)**
Source: Library of Congress
The U.S. Post Office opened its first San Francisco branch in 1848. No mail was delivered directly to the gold fields, so miners waited each morning for the post office to open. This 1850 lithograph, made after a drawing by H. F. Cox, depicts four lines at the post office, for Spanish-language service, general delivery, parcel delivery, and newspaper pickup.

The California State Register reports several interesting details about the operation of the San Francisco post office in the year 1859. The article below list the hours, postal staff, and the various routes available for mail out of the San Francisco office including:

- Atlantic Steamboats on the 5th and 20th monthly
- Great Overland Mail to St. Louis, Memphis
- Central Overland Mail to St. Joseph
- Route to Sacramento and northern mines
- Route to Stockton and southern mines
- Route to San Jose
- Route to Monterey, Santa Barbara, Los Angeles, San Diego
- Route to Acapulco, Panama, South America, West Indies
- Route to China, Sandwich Islands, and Australia

380   SAN FRANCISCO DIRECTORY.

Post-Office,

N. W. corner Washington and Battery; office hours from 8 o'clock A. M. to 5 P. M., except on the arrival of the great Atlantic Mail, when the office is opened immediately after the mail is distributed.

CHARLES L. WELLER, Post-Master.
Ferdinand Creighton, Asst. P. M.
J. A. Hinchman, Post-Master's Secretary; J. Shade Dungan, Mailing Clerk; W. W. Armstrong, Box Clerk; Samuel M. Keifer, Registry Clerk; D. D. McClelland, W. J. Bigger, T. L. Thompson, Wm. Wadhams, John Short, T. C. McCallan, Delivery Clerks; F. B. Cassas, Jr., Dead Letter Clerk; J. W. Brocas, Ladies Department; J. P. Chamberlain, Newspaper Clerk; H. W. Butler, Assistant Mailing Clerk; Manuel Simmons, Porter; Timothy Mahony, Messenger. Besides the above, temporary clerks are employed on the arrival and dispatch of the great Atlantic Mail.

Atlantic Mails.—The great mails for the Atlantic States and Europe, leave on the 5th and 20th of each month, except either of these dates fall on Sunday, when the mail leaves on the succeeding day. The mail closes at the office fifteen minutes previous to the sailing of the steamer.

Great Overland Mail, from San Francisco to St. Louis and Memphis, Tenn., *via* Los Angeles, Fort Yuma, Fort Fillmore nr El Paso, Preston and Fort Smith. leaves semi-weekly, Monday and Friday, at 12 o'clock, noon; mail closes at 11¾ o'clock, A. M.

Central Overland Mail, from Placerville to St. Joseph, Mo., *via* Carson Valley and Salt Lake, leaves Placerville weekly, on Saturday at 12 o'clock, noon; mail closes at San Francisco every Friday at 3¾ o'clock P. M.

Mails for Sacramento and the Northern Mines closes daily at 3.50 P. M.; for Benicia, Vallejo, etc., at the same hour.

Mails for Stockton and the Southern Mines closes daily at 3.50 P. M.

Mails for San José, etc., closes daily at 7.50 A. M.

Mails for Monterey, Santa Barbara, Los Angeles and San Diego, are dispatched regularly on the 1st, 10th and 20th of each month.

Mails for Acapulco, Panama, South America, and the West Indies, per great Atlantic Mail, on the 5th and 20th of each month.

Mails for China, the Sandwich Islands, and Australia, are forwarded from the Post Office by every suitable opportunity, containing all letters and papers, the inland postage of which is prepaid to San Francisco—leaving the sea postage to be collected in the ports where the mails are delivered.

The California State Register and year book of facts for 1859, page 380
Henry G. Langley & Co., Publishers
Image provided to the author from Gordon Nelson, Western Cover Society

Mail Delivery Up In the Gold Fields

In 1848 when letters eventually arrived at the new San Francisco Post Office, a problem still remained. No mail was delivered directly to the various gold fields, so miners waited each morning for the post office to open. That worked if your claim was only a mile or two from the post office in San Francisco. What if your claim was up in the hills, twenty or a hundred miles away from the nearest post office?

"Portrait of a Prospector with His Burrow"
California Historical Society Collections at USC, CHS-7810

J. H. Holiday, in his book, *The World Rushed In: The California Gold Rush* (page 310-311) writes:

> **How to get the letters to the mining camps up in the hills? Once again, Yankee enterprise took over. Sensing a profit to be made, many miners left their claims to go into the business of collecting mail at the San Francisco and Sacramento City post offices and delivering it to the camps and towns.**
>
> *These expressmen traveled everywhere, to the most remote camps, wherever a merchant kept a list on which miners could record their names. Each month the expressmen took their lists to the post offices to collect letters and newspapers for their subscribers. They charged from $1 to $2 per letter delivered and usually 50 cents for a letter taken to the post office. Through this system, which became ever more competitive as the number of ex-*

pressmen and express companies increased, the miners obtained their letters from the States."

One of the miners wrote: *"If you could have seen us when we received our letters, you would have laughed and perhaps called us fools — such hoorahing, jumping, yelling and screaming -- My hat fell into the water pail but I could not stop to pick it out until I had read my letter all through. So you will take good care and write often when I tell you that I live upon your letters -- with a small sprinkling of Pork and Bread."* [Letter of Lucius Fairchild to J.C. Fairchild, Jan. 1, 1850]

"California Gold Diggers - A Scene From Actual Life At The Mines" by John Andrew, 'Ballou's Pictorial Drawing-Room Companion,' May 3, 1856, pg. 280-281, v. 10, no. 18

Concerning Enterprising Mail Carriers in San Francisco, California

The California gold rush miners, after spending up to six or eight months traveling to arrive in the gold fields were anxious to receive mail from home.

Alden Woodruff, in a letter written on February 4, 1850, writes,

"Dear Father –

It is now almost ten months since I heard from home. On my arrival in California, I was certain of getting a letter – but have not yet received a single one. What is the reason you do not write?"

Two days later Alden Woodruff, writes in a second letter:

"I received your letter of 22nd October, 1849, on yesterday, per the express. It only cost me $2 postage to

get it; but that's nothing, for I was glad to get it at any cost. It is the first time I have heard from home since I left Fort Smith."

The "express" Woodruff refers to were the enterprising private mail carriers who picked up mail from the Post Office in San Francisco, and delivered them to the miners at the various camps out in the wilderness and mountains for fees upwards of $2 of gold per letter delivered. *[Arkansas in the Gold Rush, by Priscilla McArthur, 1986, page 126.]*

NELSON'S GOLD-WASHER AT WORK AT THE MINES.—[See preceding Page.]

"Nelson's Gold-Washer at Work at the Mines," Harper's Weekly, March 17, 1860
Wood Engraving Hand Colored, 1860, Based on a photo by Brady.

Stephen Chapman Davis, arriving at the gold fields, ran an express carrying mail into the gold fields. He had the names of 300 miners who requested him to obtain any letters at Sacramento or San Francisco. He writes in his journal:

"I just returned from below bringing some 50 letters... The postage on letters is 40¢ but we get $1.50 each... As soon as I come in sight... the miners drop their tools and run to meet me, in haste to get letters from their dear friends at home. And those who are so unfortunate as to receive no letters... look upon their fellow miners who are reading epistles... penned in fine hand of a female, frequently a tear comes... to the eye, while

the heart grieves at being thus forgotten by loved ones at home." [*Arkansas in the Gold Rush*, by Priscilla McArthur, 1986, page 127]

An Arkansan named J. Rankin Pyeatte, traveling to California seeking gold, wrote home on December 9, 1849 wondering why he had received no letters from home. He engaged an express merchant to carry his mail to him in the gold fields 200 miles from San Francisco for $1 extra for each letter:

"*Dear Companion, Children and Friends,*

Having not heard a word from you since I left home, I have become very anxious to receive something from you. It would do me more good than anything I could think of... You may think you know how anxious I am to get a letter from you, but you know nothing about it, nor cannot know unless you were in the same situation that I am in, having been absent about 8 months and not having heard a word from you. I have no doubt but you have heard from us several times, for I have written six letters to you from different points. Why have I not gotten a letter I cannot tell unless they are directed to San Francisco. This place is so far distant, 200 miles, from that, we can't get letters there.

We made arrangements with a merchant to lift our letters out of the post office there and bring them to Sacramento City for one dollar extra on the letter." [*Source: Arkansas in the Gold Rush, by Priscilla McArthur, 1986, p. 188-189*]

By 1859 California had 300 post offices scattered across the state, and the need for private mail delivery diminished.

Mail Count On the Butterfield Route

According to James H. Reed, assistant to Fort Smith postmaster W. A. Porter, the first mail pouch going west weighed 7¾ pounds - equivalent to approximately 250 half ounce letters. [*Source: Butterfield Overland Mail, Conklin, Vol. 1, page 223*]

The *Report of the Postmaster General* dated March 3, 1859 gives an estimate of the number of letters sent in 1858 from Memphis at 5,367 yielding $247.74 in postage, and letters sent from St. Louis numbered 60,800 yielding $2,723.27. The St. Louis postmaster estimated that of the 60,800 pieces of mail, 1,800 were sent free, 25,000 went all the way through with 10¢ postage *(10¢ was the rate for letters traveling over 3,0000 miles)*, and 25,000 were to destinations along the way with 3¢ postage *(3¢ was the rate for letters traveling less than 3,000 miles)*. About 22 packages were sent with each stage out of St. Louis.

Also, the stages carried for free, Memphis, St. Louis, and San Francisco newspapers to be exchanged with other newspapers along the route. This free postal service for newspapers was based on Congressional act of 1825 that allowed *"every printer of newspapers to send one paper to each and every other printer of newspapers within the United States free of postage..."*

The Congressional Globe for the 36th Congress (Appendix, p. 2461) reported on the total volume of postal business, Sept. 1858 to March 1860:

	Number	Postage Paid
Letters received from the West	244,764	$23,276.11
Letters sent to the West	441,196	$48,102.52
Total Letters	685,960	$71,378.63

The reports did not include a passenger count from any of these three cities.

At the end of that year the *Report of the Postmaster General* dated December 1, 1860, reports on page 436 that postage received on the Overland via El Paso route totaled $119,766.[76] during the past year. If we assume each letter was at 10¢ postage, that would amount to 1,197,667 letters. If we also assume they were equally distributed among the 208 Overland Mail trips during the year, it would amount to 5,758 letters in each stagecoach that year.

The volume of mail carried by Butterfield's Overland Mail Co. skyrocketed in January of 1860, because in mid December of 1859, the Postmaster General did not renew the ocean steamer contracts. So, starting at that date, the default carrier for all transcontinental mail was Butterfield's Overland Mail Co. instead of the steam ships on the ocean route to Panama Isthmus or the southern tip of South America.

Unclaimed Letters 1865

During the years of the Butterfield Overland Mail Co. the post office did not deliver door to door. Rather, individuals went to the Post Office on a regular basis and asked for their mail. If a letter sat uncalled for, the postmaster would publish a list of names, asking that they come to pick up their mail. The list shown here is from the Saint Louis paper, *The Daily Missouri Republican*, June 18, 1865. Home delivery, as we know it today, did not begin until about 1910 to 1915.

LIST OF LETTERS
Remaining Unclaimed in the Post-office at St. Louis, State of Missouri, June 17, 1865.

Officially Published in the Missouri Republican having the Largest Circulation.

——To obtain any of these letters, the applicants must call for "*advertised letters*," give the date of this list, and pay one cent for advertising.

——"If not called for within *one month*, they will be sent o the Dead Letter Office.

"*Free delivery* of letters by *carriers*, at the residence of the owners, may be *secured* by observing the following rules:

"*Direct* letters plainly to the street an l number, as well as the Postoffice and State.

"*Head* letters with the writer's *Postoffice* and *State*, *street* and *number*, sign them plainly with full name, and request that answers may be directed accordingly.

"Letters to strangers or transient visitors in a town or city, whose special address may be unknown, should be marked in the lower left hand corner, with the word 'Transient.'

"*Place* the postage *stamp* on the *upper right-hand* corner, and *leave space* between the stamp and direction for *post marking* without interfering with the writing.

"N. B.—*A Request* for the *Return* of a letter to the writer, if unclaimed within 30 days or less, written or printed with the writer's *name*, *Postoffice* and *State*, across the left hand end of the envelope, on the face side, will be complied with the usual prepaid rate of postage, payable when the letter is delivered to the writer.—Sec. 28, Law of 1863."

—— The office will be open at 7 A. M. and close at 7 P. M.—Sundays from 12 to 1 P. M.   PETER L. FOY, Postmaster.

Residence of Peter L. Foy, Postmaster of St. Louis, Missouri

Daily Missouri Republican, St. Louis, Missouri, June 18, 1865, page 4

All of the covers shown in chapters 3 to 8 are from the personal collection of the author, Bob Crossman.

CHAPTER THREE
Pre-Butterfield Overland Mail

Before the existence of Butterfield's Overland Mail route, mail was still carried to the West, however it traveled slower. This letter, shown below, traveled 529 miles in 40 days. Eight years later, the Butterfield stages, in contrast, would cover some of the same roads, but travel 2,700 miles in only 23 days.

This folded letter sheet was purchased at the 2018 Portland, Oregon Stamp Show from John F. Ullmann Collectibles of Edmonds, Washington.

This folded letter sheet above was postmarked June 26, 1850 in Jackson, TN, eighty miles due east of Memphis. There is a note on the reverse that reads: *"James P. Collins, letter June 25, 1850, Rec'd this letter, Tuesday, Aug. 6th, 1850."*

Contents of this Folded Letter Sheet

Jackson Tenn. June 25th 1850
Tuesday

D'r Robert

I am anxious to hear from Texas and to know how you are pleased with prospects. I have seated myself to draft you a few lines. *I wrote to Thomas some time ago asking information on various subjects relative to my contemplated move to your part of the country, but his reply was not of such a flattering character as to cause me to sacrifice my property here to go to a new country. Thomas has done very well, all things considered, he would not see me suffer I believe, but in the event that I sold my property on a credit here. I wanted some assurance for that assistance that I could depend on.*

That part of my letter he has passed unnoticed. This I regret as it has frustrated all my hopes of moving and being able to engage in business to my satisfaction. I certainly expected nothing, only as a loan and feel sorry that I mentioned it at all.

I would not borrow a dollar from any man without giving him ample security. I have offered my property for sale, but have not had but one offer yet for it, viz 10 annual payments each $225.00 bearing that this is what I gain, and have spent besides about $700.00 for improvements, I can not sell on such credit and have anything to start business with to carry it on successfully. Therefore for the present I am not deciding what will be my future course about that matter.

Thomas arrived at Reynoldsburg on Tennessee River a few days ago on his way to Ireland. He says he can not come to see us until he returns.

Amelia has been very unwell for about 3 months. She has the Dyspepsia, I think. I think her general health has some what improved in a few days and I hope she will continue to improve. She exercises very much. The children are well. Your children are all well and getting a long about as usual.

Mrs. Henderson and Mary are well also. Susan is here. _____, she borrowed Mr. Smith's buggy & John drove. I met them on Thursday. Susan was quite unwell with she left home with chills, but exercises good water and a scatterment of her ideas by the trip, all combined, have made her look much better and knocked the chills out of sight. She has been here 10 days and has improved in health daily. Recollect you owe me a big Doctor bill for the trip too, but this we will settle in Texas. We go today to Mr. Barns for dinner tonight. To Mrs. McWilliams, tomorrow. To Mr. Davisons for dinner then home again.

Susan speaks of starting some again next week, so you may rest satisfied that the Bairns at home are well attended to and Susan & John are in good health here. Susan has had a great many Ladies to see her, and has returned a good many visits. Her trip has added to her health and I hope will be remembered with pleasure and as it will cost only her trouble, she will not sustain any loss. Indeed I am satisfied she has escaped a spell of chills by ___ing at this time.

After you see your way pretty clear about business prospects & c **I want to hear from you how you like the country, how the business compares with your expectations, what amount you sell each month & what is the amount of your profit monthly.**

Business with me is dull. I am not making expenses, however this is the dullest time of the year. Crops are very bad generally in this country owing to incessant rains and frost.

The last letter received from you was written at Houston. Susan is expecting one from you daily. I wrote to Mary and told her to forward all letters up to the 27th to his place.

Say to John, that he must not for the present buy any cattle or anything for me, as I can't come to any decision about moving, as I can't sell my town property, but may have an opportunity after a while. Give our united love to John & Margaret. Let us know Eliza has got.

We shall be glad to hear from you to know how you are pleased & c. *Susan and all unite in love to you and best wishes for your good health & that you may be able to realize all your expectations and get into a prosperous business is the wish.*

Yours Truly, James P. Collins

Three Examples of Ocean Route Steam Ship Mail

The following group of letters could have been carried by Butterfield's Overland Mail Co. if they had written *"via overland"* or *"via Los Angeles"* on the face of the envelope.

Without these markings, until late Dec. 1859, the default transcontinental carrier was by steamship twice a month via Panama as shown on the map below.

Image source: Mails of the Westward Expansion, 1803 to 1861
by Steven C. Walske and Richard C. Frajola, Western Cover Society, 2015, Chapter Six

1858 Eastbound Ocean Steam Ship Cover to Maine

The sender used a US postal stationary envelope, embossed with a green U16 on buff paper. Note on the reverse reveals letter was written by S. S. Bradford on Sept. 20, 1858. Cover was canceled at the San Francisco, California Post Office the following day, Sept. 21, 1858.

This cover was mailed one week after the beginning of Butterfield's Overland Mail Co. route. The sender could have, for no additional postage, requested for this letter to be carried *"overland via Los Angeles"* by stagecoach. Instead this letter traveled by ocean steam ship to the Isthmus of Panama, because in all of 1858 and 1859, the default route for all transcontinental mail was by ocean going ship.

This cover was purchased at the 2014 APS Little Rock Show
from Roger Gutzman, R. G. Stamps of Bigg, California.

This cover was postmarked on Sept. 21, 1858, at San Francisco, California, addressed to: J. W. Webb Esq., Care of Farris & Webb, Bangor, Maine.

At the time of this letter, the steamships departed New York and New Orleans twice a month with the mail. The port of San Francisco was packed with sailing ships that had arrived with mail or passengers. There were very few passengers seeking passage back east, so the empty ships accumulated in the harbor.

1851, Port of San Francisco

Port of San Francisco

1858 Westbound Steam Ship Cover to San Francisco's Mint

Based on the postmark the cover shown below was mailed from either Carmichael or Carbondale, Pennsylvania. Postmarked Aug. 4, this 1858 letter from Pennsylvania was carried by oceangoing steamship. Since the letter was in transit only 5 to 6 weeks, arriving Sept. 17-19, 1858 it must have crossed at the Panama Isthmus on its way to San Francisco. If it had been carried further south past the tip of South America, it could not have made that longer journey in only 44 to 46 days.

Traveling over 3,000 miles, it carried the correct postage paid with a ten cent stamp.

Purchased at the 2021 APS show in Chicago
from Mark C. Reasoner of Prospect Heights, Illinois.

This cover was received at the U.S. Mint in San Francisco on Sept. 17-19, 1858, addressed to Stephen L. Merchant Esq. This might be the Stephen L. Merchant who was born Sept. 3, 1834 in Georgia, and died June 6, 1901 (age 66), son of Huntington W. and Elizabeth Merchant.

"The First San Francisco Mint, 1854" Artist unknown. Image is in the public domain.

In 1849, the California Gold Rush brought a flood of people west for the chance to get rich. Transporting the gold east all the way to the Philadelphia Mint was time-consuming and fraught with risk. The San Francisco Mint, shown above, operated from April 3, 1854-1873 and was eventually torn down.

In the first year of operation alone, the San Francisco Mint turned miner's gold into coins, producing \$4,084,207$\underline{.00}$ in gold pieces in its first year (1854) alone. In 1857, more than two tons of gold dust, nuggets, coins and ingots from the California Gold Rush were loaded onto the *S. S. Central America*, which regularly transported gold from California to the east coast. After being caught in a hurricane off the coast of the Carolinas, the *S. S. Central America* sank and the human and financial loss was felt around the world.

Five Dollar Gold Coin From the Estate of Paul J. Crossman

1861 Eastbound Ocean Steam Ship Cover

In late Dec. 1859, Butterfield's Overland Mail Co. became the default carrier of all transcontinental mail. This particular letter shown below would have traveled by stagecoach on the Butterfield, except that the sender specifically wanted this letter to travel by ocean steam ship, and marked on the cover *"Via Panama."*

Postmarked Jan. 10, 1861 in Sacramento City, California. This postmark [SAC-1850] was used Sept. 19, 1856 to Sept. 24, 1862 *[John Williams, Western Express, Jan. 1994, page 41]* Addressed to Robert McCaull, Cayuga Bridge, Cayuga County, New York, it traveled over 3,000 miles, with the correct postage paid with a ten cent Scott #35 stamp.

This letter was sent to the address of *"Cayuga Bridge"* in Cayuga County, New York. That county is located in the west central part of New York state, in the Finger Lakes region, with Lake Ontario on the northern border of the county.

Purchased at the 2021 APS show in Chicago
from Paul and Becky Huber of Beaufort, North Carolina.

As you will note in the front lower left, the sender explicitly wanted this letter to be carried across the Isthmus of Panama, instead of on a ship going around the southern tip of South America to reach New York. *"Via Panama"* also indicated the sender did not want his letter to be carried by Butterfield's Overland Mail Co.

Cayuga Bridge, Cayuga County, New York, from Memoir by Cadwallader Colden, 1825

Cayuga bridge, shown above, was no longer in operation at the time this letter was mailed. Perhaps Robert McCaull lived in the old watchman's quarters, or in a home near the foot of the bridge on the Cayuga County Side. The original Cayuga Long Bridge opened on Sept. 4, 1800. At a length of 1 mile and 8 rods (5,412 feet), it was the longest bridge in the Western Hemisphere at that time. The bridge was 22 feet wide, making it possible for wagons to pass in opposite directions. Tolls were $1 for a four-wheel carriage, 75 cents for a wagon and horses, 50 cents for a one-horse cart and 2 cents for each sheep or hog. Local residents were exempt from the tolls.

Cayuga Long Bridge Marker, Photo 2019

Unfortunately, because of the nature of its construction, the bridge lasted only a few years. A replacement was completed in 1807, at a new site about 2 miles north of the first Cayuga Long Bridge.

A new (third) Cayuga Long Bridge was constructed in 1833 on the north side of the second Cayuga Long Bridge, at a cost of about $15,000. Toll revenues on this third Cayuga Long Bridge amounted to $10,000 a year until the railroad line began operating in 1841. Competition with the new railroad line caused a sharp decline in bridge toll revenues. In 1856, the bridge's total revenues were only $1,073. No repairs were made to the Cayuga Long Bridge and it fell out of use in 1857.

This letter was mailed in 1861, but perhaps remnants of the old bridge were still standing - enough to serve as a postal address for Mr. Robert McCaull.

NOTE: I have three university degrees, but I was never an English major. Today, however, looking through a newspaper from 1860 I found a poem that touches a subject of great interest to me. In the middle of a larger work, the author waxes poetic about traveling on trains and upon sailing vessels — he writes what I have entitled: *"Untitled Overland Mail Stagecoach Poem from the pages of The Van Buren Press."* *Bob Crossman*

The Van Buren Press • J. S. Dunham, Editor
Van Buren, Arkansas • Friday, September 7, 1860

...Venerable stage; memento of other days. So full of respect for persons and monuments! Silently moving near some sacred spot; sometimes halting near some national monument. Venerable stage of olden times, with all the faults and virtues of man's home.

As long as you are outside of the stage, an unknown pilgrim, the passengers already ensconced in their narrow places, would be glad if you would not encroach on their little domain; but boldly step in, be seated, look round, meet the glances of all, and soon you are one of the happy family!

Venerable stage! Home of the happy family! Once, as I went sight-seeing, I was shown a very large cage; within were all manner of unfortunate animals, living and traveling together; they came from different climes; birds, cats, dogs, rats, foxes – a curious assortment having nothing in common, but some native instincts which, undoubtedly made them wish for the end of their journey! We were kind of happy family in the **Overland Mail Stage.**

There was a **miner**, fresh from the lower stratifications of mother earth.

There was a **stage conductor** from the vast plains stretching to our west; accustomed to the air of the plain, he longed for the open air, as yonder bird, in yonder "happy family" longs for the tree in the illimitable forests of his first home.

There was **another man** – a type of the unknown; whence he came and whither he went, was a mystery to me and oftentimes I would have wished to trace a few pathways of his life, for, no doubt, his human heart had been attuned to sorrow's sad notes and to joy's lofty songs, thus we were a happy family.

A **female traveler** from California's gold diggings completed the picture; a string of gold plates surrounded an ample neck, and testified of those belts of gold which loving nature has placed upon our earth.

There the brilliant drops of perspiration produced by a hot! July sun, and gathering into substantial soil the loose clouds of dust which every movement of the lumbering stage threw up, contrived to make of that neek a kind of stratified specimen of geology; however, kind hearts were there – noble thoughts dwelt there – and a noble helping hand could have been found there! Oh! The Magnificent evil!

Nine persons in the stage, with a sun 120 degrees hot pouring its overflowing tide of warmth upon us; no doubt, Dante who has so graphically portrayed to man the abodes of the wicked, had he known something of modern traveling, would have placed in his "Purgatorio" an **underland mail**, especially at night, dashing and clashing amidst the rocks, ravines and dry rivers of the Ozark mountains, where everybody's head, searching for a pillow, or, at least, for some immovable position and finding none, clashed against another cranium or awoke in alarm the unsuspecting neighbor.

However, onward we went; north of us; the sugar cane seemed to be largely cultivated; in Missouri, the hungarian grass waved coolly to the breeze whilst in northern States timothy and clover prevail everywhere... ———

CHAPTER FOUR
Butterfield Mail
Carried on the
Memphis to Fort Smith Route

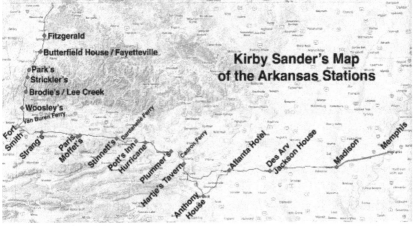

Butterfield Overland Mail Stagecoach Stops in Arkansas
Map by Kirby Sanders
To learn about the STAGECOACH LAND ROUTE across Arkansas,
see Bob Crossman's 2021 book: "Butterfield's Overland Mail STAGECOACH Route
Across Arkansas: 1858-1861"

Memphis Route - Quincy, California to Fort Valley, Georgia

Below is one of just a handful of Memphis route covers that have survived.

The cover shown below was mailed from Quincy, California on Feb. 26, addressed to Fort Valley, Georgia - a distance of over 3,000 miles requiring postage of 10¢. The Quincy postmaster wrote *"Paid 10ᶜ"* in the upper right to indicate that the sender had paid the postage at the Quincy Post Office. This cancellation [PLU-1000] was used May 13, 1856 to Oct. 29, 1868.

[John Williams, Western Express,Oct., 1990, page 70]

John Birkinbine II, of American Philatelic Brokerage in Tucson, Arizona believes there is a 95% probability that this letter, with a Georgia destination, traveled the Memphis leg of the Butterfield route instead of the St. Louis route.

This cover is postmarked Feb. 26 Quincy, Cal., addressed to: Rev. Whitman C. Hill, Fort Valley, Houston Co. Georgia. The 1860 census shows W. C. Hill, age 70, in Housion City, Georgia had 43 slaves. The Rev. Whitman C. Hill, born 1790 and died 1861, was admitted as a Methodist minister in 1809. He married Jane Smith on Jan. 11, 1816, a daughter of Rev. Isaac Smith. *"He was a man of more than ordinary ability, and achieved much success in the fields he served."*

Rev. Hill was pastor of Alabama's Indian Mission at Asbury from 1825 to 1828. He was one of three witnesses on the Treaty with the Creeks on Nov. 15, 1827 when they ceded all their lands in Georgia. Some time between 1828 and 1860, W. C. Hill moved about 150 miles northeast from Asbury, Alabama to Fort Valley, Georgia - where he received this letter.

This is one of just a handful of Memphis route covers that have survived.
From the Quincy, California Post Office, this letter would have traveled on Feb. 26 or 27th by horseback or wagon south to catch the noon Monday or Friday Butterfield Stage out of San Francisco.
From San Francisco via Los Angeles,
Fort Yuma then to Gila River, Arizona.
Then from Gila River to Tucson, and to Soldier's Farewell, Texas.
Then to El Paso, Pecos River Crossing, Fort Chadbourne, to Fort Belknap.
Then to Sherman, Texas to Fort Smith, Arkansas, then to
Little Rock and by stage or steamboat to Memphis.
At Memphis a train would have completed the journey to Georgia.

If this Feb. 26th cover, shown above, was mailed in 1859, it would have traveled by Butterfield's stagecoach from San Francisco arriving in Little Rock on March 22nd to transfer to John Butterfield's steamboat *Jennie Whipple* headed down the Arkansas and Mississippi Rivers to Memphis.

If this cover was mailed in 1860 or 1861, the *Jennie Whipple* was unavailable – grounded above Fort Smith due to low water. So then, the letter would have then traveled by stagecoach all the way from Fort Smith across Arkansas directly to the Mississippi River ferry to Memphis, Tennessee.

Nov. 1858 Butterfield's Overland Mail Cover to Kentucky

The first eastbound batch of Butterfield's Overland Mail left San Francisco on Sept. 16, 1858. Just sixty days later, the cover shown below was postmarked in Nov. of 1858 in San Francisco, Addressed to Miss Mary Ann Steward, Columbus, Adair County, Kentucky.

While most of the transcontinental mail in 1858 was carried by ship to the Isthmus of Panama, transported over the Isthmus by train, then boarded onto a second ship for the trip north to the states. This sender, however, preferred that the letter travel by stagecoach so the sender wrote instructions to the postmaster in the lower left: *"via Overland Mail Los Angeles."*

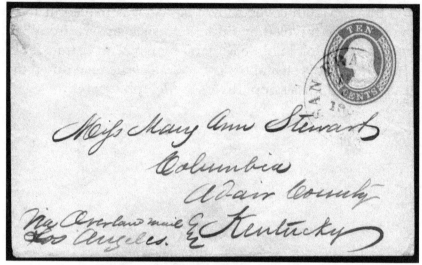

US postal stationary envelope: Scott # U15
This cover was purchased at the 2018 Little Rock Pinnacle Stamp Show.

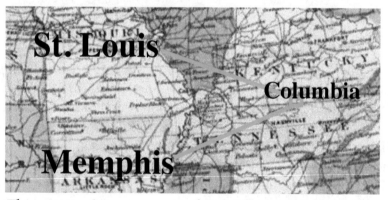

This particular cover may have been carried by Butterfield's Overland Mail Co. to either Memphis or St. Louis, since its final destination is about the same distance from either eastern terminus of the Overland Mail route.

Headstone for four siblings (Mary, William, Elizabeth and Sallie) found in the Columbia Cemetery, Adair County, KY.

The recipient of this letter may be the Mary A. Stewart (1834-1873) who is buried in the Columbia cemetery. She was the daughter of John and Elizabeth Slater Stewart. She was the sister of Joseph, Elizabeth, William, Josephine and Sallie. The letter may have been from a brother or boyfriend among the Gold Rush 49ers. Mary was 25 at the time this letter was written.

This photo was taken about 1884 when the Adair County Court House in Columbia, Kentucky was constructed.

1859 Memphis Route of Butterfield's Overland Mail Co. This is another example of just a handful of Memphis route covers that have survived.

The sender of the cover shown below paid the 10 cents postage for a half-ounce letter traveling more than 3,000 miles. The sender wrote instructions to the postmaster in the upper left of the envelope: *"Overland via Los Angeles."*

Based on the postmark date of April 8, 1859, this cover departed San Francisco by stagecoach on Monday, April 11, 1859, arriving in Little Rock on May 6, where it was transferred to Butterfield's steamboat, *Jennie Whipple*, for the balance of the trip to Memphis. On May 9th at Memphis, this cover was transferred to a mail steamboat headed south on the Mississippi River toward its Natchez, Mississippi destination.

This cover was postmarked at San Francisco, April 8, 1859 This cancellation [SAF-295] was used July 20, 1857 to Aug. 7,

1861. *[John Williams, Western Express, March 1995, page 16]* The sender designated in the upper left: *"Overland via Los Angeles,"* addressed to: Miss Zoe LaCrozer, Natchez, Mississippi.

This cover was purchased at the Little Rock Pinnacle Club Stamp Show in 2018. ex Allen

The Natchez Steamboat Landing, ca. 1910

Most likely Zoe was the girlfriend or sister of a Gold Rush 49er. We do not know Miss LaCrozer's residence, however the city of Natchez is known for its old beautiful homes. The Elms, for example (shown below) has a colorful history. For a 10-year period between 1825 and 1835, it served as the Presbyterian manse and, for a few years in the early 1840s, as a young ladies' boarding school. Tutors advertised that the site was *"sheltered, retired, with extensive pleasure grounds."* The house has been known as The Elms since 1843. In 1878 Mosely John Posey and Caroline Agee Drake purchased the property, and their descendants have occupied the house since then.

The Elms, Natchez, Mississippi

1859 Memphis Route to East Tennessee
This is another example of just a handful of Memphis route covers that have survived.

The cover shown below was mailed from Iowa City, California, postmarked July 14, 1859. The Iowa City postmaster stamped a circular "PAID 10" to indicate the sender paid the 10¢ postage due for letters traveling 3,000 miles or more. Leaving Iowa City, California and traveling about 140 miles south to San Francisco this cover boarded Butterfield's Overland Mail Co. stagecoach to Fort Smith, then on to Little Rock. Arriving in Little Rock, Arkansas about Aug. 1 or 2, 1859, this letter departed on John Butterfield's Arkansas River steamboat *Jennie Whipple*, arriving at Memphis Aug. 5, 1859. From Memphis this cover traveled another 400 miles due east by train to Philadelphia, Monroe County, Tennessee.

On Aug. 10th, the *Jennie Whipple* departed Memphis for Cincinnati to have *"her hull thoroughly over hauled and painted... As she draws but sixteen inches water, she will suffer no detention from low water. No boat of her class has better accommodations, and no boat of any class has better officers..."* Jennie Whipple returned to the mail route on Sept. 5th. Sadly, the next day, *"the Jennie Whipple met with an accident while ascending the Arkansas River a few days ago, about forty miles above Napoleon. She struck a snag, which knocked a hole in her bow, causing her to fill rapidly. Captain Gray found it necessary to run her on a bar. She was afterward pumped out, and proceeded on her way to Little Rock.* [*Source: Sunday, Aug. 6, 10 and 28, 1859, and Sept. 14, 1859 Memphis Daily Appeal*]

This letter was probably sent by Robert R. Cleveland to his wife, Sydney G. Nelson Cleveland (born July 15, 1811 - died Oct. 23, 1884). Robert R. Cleveland's ancestors moved from Virginia to Blount County, Tennessee after the Revolutionary War, and the Cleveland children scattered through Eastern Tennessee.

This cover was purchased on ebay from andrew2u, Nov. 28, 2021. Starting in early spring 1859, printed envelopes with a simple overland directive began to appear, almost exclusively on eastbound mail. Within a few months they became more elaborate as shown here.

This cover was postmarked: Iowa City, Cal., JUL 14, 1859. This cancellation [PLA-1101] was used Oct. 19, 1856 to Sept. 21, 1859. *[John Williams, Western Express, Jan. 1991, page 78]* This 6 Horse illustrated cover contains the instructions: *"Overland Mail To all parts of the Union From San Francisco via Los Angeles."* Addressed to: Mrs Sydney G. Cleavland, Philadelphia, Monroe County, East Tennessee.

Arriving in Little Rock, Arkansas about Aug. 1 or 2, 1859, this cover departed on John Butterfield's Arkansas River steamboat *Jennie Whipple*, arriving at Memphis Aug. 5, 1859.

The 6-horse illustrated cover above was printed by *"Hutchings & Rosenfield, No. 146 Montgomery Street, San Francisco."* The same company also printed the engraving below of San Francisco in 1858.

San Francisco, 1858, printed by Hutchings & Rosenfield

1860 Memphis Westbound Route - Baton Rouge to California
Below is an example of just a handful of westbound Memphis route covers that have survived.

Purchased Nov. 7, 2022 from Ron Trosclair, 1713 Live Oak St, Metaire, LA 7005

The cover shown above was postmarked in Baton Rouge, La on June 11, 1860, addressed to Mrs. Julia M. Fraser, In care of Rev. Thomas Frazer, Santa Rosa, California.

This cover is franked with a 3¢ dull red Scott #26 postage stamp. Since the correct postage for distances over 3,000 miles was 10¢, postmaster J. McCormick marked the cover *"Due 7"* indicating that the recipient would need to pay 7¢ when picking up this cover at the Santa Rosa, California Post Office.

Leaving Baton Rouge June 11th, this cover would have traveled by mail steamboat north to Memphis. Arriving in Memphis, it would have departed Memphis on June 14 or 18th on the Overland Mail westward toward Fort Smith and on to San Francisco about July 12th. We know this cover was carried by Butterfield's stagecoaches across Arkansas because during the entire summer of 1860 his steamboat *Jennie Whipple* was stuck aground beyond Fort Smith and was unavailable to carry the Overland Mail.

Arriving in San Francisco, about July 12, 1860, the cover left the care of the Overland Mail Co., and was carried north about 60 miles to the Santa Rosa Post Office to wait for the Frazers to call for their mail.

1876 Panoramic View of Santa Rosa, Sonoma County, California
Drawn by E. S. Glover, Published by Wm. E, Evans
Caption reads, *"Santa Rosa - The County Seat of Sonoma County; has a population of about 4,000; it publishes two weekly papers and one daily; has two Banking Houses; several First-class Hotels, and numerous Mercantile Establishments."*
View notes the location of: Pacific Methodist College, Public High School, Christian College, Boys' Academy, Methodist Episcopal Church, Presbyterian Church, Methodist Church South, Christian Church, Catholic Church, and the Seventh Day Adventist Church. Engraving also notes that the *"Great Redwood Forest is 18 miles distant."*

The cover shown above is addressed to Mrs. Julia M. Fraser in care of Rev. Thomas Frazer of Santa Rosa, California. Rev. Fraser (1820-1902) was a Presbyterian home missionary in Southern California and Wisconsin. He previously served congregations in New Bern, North Carolina; Little Rock, Arkansas; and Portland, Oregon. From 1887-1892, he was a Professor of Systematic Theology at San Francisco Theological Seminary. Julia M. Fraser died in 1882.

Dec. 1860 Butterfield Cover to Kentucky

Alex Norman *(see name on lower left margin of the envelope)* mailed this letter from San Pablo, California on Dec. 20, 1860 in a pre-printed cover. The original stamp either fell off in transit, or was removed at some point by a postage stamp collector. A Scott #35, ten cent Washington stamp was added for the purpose of display.

Purchased at 2021 APS show in Chicago from
Phillip Sager, Geezer's Tweezers, of Pikesville, Maryland.

The red stagecoach bears the same wording that is printed below the team of horses: *"Overland Via Los Angeles."* This cover was first carried from San Pablo a few miles south across the bay to San Francisco. Based on the letter's date of Dec. 20, 1860, the cover was placed on the stage departing at noon, Monday, Dec. 24, 1860 to Fort Smith. With a Kentucky destination, this cover may have traveled the Memphis Route.

The town of Owingsville was founded by Colonel Thomas Dye Owings. In 1795, Mr. Owings was sent from Maryland to Kentucky by his father to operate some of the first iron furnaces in the region. Within 15 years, Owings had amassed a good deal of wealth and land. Along with Colonel Richard H. Menefee, Owings founded the community that took his name, Owingsville.

Owings and Menefee each owned significant parcels of land in what would become the town of Owingsville. To select whose name the community would take, the two men wagered that the man who built the finer home the quickest would be the namesake of the town. For the sum of $60,000, Owings won the contest. Owingsville was then founded in 1811.

Most likely this letter was carried on the Memphis Route to Owingsville, Bath County, KY
On the cover the Bath County town of Owingsville is misspelled "Owensville."

This is one of the grand old homes in Owingsville built in 1845.

Butterfield's Mail Bags

No Butterfield used mail bags have survived. We do know, however, that the bags were locked, since newspapers reported that robbers had to **cut open** the California Overland Mail mail bags.

"*Mail Robbers Arrested - Mr. S. H. Shock* [Butterfield] *agent in this city* [Memphis] *of the California Overland Mail route, received news on Tuesday, that the mail bags, which reached Madison, Arkansas, last Sunday night, had been* **cut open** *and robbed of their contents...*" [Memphis Daily Avalanche, Aug. 9, 1860, page 3]

Another interesting mention of the mail bags is found in the newspapers reporting the cake that was made for John Butterfield at Fort Smith when the first stagecoach arrived from California.

"*The arrival of the first overland mail from California was celebrated at Fort Smith. ...A large cake in the precise shape of the* **mail bags** *endorsed 'Overland Mail, San Francisco' in gilt letters was on the table, which when cut open, had in its center a letter, postmarked San Francisco, stamped in exact imitation, directed to Mr. John Butterfield, President Overland Mail Company.*

Mr. B. opened the letter and read it to the ladies and gentlemen present, which was greeted with shouts of laughter, and applause. The cake is a faithful representation, and since I commenced this letter to you, I have had a good view of it, and truly, it was surprising how exact in imitation of a **mail bag** *has been made with dough.*

The old Admiral says the first **mail bag** *has been opened and robbed at Fort Smith, and he shall keep a sharp look-out in future.*"
[Commercial Advisor, Oct. 25, 1858

This 1859 US Mail padlock is on display at the Smithsonian Postal History Museum Washington DC

This canvas locking mail bag from 1850-1860, may bear some resemblance to the bags used by the Overland Mail Company. This 15" wide and 20" long bag is owned by an antique collector in Webster, New York.

The lock on this russet leather stagecoach bag has patent dates of 1858, 1860 & 1866.

Antique Roadshow • Overland Mail Co. Shotgun

In season 24, episode 20 of the Antique Roadshow, Paul Carella of Bonhams, San Francisco, California appraised a shotgun that was brought to the show. The shotgun is reported to have been owned by George Washington Boyd, former 'stagecoach guard' and 'station master' for Butterfield's Overland Mail Company.

Appraiser Paul Carella identified it as made about 1840 in Burmingham, England. The shotgun was then shipped to a famous arms dealer, *(see image below)* A. J. Plate in San Francisco, California. Carella said that A. J. Plate then sold the shotgun to the Overland Mail Company, and then the brand "O.L.M.Cº" was placed on the stock *(see image below)*. Carella said that most "stagecoach" rifles are fake, however this rifle is genuine. While the rifle is only worth $300, with the provenance and Overland Mail Co. brand on the stock it would auction for at least $3,000.

Note: Lou Pipper discovered a reference to the rifles in the *"New Orleans Daily Crescent"* Aug. 16, 1859, page 1, col. 3: *"The Indians are mounted on fine American horses, and armed with rifles and six shooters, which they say were **bought by them***

Initials on the stock of the rifle.

CHAPTER FIVE

Butterfield Mail Carried on the St. Louis to Fort Smith Route

Butterfield Telegraph Mail On The St. Louis Route
Butterfield's Overland Mail Co. was the first contract to connect with the west coast by telegraph.

The two examples below are from exhibits of George Kramer. Once this envelope arrived in St. Louis from San Francisco, the contents were immediately telegraphed to the east coast. Kramer wrote, *"The best telegraph facilities were conducted by the National Telegraph Company in St. Louis; the two companies* **[Overland Mail & National Telegraph]** *had a working arrangement whereby the sender could have their message telegraphed eastward if the preprinted envelope were used. Use of this envelope authorized the National Telegraph Company to open the letter and telegraph the contents, thereby saving about three days."*

The example below came from *"Butterfield Overland Mail National Telegraph Exhibit,"* by Kramer.

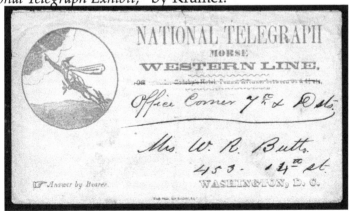

Purchased Oct., 2022 from
Marc S. Bedrin, 5314 S. W. 33rd Ave., Fort Lauderdale, FL 33312-5578

The example below is from Kramer's exhibit: *"The But-*

terfield Overland Route." A stamp was added to the envelope below for purpose of display in Kramer's exhibit.

Via Los Angeles, Overland.

CHAS. J. OSBORN,

NATIONAL TELEGRAPH OFFICE,

ST. LOUIS,

MISSOURI.

Purchased Oct., 2022 from
Marc S. Bedrin, 5314 S. W. 33rd Ave., Fort Lauderdale, FL 33312-5578

These two examples above came from exhibits prepared by George J. Kramer, one of America's most accomplished collectors, exhibitors and philatelic researchers. He received the 2018 Alfred F. Lichtenstein memorial award for his distinguished service to philately.

1860's Telegraph Key

George J. Kramer
Role of Distinguished Philatelists,
and the Luff Award

1858 Butterfield Mail On The St. Louis Route
One of the first pieces carried by Butterfield's Overland Mail

When Butterfield's Overland was only 60 days old, this cover was carried by stagecoach from San Francisco 8am Monday, Nov. 22, 1858. The stage arrive in Tipton, Missouri on Dec. 21st when it transferred to a train arriving in St. Louis Wednesday, Dec. 22, 1858* at 8:40 am, and continued by train toward its destination in Dorchester, Massachusetts to wait at the post office for Holly Wales pick up her mail. *[*Source: Mails of the Westward Expansion, Walske/Frajola, Appendix F, p. 299]*

1852 Street Map of Dorchester, Mass.

1852 Map of Dorchester, Massachusetts

Stagecoach image by Nathan A. Wright from Pixabay

Purchased Feb. 22, 2022 from Michael Heller, Mount Kisco, New York

The cover above was postmarked at San Francisco, California on Nov. 19, 1858, addressed to Miss Hollie L. Wales of Dorchester, Massachusetts - a distance of over 3,000 miles requiring postage of 10¢. This cancellation [SAF-295] was used July 20, 1857 to Aug. 7, 1861. *[John Williams, Western Express, March 1995, page 16]*

Miss Wales was most likely a girl friend or sister of one of the Gold Rush 49ers. Across the top, the sender wrote: *"Per Southern Overland Mail via Los Angeles,"* indicating the sender did not want it to be carried by ocean steam ship via Panama.

1859 St. Louis Route - Overland Mail Cover to Michigan

The cover shown below was mailed from Green Springs, California on Feb. 22, 1859, addressed to Richland, Michigan - a distance of over 3,000 miles requiring postage of 10¢. The original stamp either fell off in transit, or was removed at some point by a postage stamp collector. A Scott #35 ten cent Washington stamp was added for the purpose of display.

The original letter is missing, but it does contain a note that was sent with the letter:

Friend James,   *Reil Mountain, February 21st, 1859*

Will you please hand the enclosed to your sister and oblige.

                   Yours Truly, James Rowley, Esq.

Mr. Thompson was most likely one of the Gold Rush "49ers" - men who rushed to California seeking gold. The Gold Rush began on Jan. 24, 1848 when gold was found by James W. Marshall at Sutter's Mill in Coloma, California. The news of the gold rush brought approximately 300,000 people to California from the rest of the United States and abroad. These men were anxious to write home to their sweethearts and wives, and to receive return mail from them with love and news from home.

This cover and enclosed letter was purchased from
Labron Harris, P.O. Box 739, Glen Echo, Maryland

This cover was mailed from: Green Springs, California on Feb. 22nd. The sender designated in the lower left corner: *"Overland mail via Los Angeles,"* addressed to: James Rowley Esq., Richland, Macomber Co., Michigan.

1859 St. Louis Route - Overland Mail Cover to Maine

The cover shown below was mailed from Columbia, California on March 10, 1859, addressed to North Castine, Maine - a distance of over 3,000 miles requiring postage of 10¢. The sender wrote instructions to the Postmaster in the lower left of the cover, *"Over Land / By Via Los Angeles"* to indicate that the sender wished this cover to be carried by Butterfield's Overland Mail Company instead of carried by ocean steam ship via Panama or South America.

This March 10, 1859 cancellation [TUO-275] was used Dec. 18, 1856 to June 12, 1866. *[John Williams, Western Express, April 1993, p.42]*

This cover was purchased on Aug. 28, 2022
from Alex Benenson, California Covers, 4802 Queen Palm Lane, Tamarac, Florida

The recipient, Reuben Dunbar, North Castine, Maine is probably the Reuben Dunbar, who was born Feb. 5, 1798 in Penobscot *(just six miles from North Castine)*, Hancock County, Maine son of David Dunbar (1756-1841) and Elisabeth Ellms (1743-1791). Reuben Dunbar married Elizabeth Parker (1803 - 1878) and had 6 children. Reuben passed away on Aug. 15, 1881 in Penobscot, Hancock, Maine. His children were: Sally Sarah Dunbar (1821-1904); Bennett Roland Dunbar (1829-1919); Joel P. Dunbar (1832-1862); George H. Dunbar (1843-1860); Elizabeth "Lizzie" Dubar (1845 -1901); and Samuel Jerrish Dunbar (1847-1908).

The sender is most likely a "Gold Rush 49er" since it was mailed from Columbia, California - perhaps even from one of his sons: Bennett (age 30), Joel (age 27) or George (age 16). Columbia is located in the Sierra Nevada foothills, Tuolumne County, California. It was founded as a boomtown in 1850 when gold was found in the vicinity, and was known as the *"Gem of the Southern Mines."*

Today Columbia *"is a living gold rush town featuring the largest single collection of existing gold rush-era structures in the state.*

Visiting Columbia is like traveling back in time to the sights, smells, and sounds of a 19th century mining town—merchants dressed in 1850's attire, a whiff of coal smoke from the blacksmith shop, and the rumble of a stagecoach pulling into town! Spend the day enjoying fun activities for the whole family. Pan for gold, explore exhibits, ride the stagecoach, discover unique shops, and learn about the rich history of the California gold rush on a guided town tour."

Columbia, California as it appears today. Photo by visitcolumbiacalifornia.com

1859 St. Louis Route - Overland Mail Cover to Massachusetts

The cover below was mailed from San Francisco, California on May 22, 1859, addressed to Framingham, Massachusetts - a distance of over 3,000 miles requiring postage of 10¢.

This cover was purchased from Gary Kunzer of Webster, New York

The original stamp that was affixed to this envelope either fell off in transit, or was removed at some point by a postage stamp collector. Shown here in it's place is a 10¢ Scott #33 postage stamp, with flaws, that has been attached to this cover to give the reader a better idea of what the cover once looked like. This cover left San Francisco on Butterfield's stagecoach Monday, May 23 at noon, and arrived at Shackleford's Station in Syracuse, Missouri at 10:30 pm on Wednesday, June 13 for transfer to a train arriving in St. Louis June 14, 1859* at 8:40am, and on to Massachusetts by train. [*Mails of the Westward Expansion, p. 300]

This cover is postmarked: San Francisco, May 22, 1859, on a preprinted envelope by Hutchings & Rosenfield, "From San Francisco via Los Angeles," addressed to: Ezra Dyer Esq., Framingham, Massachusetts. This cancellation [SAF-295] was used July 20, 1857 to Aug. 7, 1861. [John Williams, Western Express, March 1995, page 16]

The recipient, Ezra Dyer, was born Nov. 11, 1776 and died June 28, 1870 at the age of 96.

Ezra was married to Anne, who was born Feb. 7, 1779 and died Aug. 5, 1845. They had a daughter, Elizabeth W. Dyer, born April 5, 1818 and died Sept. 22, 1913.

Ezra Dyer was the son of Asa Dyer (who was the son of Joseph, grandson of William, and great grandson of Christopher, and great great grandson of William Dyer).

Ezra's father, Asa, was born on July 26, 1739 in Weymouth, Norfolk and died on May 3, 1831 in Weymouth, Norfolk at the age of 91. Ezra's mother was Ruth Whitmarsh Dyer, who was born Jan. 4, 1744/45 in Weymouth, Norfolk and died on Sept. 21, 1807 in Weymouth, at the age of 62. Ezra's siblings were Jane, Rebecca, Asa Jr., Rebecca and Ruth.

"View of Framingham Common in 1808," painting in water colors by D. Bell Lithographed by the New England Lithographic Co., Boston, 1872

Framingham was first settled in 1647. About the time this letter was mailed, Framingham was known for its an annual gathering for members of the abolitionist movement. Each Independence Day from 1854 to 1865, the Massachusetts Anti-Slavery Society held a rally in a picnic area called Harmony Grove near what is now downtown Framingham.

In 1854 at the first rally in Framingham, William Lloyd Garrison burned copies of the Fugitive Slave Law of 1850, judicial decisions enforcing it, and the United States Constitution. Other prominent abolitionists present that day included William Cooper Nell, Sojourner Truth, Wendell Phillips, Lucy Stone, and Henry David Thoreau.

1859 St. Louis Route - Overland Mail to Massachusetts

The cover below was mailed from San Francisco, California on June 27, 1859, addressed to Boston, Massachusetts - a distance of over 3,000 miles requiring postage of 10¢. The Butterfield stage departed at noon Monday, June 27, 1859, traveling east by stagecoach for 21 days, arriving at Syracuse, Missouri July 18 at 10:30pm. Then by train to St Louis arriving July 19, 1859* at 8:40am *[*Mails of the Westward Expansion, p. 300]* It then took 14 days by train to travel through the postal system from St. Louis to Boston, arriving in George Simmons hands on Aug. 4, 1859, 38 days in transit from San Francisco.

This cover is postmarked: San Francisco, California, June 27, 1859 , using a US postal stationary envelope: Scott #U17, Die 2, pale green on white, addressed to: George A. Simmons, Esq.., 21 Long Wharf, Boston, Massachusetts. This cancellation [SAF-295] was used July 20, 1857 to Aug. 7, 1861. *[John Williams, Western Express, March 1995, page 16]*

The recipient of this letter, George A. Simmons, was a manufacturer of sperm whale oil and sperm candles, located on Newton St., Counting Room, No. 21 Long Wharf, Boston.

1859 St. Louis Route - Overland Mail Cover to Ohio

The cover shown below was postmarked Aug. 7, 1859 in San Francisco, addressed to Powell & Van Deman, Attorneys at Law, Delaware, Delaware County, Ohio. This cancellation [SAF-295] was used July 20, 1857 to Aug. 7, 1861. *[John Williams, Western Express, March 1995, page 16]*

According to the *"Delaware County Historical Society"* (1955) more than 150 residents of Delaware County traveled west as a Gold Rush 49er. This letter was probably written by one of those prospectors back home to their attorney.

Postage was paid with a Scott #31 ten cent stamp since destination was over 3,000 miles. Butterfield's stagecoach departed noon Monday, Aug. 8th, arriving at the Shackleford's station in Syracuse, Missouri on Wednesday, Aug. 28th at 10:30 pm. There it was transferred to a train arriving in St. Louis Aug. 29, 1859* and on to Ohio where attorney Powell would pick up his mail at the local post office. *[*Mails of the Westward Expansion, p. 300]*

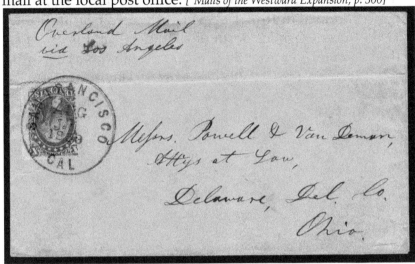

Purchased at the 2021 APS show in Chicago from
Don Tocher, U.S. Classics, of Sunapee, New Hampshire.

In the *"Delaware City Directory, 1859-1860,"* among the attorneys at law, the firm of Powell & Van Deman is listed. Thomas W. P Powell & Van Deman offices were located on East Sandusky, between North and Bumford Streets in Delaware. Thomas Powell died on Dec. 12, 1882.

Downtown Delaware image of Collins Banks store, located on South Liberty Street
Image source: Delaware County Historical Society

Delaware, a city in Delaware County, was founded in 1808 and incorporated in 1816. Delaware is located near the center of Ohio, about 30 miles north of Columbus, and is now part of the Columbus metropolitan area made famous as the birthplace of the 19th President, Rutherford B. Hayes.

The birthplace of the 19th President, Rutherford B. Hayes, (born 1822) is located in Columbus, Ohio. Image source: Library of Congress

1859 St. Louis Route - Overland Mail Cover to New York City

The sender of the cover shown below paid the 10¢ postage for a ½ ounce letter traveling more than 3,000 miles by using a 10¢ postage paid envelope Scott #U18. This cover was postmarked at San Francisco on Nov. 14, 1859 and received a clear strike of a circular postmark. This cancellation [SAF-295] was used July 20, 1857 to Aug. 7, 1861. *[John Williams, Western Express, March 1995, page 16]* The letter is addressed to Mr. Henry Biers, Care of Box 2586 Post Office, New York. The sender wrote instructions to the postmaster across the lower left edge of the envelope: *"Overland Mail via Los Angeles to St. Louis."*

This is the only cover in the author's collection (Bob Crossman) with the addition of "St. Louis" explicitly mentioned along with *"via Los Angeles."*

The Butterfield stage left San Francisco at noon Nov. 14,

1859, arriving at Syracuse, Missouri at 10:30 pm on Dec. 5th then by train to St. Louis arriving Dec. 6, 1859* and on to New York City for Mr. Henry Biers to pick up his mail at Box 2586 in his local post office. [*Mails of the Westward Expansion, p. 300]

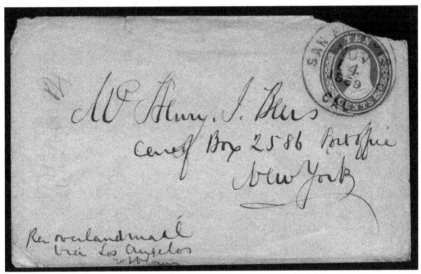

Purchased from Eliseo Temproano, Ottawa, ON, K1V1H1, March 13, 2022

*1858: New York City, Looking South from Chatham Square
Lithograph by A. Weingärtner's Lithography, 1858*

1870 Bird's Eye View of Lower Manhattan, NY, Currier & Ives, Library of Congress

1860 St. Louis Route - WESTBOUND Way Mail to Texas

The cover shown below was mailed from St. Louis, Missouri on March 7, 1860 to Jacksboro in north central Texas. Jacksboro was located on the route of the Butterfield Overland Mail. Regular postal service began at Jacksboro in 1859. Overland Mail, such as this, traveling less than 3,000 miles, therefore paying 3¢ rate, are much less common than 10¢ rate.

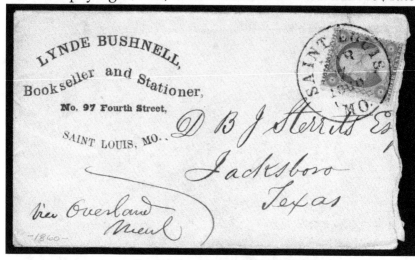

Purchased on Nov. 14, 2021 from
Thomas Stewart, Elgin, TX Hipstamp.com

This cover was postmarked at St. Louis, on March 7, 1860, addressed to D. B. J. Sterrets, Esq., Jacksboro, Texas. Notation on reverse side: *"Bushnel March 6, 60"* indicating that the cover once enclosed a letter written on March 6, 1860 from Lynde Bushnell Bookseller.

This cover was placed aboard the Butterfield stagecoach at 6 pm on Thursday, March 8th at Syracuse, Missouri. The stagecoach was scheduled to arrive in Jacksboro, Texas about March 20th.

The envelope was roughly opened along the right edge, but the tear did not affect the stamp affixed. The sender used a Lynde Bushnell Bookseller and Stationer advertising cover.

There is a contemporaneous manuscript notation at the bottom left requesting it be carried *"Via Overland Mail."* This envelope is addressed to the early Jack County pioneer, D. B. J. Sterrets, Esq. in Jacksboro, Texas.

"West Side Square, Jacksboro, Texas"

Jacksboro, Texas was first settled in the 1850's, with newcomers attracted by land offers from the Texas Emigration and Land Office. Originally called "Mesquiteville," the community grew up along the banks of Lost Creek and spread out over the pasture land between Lost Creek and the waters of the West Fork of Keechi Creek. The town was renamed "Jacksboro" in 1858, when it became the county seat, in honor of brothers William and Patrick Jack, veterans of the Texas Revolution. The county was one of the few in Texas to vote against secession before the Civil War.

1860 St. Louis Route - Overland Mail Cover to Wisconsin

The cover below was postmarked in Michigan Bluff, (DPO) Placer County, California on Sept. 10, 1860. This may be the earliest use of this cancellation. John Williams only records its use [PLA-1336] from Aug. 19, 1861 to Feb. 26,1867. *[John Williams, Western Express, Jan. 1991, page 82]*

The Postal System carried this mail 150 miles southwest to San Francisco, where it was placed aboard Butterfield's Overland Mail Co.'s stagecoach at noon on Friday, Sept. 14, 1860 arriving at Fort Smith Oct. 4th,* *[*Mails of the Westward Expansion, p.302]* then on to Syracuse, Missouri at 10:30 pm Saturday, Oct. 6, 1860, and then by train to Westford, Massachusetts.

This cover was purchased on Feb. 20, 2022 from
Tom Heisey, P.O. Box 490, Susanville, California.

The sender of this cover paid the 10¢ postage for a ½ ounce letter traveling more than 3,000 miles, using a Scott #35 stamp. The sender wrote instructions to the postmaster across the left of the envelope: *"via Los Angeles."* This envelope is addressed to Mrs. Susan Amelia Leland of Westford, Massachusetts. She was born in 1834 and died in 1862. Its likely she was the sweetheart, wife or daughter of a Gold Rush 49er.

The town of Michigan City, California was founded in 1850. In 1858 the town became undermined and unsafe so it was moved half a mile, and renamed Michigan Bluff two years before this cover was mailed.

Westford, Massachusetts, 1886, engraving published by L. R. Burleigh, Troy, NY showing 1-Uniterian Church, 2-Congregational Church, 3-Westford Academy, and 4-Town Hall

The town of Westford, Mass. was incorporated in 1729, and is located northwest of Boston.

1860 St. Louis Route - Overland Mail Cover to California
This is Bob Crossman's first Butterfield Cover. It was purchased from Rainer Gerlach at Tulsa's Sooner Stamps.

At the time the cover shown below was mailed, Butterfield's Overland Mail Co. was the default carrier for all transcontinental mail - therefore Mrs. Wheeler did not need to express her personal preference to avoid the ocean bound steam ship route by writing *"Overland"* in the upper left.

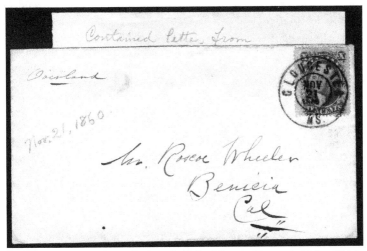

This cover was purchased from Rainer Gerlach of Sooner Stamps in Tulsa, Oklahoma.

This letter was written by Mrs. Wheeler at Pigeon Cove, Massachusetts on Nov. 20, 1860. This cover was postmarked six miles away at the Gloucester, Massachusetts Post Office on Nov. 20, 1860, addressed to her husband, Mr Roscoe Wheeler of Benicia, California - a distance of over 3,000 miles requiring postage of 10¢. The sender wrote directions in upper left: *"Overland,"* and paid the postage with a 10¢ Washington, Scott #35, Type V.

According to western postal history expert John Birkibine II of Tucson, Arizona, it is highly likely that Mr. Roscoe Wheeler moved to Benicia, California as part of the gold rush.

According to the records of John Birkinbine II: Leaving Gloucester, Massachusetts on Nov. 21, 1860 it arrived at St. Louis by train at 8 am on Thursday, Nov. 22, 1860. The cover was then carried by train to Syracuse, Missouri where it continued west on Butterfield's mail stagecoaches. The route west involved these stations:*(Overland Mail's 1859 Schedule)*

St. Louis, Missouri train station, departing for a 10 hour trip covering 160 miles to
Syracuse, Missouri, departing at 6 pm for a 37 ¾ hour trip covering 143 miles to
Springfield, Missouri, departing at 7:45 am for a 26½ hour trip covering 100 miles to
Fayetteville, Arkansas, departing at 10:15 am for a 17½ hour trip covering 65 miles to
Fort Smith, Arkansas, departing at 3:30 am for a 45 hour trip covering 205 miles to
Sherman, Texas, departing at 12:30 am for a 32½ hour trip covering 146½ miles to
Fort Belknap, Texas, departing at 9:00 am for a 30 ¼ hour trip covering 136 miles to
Fort Chadbourne, Texas departing at 3:15 pm for 36½ trip covering 165 miles to
Pecos River Crossing, TX departing at 3:45 am for a 55 ¼ hour trip covering 248½ miles to
El Paso, Texas, departing at 11:00 am for a 33½ hour trip covering 150 miles to
Soldier's Farewell, Texas, departing at 8:30 pm for a 41 hour trip covering 184½ miles to
Tucson, Arizona, departing at 1:30 pm for a 31½ miles trip covering 141 miles to
Gila River, Arizona, departing at 9:00 pm for a 30 hour trip covering 135 miles to
Fort Yuma, California, departing at 3:00 am for a 53½ hour trip covering 254 miles to
Los Angeles, California, departing at 8:30 am for a 23 hour trip covering 96 miles to
Fort Tejou, California, departing at 7:30 am for a 28 hour trip covering 127 miles to
Visalia, California, departing at 11:30 am for an 18 hour trip covering 82 miles to
Firebaugh's Ferry, California, departing at 5:30 for a 27 hour trip covering 163 miles to
San Francisco, California, arriving on Dec. 16, 1860 at 8:30 am.
After arriving in San Francisco on Dec. 16, 1860
it was carried 36 miles north by the Postal System to the post office at Benicia, California
where it was held until Mr. Roscoe Wheeler came to pick up his mail.

The original letter has been removed, but this cover still contains a handwritten note: *"Contained letter from Mother to Papa dated Nov. 20, 1860 written just before leaving Pigeon Cove for California."*

The Following Eleven Covers Are Butterfield Mail NOT marked *"Overland via Los Angeles"*

On Dec. 17, 1859, the postmaster General ordered that unless otherwise directed, the new default method for transporting transcontinental mail would be by Butterfield's Overland Mail Co. instead of by ocean ship. Prior to 1860, only letters specifically directed on the face of the envelope: *"overland"* or *"via Los Angeles"* were carried by the Butterfield Overland stagecoaches.

1860 St. Louis Route - Overland Mail Cover to Ireland

The cover shown below received a red circular postmark on May 5, 1860 in San Francisco.

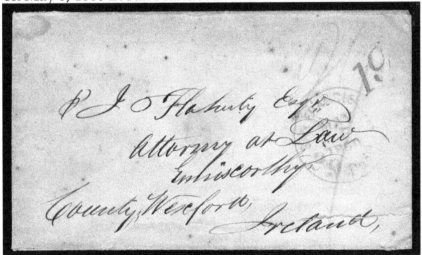

There are no backstamps to indicate what ship this cover was carried on.

This cover was loaded onto the Butterfield stagecoach at 8:00 am Monday, May 7, 1860 arriving at Syracuse, Missouri Monday, May 28th at 10:30 pm From Syracuse, it traveled by train to St. Louis arriving Tuesday, May 29, 1860* *[Mails of Westward Expansion, p. 301]* and on to New York City where it transferred to a ship to reach P. J. O'Flaherty in Enniscorthy, Wexford County, Ireland. This cover is addressed to J. O. Flaherty Esq. Attorney at Law, Enniscorthy, County Wexford, Ireland.

According to James W. Milgran, (Stampless Cover Editor for The Chronicle of the Classic United States Postal Issues):

"The transcontinental passage of a letter was increased from 5 cents to 10 cents in the crediting of any transatlantic cover whether it was carried by a British ship or an American ship. This cover has a red crayon 29 indicating a payment of 29 cents in San Francisco. The New York red exchange marking clearly states that 29 cents was paid. The 19 in red is the credit that the United States gave to Great Britain, 16 cents for ocean postage and 3 cents for internal British postage. Most covers from towns such as Boston or Philadelphia going by New York would have had PAID 24 exchange markings, but the rate was higher, 29 cents, because this was a west coast usage."

1860 St. Louis Route - Overland Mail Letter to Maine

The cover shown below was addressed May 30, 1860 at Clipper Mills, California. James Manter had to carry his letter four miles to the nearest post office at Strawberry Valley. There it was postmarked, on the left front center, with a faint red circular cancellation on June 1, 1860. This cancellation is not reported by John Williams. *[Western Express, Sept. 1994, p.68]*

From Strawberry Valley, the postal system carried this letter 170 miles southwest to San Francisco. At noon on Monday, June 4, 1860 it was placed on Butterfield's Overland Mail stagecoach for an 18 day trip to Fort Smith, Arkansas. At Fort Smith, it merged with the Memphis mail, and arrived at Springfield, Missouri June 24th.* *[Mails of the Westward Expansion, p. 301]* Arriving at Syracuse at 10:30 pm on June 27th, it was then transferred to a train for the balance of its trip to Maine.

This letter was written by James A. Manter (1802-1882), son of Benjamin (1773-1868) and Abigail West Manter (1777-1814). He was married twice: Maria Norton (1804-1864) and Nancy Russell Gray (1825-1911). They had six children: Benjamin Frankin Manter (1827-1920); Amy Allen Manter (1849-1925); Charles Manter (1843-1931); James Murray Manter (1838-1838); Harriet Maria Manter 1828-1916); and Hiram Manter (1836-1916).

James addressed this letter to one of his children, Hiram Manter, Esq. Hiram Manter was born in Industry, Franklin County, Maine on April 3, 1836 to James Manter (1802-1882) and Maria Norton (1804-1864). Hiram Manter married Frances Weymouth (1843-1902) and had 2 children - John Lyman Manter (1879-1935) and Mary F. Manter (1864-1900). Hiram Manter passed away on Oct. 30, 1916 in Fort Fairfield, Aroostook County, Maine.

Purchased March 25, 2022 from
Mark Baker, California Covers, Pollock Pines, California. Ex Chandler

This cover still contains the original letter, which reads:

Folks at Home,   *Clipper Mills, May 30, 1860*
     When I last wrote Home about 2 weeks ago, I was down on the plains at work for the Boys, I was then about to start for this place. I am now in the employ of a large Mill Company - Willey, Hudson, Craine & Co. and my business is Watchman. Watch the mill nights. My health is very good. As was the rest of the boys when I left the Valley. Stephen Holbrook is Clerk of the Lumber Yard here. It is a Steam Saw Mill. Consequently there is considerable danger from fire. At night I am boarded in the House with the family, and have a room and bed of my own.

It is 60 miles from here to where John lives. There is lumber here that would astonish the log choppers of Maine. Pine trees, as thick together as the maples in Your Grove, and from 3 ft to 10 foot through, and from 100 to 200 ft high and straight as a rifle. I have seen trees called Sugar Pine (like our best pine at home) that was free from limbs for more than 100 feet from the base. When they fall it makes the old woods tremble.

Pay in California is not so high as at home. My Chance [job] of Watchman is not hard, as work to do at all. Nothing but go my rounds for hours. And then do what I please. I suppose you're curious to know how much I get per month. Well I get $40.⁰⁰ and food. So now you can rest easy.

Adelaide thinks she had better come here. I think she had better stay at home. A time may come when I can find her a Chance [job], and then if she wants to come I will try to help her to get here. There is no society here. So far as I have seen. She would, well I don't know what she thinks she can do.

I want you to put my watch tools and fixens together for I may strike a Chance [job] yet, and send for them. Watch cleaning and ring making pays big here in some places. I have seen men pay from five to ten dollars to have their watch cleaned. I scant do any thing at it unless I have a big Chance [job].

I have not heard from home for 2 months. If you write one direct at Strawberry Valley Yuba County. That is the nearest post office. When I was at Marysville on my ways here I saw Daniel Taylor and Kendrick Moose. They were on their way to Camptonville. Had hired out, going to mining. Looked well and rugged.

Hiram, you must write to me every time __ ___ for I think that your letters are a little better than the rest. Has your sheep got a lamb yet? Tell father if H. E. grants you to stay at home and be contented. You must have something to call your own. I suppose your just finishing up spring lambs.

Well I have been doing Spring Work all winter and now here lambing is about done, and Thanksgiving will come and shortly. I suppose that by this time Jim Manter is entirely forgotten, but should some one accidentally ask of me, give them my post office address together with my respects and tell them to write and find out. As time is passing and I must close. Farewell,

James A. Manter
Strawberry Valley, Yuba County, Cali.

1860 St. Louis Route - Overland Mail Letter to Maine

The cover shown below was postmarked 22 days after the cover above, and was written to the same address. This cover however is addressed to A. A. Manter instead of Hiram Manter. Apparently James A. Manter was addressing this letter to another one of his children, Amy Allen Manter (1849-1925).

This cover was postmarked, on the left front center, with a faint red circular cancellation at the nearest post office – Strawberry Valley, California on June 21, 1860. This cancellation is not reported by John Williams. *[Western Express, Sept. 1994, p.68]*

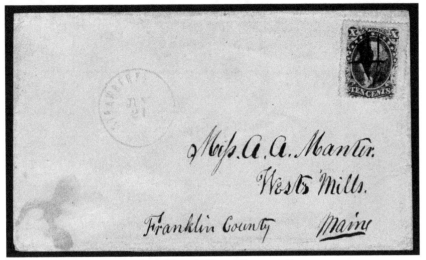

Purchased Feb., 2023 on Hipstamps from
Doyle Tillma, Doyle's Stamps, Lakewood, WA Ex Chandler

Entering the postal system at Strawberry Valley, this mail was carried 170 miles southwest to San Francisco. Departing 8 am June 25, 1860, Butterfield's stagecoach arrived at Fort Smith, Arkansas in 18 days. At Fort Smith, after transferring Memphis bound passengers and mail to a second stagecoach, this cover passed through Fayetteville, Arkansas July 14, 1860.* [*Mails of the Westward Expansion, p. 301] Scheduled to arrive at Syracuse, at 10:30 pm on July 18, this cover was transferred to a train for the balance of its trip to Maine.

Central Route used by the Pony Express '60-'61, and Butterfield '61-'64

The town of Strawberry Valley was a station along the Central Overland Pony Express between Yank's Station and Webster's, Sugar Loaf House Station. **If this letter had been mailed in 1862, it could have been handed to the Overland**

Mail stage as it passed by on its way from Placerville, California to the eastern terminus of the Central Overland Trail.

During the Gold Rush, Strawberry Valley was a major trading outpost for the gold miners. Hydraulic mining was done extensively in Strawberry Valley.

1860 Cleveland, Ohio to California via Overland Mail

The cover below received a red postmark at the Cleveland, Ohio Post Office on June 13, 1860, addressed to Mr. Thomas Cullen, Oroville, Butte County, California. This letter's destination was more than 3,000 miles, so only 10¢ postage was required. However, its weight was more than ½ ounce, so double postage was paid with a horizontal pair of 10¢ green type II (Scott #32) affixed to the left side of the envelope.

Purchased April 24, 2022 from Northland International of Verona, New Jersey on ebay.

This westbound letter was addressed to Oroville, were gold was found at Union Cape, just north of Oroville. This was one of the most successful mining operations in the entire state of California. A trench of about 5,000 feet long was built to divert the Feather River for the mining at the claims.

This letter would have traveled by train from Cleveland to Syracuse, Missouri where it would have been placed on Butterfield's Overland Mail Co. stagecoach to begin the 21 to 23 day journey to San Francisco. Arriving in San Francisco, this letter would have been carried the final 150 miles north to Oroville, California by the postal system. *In 1856 Oroville's population was 4,000, the 5th largest city in California.*

In the spring of 2022, this letter was examined by the expertizing committee of the American Philatelic Society. They determined that *"United States, Scott 32, horizontal pair with centerline in selvage, type II, position 9-10L1, tied by red Cleveland Ohio cancel to California, cover tear at top. Can not determine year or how carried to California. Genuine."* [APEX certificate # 243689]

There are two men by the name of Thomas Cullen buried in Cleveland. One was born 1843 and died 1886. Another was born 1844 and died 1865.

Photo No. 1.—Rock crushing plant of the Natomas Consolidated of California at Oroville. Capacity 1000 tons of crushed rock per day.

View of the Natomas Consolidated at Oroville, California during gold rush years. ca. 1909.

July 1860 - St. Louis Route - Middle Yuba , CA to Fairplay, WI

The cover below was written July 7, 1860 in Middle Yuba, California by John, brother of Mary Deawitt.

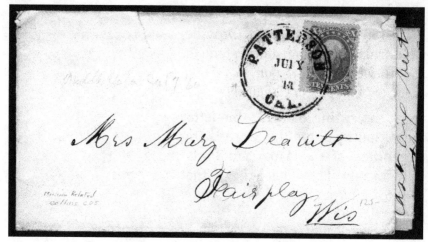

Purchased Feb. 15, 2023 on Hip Stamps from
Doyle Tillman, of Doyle's Stamps, Lakewood, Washington.

The Middle Yuba River was a major mining site during the California Gold Rush. It was one of the areas most heavily affected by hydraulic mining, which washed large volumes of loose sediment into the river channel. The Middle Yuba River drains a remote portion of the Tahoe National Forest.

This letter was carried from Middle Yuba, to the post office at Patterson, Nevada County, California where it received a postmark on July 13, 1860. This may be the latest use of this cancellation [NEV-1075]. John Williams only records its use from May 5 to July 1, 1857. *[Western Express, Jan. 1991, p.52]*

The Butterfield stagecoach departed San Francisco at noon on Friday, July 16, 1860 and headed south.

Based on the postmark, this letter would have been carried from Patterson 49 miles south to the Firebaugh's Ferry Station where it was placed on the Butterfield Overland Mail stagecoach on Tuesday, July 17, 1860 when the stage stopped for a change of horses. The stage was scheduled to arrive in Syracuse, Missouri on Aug. 8th, where it was transferred to a train toward its destination at the post office in Fairplay to wait for Mrs. Mary Deawitt to pick up her mail.

The Patterson, California postmark is considered rare by John Williams.*[Western Express, Jan. 1991, p.52]* A complete city-date cancellation on the cover, ties the XF Scott #35 green Washington stamp to the cover. The stamp is sound and well adhered and the cover is very clean despite pencil notations by previous dealers on the reverse. There are a couple of tears along the upper edge of the envelope. In addition, the folded letter which was conveyed in the cover is also included. The enclosed letter reads:

Middle Yuba, Cal July 7th 1860

Dear Sister Mary,

Your letter May 14th has been received more than a week ago. I have been working very hard in the mines trying to make things go right and have not written to anyone for several weeks on that account, not even to Effie. We got your letters announcing Father's death some time before the last one but I had previously heard of it through William. I can offer no comments on that occasion. I leave you to judge what my feelings are and hope he is better off now than he was here.

I hope Agnes may get along well. I do not see how she could imagine that the Money was for work done on the diggings. She ought to know that I owed nothing on that. I cannot see why it is that because I owed one farthing to them that I should be made to bear the whole expense of their working.

I hope she knows before this time how it is. I sent the Money to Father because he asked for it. Not because I owed him for a cause. You, and every one else who knows anything about our affairs, knows it was as I say. What I said in the letters was true and, although I felt sad that when I heard that I had probably written it while Father was on his death bed, yet I had hoped to hear things from him. I wish you had kept the letter or burned it as James tells me she will be likely to show it to every one. I have a good mind to demand that the letters should be returned for she has no right to it. But as it is likely all the people in Fairplay and half the people of Dubous had read it by this time. I suppose it is hardly worth while. Had I known that Father was in the habit of showing my letters, as I now know, I would hardly have written to him at all and I am sure I would cut my correspondence when I had any reason to suspect for such work.

You will see Mary, that so far I have been writing in bad humor, and I am sorry for it. I should never give way to such moods but I am all impulse, and as I feel when I sit down to write my letters will show exactly.

I am glad to see that you are in good spirits. I can not see why you could not get along well enough on the place. I know you will have hard work, and many trials, but that appears to be the lot of us all and I hope and trust you may have as few of them as any of us for I am sure you have had your share and more. Go along and never mind what any one says - may go best if you can stand to what you said in your last letter with regards to minding your own business. Remember that we have not in trust at Fairplay any longer and there are more than one Eye looking to your welfare.

It is altogether likely you will see some change in affairs at Fairplay before a years time at all. I should feel like a stranger there, and consider myself as such now, not that I wanted anything to do with anything there but what belonged to the Family should not have gone - especially when it did not belong to the one who pretended to give it.

But I am as well satisfied as things are, if I can ever get clear of that infernal Debt on the Diggings. Curse the day I ever had anything to do with them. She can surely claim no more. As for the Diggings, you had better sell them or do what ever else you like with them. I don't want to hear anything more about the matter. They have cost me all they ever shall.

I am glad to hear you contemplate improving your place this summer. Let us know how you expect to do the fencing as you have given us a hint as to the trees.

I hastily wish indeed that I could have been one of the party to pay you a visit but I hope you all enjoyed yourselves well and it may be my turn after a while.

I hear Effie will be thinking I am slow about writing to her this time, but I cannot help it and hope she will forgive me.

I can appreciate all your kind wishes and believe your are sincere with regard Effie and me but I think it might as well be left out for there is no telling what may happen and as for happiness it is something not to be looked for with any one. My love to all
from your Brother John

1860 Little Rock to Connecticut via Overland Mail

The cover below contained a letter written July 15, 1860, mailed at Little Rock, Arkansas, addressed to George O. Hoadley, Esq., of Hartford, Connecticut. The recipient wrote on the face, *"July 15, 1860 Ans. Dec. 7th 1860."*

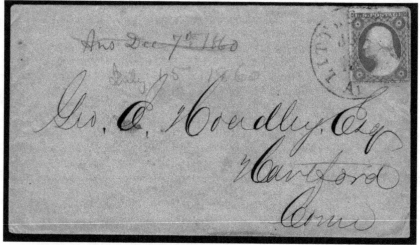

Purchased May 3, 2022 from Larry A. Dobbs of Hoxie, Arkansas on ebay.

This letter's destination was less than 3,000 miles, so only 3¢ postage was required.

This letter was placed on Butterfield's Overland Mail stagecoach on Tuesday, July 17 at Little Rock's Anthony House, and arrived at the Memphis Post Office on Thursday, July 19, 1860, where it would have been transferred to an eastbound train bound for delivery to the Hartford, Connecticut Post Office to wait for George Hoadley to call for his mail.

This letter is addressed to the capital city of Connecticut, and most likely it was intended for the George Hoadly (July 31, 1826 – Aug. 26, 1902), who was a Democratic politician who served as the 36th governor of Ohio Jan. 14, 1884 until Jan. 11, 1886.

Governor Hoadly was born in New Haven, Connecticut, on July 31, 1826. As the son of George Hoadley and Mary Ann Woolsey Hoadley, his birth name was "Hoadley", but he later dropped the "e."

Governor Hoadly married Mary Burnett Perry in 1851, a descendant of Dr. William Burnet, a surgeon on the staff of the Continental Army. Their son, George, earned degrees at Harvard University, and their so, Edward M., graduated from Rensselaer Polytechnic Institute. Their daughter, Laura, married a second cousin, Theodore Woolsey Scarborough.

Governor George Hoadly
Source: National Governors Association

1860 St. Louis Route - Overland Mail Cover to Illinois
Stampless Cover from Butterfield Station at Visalia, California

The cover below was postmarked in Visalia, Tulare County, California July 24, 1860. John Williams records this as the earliest use of this cancellation [TUL-2385] that was used July 24, 1860 to Aug. 15, 1863. *[Western Express, Jan. 1993, page 60]*

It was placed on the Butterfield Overland Mail Co. stage when it stopped at the Visalia swing station 228 miles south of San Francisco on July 29, 1860, scheduled to arrive at Shackleford's Station in Syracuse, Missouri on Saturday, Aug. 18 or Wednesday the 22nd where it was transferred to a train for Decatur, Illinois.

Instead of affixing a stamp, when the sender paid the required 10¢ in cash, the Postmaster marked the envelope "10¢" and affixed a black oval "PAID" rubber stamp in the upper left corner.

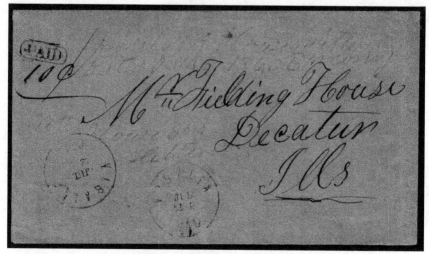

*This cover was purchased on ebay from
Mark Baker Enterprises, Pollock Pines, California on Aug. 31, 2022.*

The recipient wrote across the face of the envelope in faint pencil, *"Fielding House Letter Dated ... 1860 ..."*

The article on Visalia in Wikipedia reports, *"Early growth in Visalia can be attributed in part to the gold rush along the Kern River. The gold fever brought many transient miners through Visalia along the way, and when the lure of gold failed to materialize, many returned to Visalia to live their lives and raise families. In 1859, Visalia was added to John Butterfield's Overland Stage route from St. Louis to San Francisco. A plaque commemorating the location can be found at 116 East Main Street."*

*Early photo of Visalia, Tulare County, California. Sign on the second floor reads, "New St. Charles 25 Meals - Lodging." Signs on the first floor read,
"Woo Kee Washing Ironing," "Lodging 25ᶜˢ," "St. Charles Saloon," "Meals 25ᶜˢ."*

This envelope is addressed to Mr. Fielding House of Decatur, Illinois. The city of Decatur was founded in 1829 and is situated along the Sangamon River and Lake Decatur in Central Illinois.

1860 Westbound from New York to California

The cover below was mailed to San Jose, California which was a regular stop on the Butterfield route. Edward (abbreviated Edw.) Huntington mailed the cover, shown below, from Rome, New York on Nov. 2, 1860 to Henry W. Coe. The distance was over 3,000 miles and required ten cents postage, paid here with three 3¢ and one 1¢ stamp.

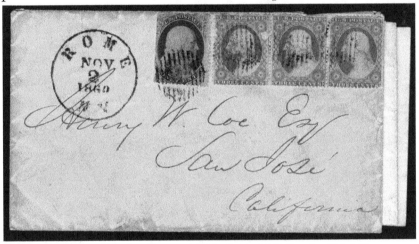

This is one of the few covers carried by Butterfield's Overland Mail Co. whose postage was paid with four stamps instead of one 10¢ stamp.

The Nov. 2, 1860 letter is not enclosed, but two other letters between these correspondents are still enclosed in the envelope above: April 4, 1859 and Dec. 3, 1858.

Butterfield's San Jose station was about 50 miles south of San Francisco. San Jose was officially founded as California's first civilian settlement on Nov. 29, 1777, as the Pueblo de San José de Guadalupe.

The recipient of this cover, Henry W. Coe, Sr. was born Feb. 6, 1820 in Northwood, N. H, and died June 17, 1896. He moved into California in 1848. He settled in San Jose, where he purchased 150 acres in the section known as The Willows. Here he established a beautiful country residence, the hospitality of which was nowhere surpassed. He cleared his tract, and was the first man to plant fruit trees and hops.

Henry W. Coe Sr.
Source: Hamiltonhistoricalrecords.com

Mr. Coe was the first extensive shipper of hops to New York, Liverpool and Australia, and he grew the first tobacco in California, from which he made cigars, and the first silk grown and manufactured from the native product of the United States. His experimental crop demonstrated the possibility of silk culture in Santa Clara Valley, both soil and climate being admirably adapted to the mulberry and cocoon production.

Henry was exceptionally well read, with a memory that was remarkable, and he retained his faculties up to within an hour of his death. He remembered perfectly General LaFayette's visit to this country. He and his brother Eben had stood watching on the banks of the Hudson when Fulton first ran his steamer on its waters. He knew San Francisco when it contained a population of only five hundred.

Henry W. Coe acquired the San Felipe Ranch and had his two sons, Henry Coe Junior and Charles Coe. In 1892, the brothers vastly expanded the property owned by their family, by acquiring 6,000 additional acres within the bodies of water and hills of the Diablo Valley. In 1958 the deed of the ranches were deeded to California which allowed the state to convert the property to a state park, named The Henry W. Coe Sr. State Park.*[Source: Hamilton Historical Records, by Phillip Hamilton and A History of New California, 1903, page 173-ff.]*

Dec. 1860 Honolulu, Hawaii to Boston, Mass.
Below is one of just a handful of Hawaii via Butterfield Overland covers that have survived.

The cover below was postmarked on Monday, Nov. 26, 1860 in Honolulu, Hawaii, addressed to Judson Shute of Boston, Massachusetts. This letter was carried by ship to the USA, arriving at San Francisco on Friday, Dec. 21, 1860.

Purchased Oct. 21, 2021 on ebay from larrysellcovers of Hornell, New York

Left: Kanaina, a chief of the Sandwich Islands, one of the two chiefs to greet Captain James Cook at Kealakekua Bay by John Webber. ca 1800
Right: Ka'ahumanu, Queen of the Sandwich Islands, engraved by G. Langlume, 1822

The Francis Palmer, 1886 — Ocean Steam Ship — Butterfield's Stagecoach — Stagecoach — Train to Boston

According to the Honolulu paper, *The Pacific Commercial,* the only mail ship departing for San Francisco between Nov. 26 and Dec. 20th was the *Francis Palmer,* departing on Dec. 8th. Typically it took about 12 days to sail to San Francisco.

The large "12" in the San Francisco postmark indicates that the recipient needs to pay the 12¢ due – 10¢ for the transcontinental rate, and 2¢ for the ship fee.

Following the Dec. 17, 1859 order of the Postmaster General that the default carrier of transcontinental mail would be Butterfield's Overland Mail Co (instead of by Ocean Steamer), this letter would have been held at the San Francisco Post Office over the weekend, and placed in a mailbag departing on Butterfield's Overland Mail stage. The next stage departed San Francisco on Monday, Dec. 24, 1860 at noon, and scheduled to arrive in St. Louis on Jan. 17, 1861. Christmas Day did not keep the Butterfield stagecoach from keeping its scheduled departure on Dec. 24th. [*Mails of the Westward Expansion, p. 302]

From St. Joseph, this letter would have continued eastbound on a train for delivery to the Boston, Massachusetts Post Office to wait for Judson Shute to stop by to ask if he had any mail. The recipient, Judson Shute was born in Montgomery, Alabama, on Aug. 20, 1837 to William M. Shute (1804-1870) and Martha Chaplin (1806-1882). He passed away on Dec. 29, 1911 in Boston, Suffolk County, Massachusetts. Judson Shute had two children: Katherine Hamer Shute (1862-1939) and Mary Chaplain Shute (1871-1954).

1860 St. Louis Route - Butterfield's Overland Mail Cover to Maine

The cover shown below was postmarked at the gold rush town of Camptonville, California on Dec. 12, 1860. This cancellation [YUB-235] was used Dec. 18, 1859 to Feb. 1, 1863. [John Williams, Western Express, Sept. 1994, page 60]

The Postal System carried this letter 170 miles to San Francisco. The Butterfield stage departed Dec. 17, 1860, scheduled to arrive 23 days later in St. Louis. Then by train to the Brunham Village, Maine Post Office to wait for Miss Eliza A. Berry to pick up her mail. No designation of *"via overland"* or *"via Los Angeles"* was needed since Butterfield's Overland Mail was the default carrier of all transcontinental mail in all of 1860.

Purchased at the 2021 APS show in Chicago from Labron Harris or Glen Echo, Maryland

Camptonville, California is about 170 miles northeast of San Francisco. Gold was discovered at that location in 1850, and the place first became known as *Gold Ridge*. In 1854, when the community received its first post office, the name *Gold Ridge* was changed to *Camptonville,* honoring the town blacksmith, Robert Campton.

Camptonville, California "Horse Drawn Wagon" ca 1915, courtesy Yuba County Library

During the gold rush years, Camptonville was a frequent stop for travelers and freight wagons since it was on the Henness Pass Road, a major route over the Sierra Nevada via Henness Pass. There is a plaque in Camptonville revealing that the town had over 50 saloons, brothels and even a bowling alley once upon a time. By 1863, William H. Brewer passed through

Camptonville and described it in his journal as follows:

> *"September 10 we started on our way--first to Nevada [City], a few miles, a fine town in a rich mining region, then to San Juan North (there are several other San Juans in the state), then to Camptonville, a miserable, dilapidated town, but very picturesquely located, with immense hydraulic diggings about. The amount of soil sluiced away in this way seems incredible. Bluffs sixty to a hundred feet thick have been washed away for hundreds of acres together. But they were not rich, the gold has 'stopped,' the town is dilapidated--but we had to pay big prices nevertheless."*

When the gold mining in the area diminished, the local economy turned to the timber industry. When Sierra Mountain Mills closed in 1994 it put 75 people out of work, and the population of Camptonville plummeted. Today the only businesses in town are the Lost Nugget gas station/convenience store, a post office, an elementary school, Burgee Dave's bar and restaurant in the old Mayo Saloon building, and the district office of the Yuba River Rangers and fire crew.

1860 Austin, Texas via Butterfield Overland to Pennsylvania
Overland Mail traveling less than 3,000 miles, therefore paying 3¢ postage, are much less common than 10¢ rate.

John Simpson wrote this letter and had it postmarked at Austin, Texas on Dec. 18, 1860.

From Austin the Postal System carried this mail north to Fort Belknap Station. At Fort Belknap, Texas it most likely was placed on the Butterfield Overland Mail Co. stagecoach since it was transcontinental mail. From St. Louis this cover traveled by train to T. C. Simpson Esq. of Norristown, Montgomery County, Pennsylvania.

No designation of *"via overland"* or *"via Los Angeles"* was needed since Butterfield's Overland Mail Co. was the default carrier of all transcontinental mail in all of 1860. The attached postage is only 3¢ since its destination was less than 3,000 miles from Austin.

This cover was purchased from Kurt Harding, of Boerne, Texas,
at the Oct. 2021 Pinpex Stamp Show in Jacksonville, Arkansas

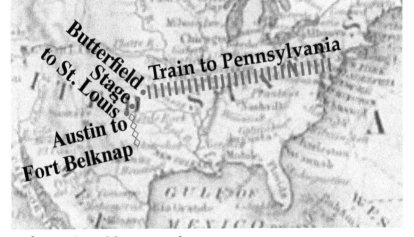

The enclosed letter reads:
Austin, Texas, Dec. 18, 1860

Dear Friend,

I suppose you will think I have forgotten you entirely but it is not so. I have been very busy for the last two months.

First I had to go up country with the paymaster to pay off some companies which are up there. When I came back I had to start out to buy horses for the Regiment M. Many having the contract for supplying them, we have got through now.

Well, here we are not yet – instead I have been out fighting Indians, but I expect to leave the last of this week to go to the Jackson's. A place about three hundred miles from here where we will shall stay all winter, then in Spring occupy the posts along the Frontier.

I haven't much news to send you. The officers gave a ball a few evenings ago which I attended and had a very pleasant time. It was held in the State Capital. The Governor and ___ were there and all the first families of Austin. Everybody enjoyed themselves very well.

There has been a good deal of cholera here this fall. Quite a number of the Soldiers died. *I have had very good health since I have been out here.*

I wish you would inquire how I stand in the lodge and pay up whatever dues may be against me and leave me know [if you] have heard anything from my Father lately. Tell Jake Frick that I am all O. K. and if he promises not to reduce me, I shall write him soon. Remember me to Joseph. Although tell him to pick me up some nice young gal. Write soon and give all the news. Send me a paper. Express my love for Mrs. Simpson's baby and self.

I wish you all a Merry Christmas & happy New Year.

Yours Truly, John Simpson
To T. C. Simpson, Esq., Direct Care of D. A. Wray
6th U.S. Calvary, Austin, Texas

*A VERY early photo (1860s) of Congress Ave. in Austin, Texas
looking north toward the old capitol building. Note the foot bridges crossing the street.
Those were to keep the mud and slop off of people as they crossed. The streets were subsequently bricked over and then, in the early 1900s, paved. Source: Traces of Texas*

*1853 Texas State Capitol, photo taken in 1875
By 1850, Texas had become a part of the United States. The state legislature appropriated the funds for a more permanent capitol, this time on the original site of Capitol Square. Finished in 1853, the new Texas Capitol was built of local limestone at a cost of $150,000. With its small crowning dome, it overlooked Congress Avenue and the town of Austin. Image courtesy of University of Texas at Austin*

One of the Last Envelopes Carried by Butterfield on the Southern Ox Bow Route

Feb. 24, 1861 Sacramento, Cal. to Wilmington, Ohio

The cover below was carried on the Southern Ox Bow Route one week before it was closed by the Act of Congress passing the Post Office Appropriation Bill on March 2, 1861, ending the southern Overland Mail Route.

At the time this letter was mailed, Butterfield's Overland Mail Co. was the default carrier for all transcontinental mail - therefore Mrs. Wheeler did not need to express her personal preference to avoid the ocean bound steam ship route by writing *"Overland"* in the lower left.

This cover, postmarked in Sacramento, California on Feb. 24, 1861 was addressed to Mr. M. Ronback of Wilmington, Ohio. This cancellation [SAC-1850] was used Sept. 19, 1856 to Sept. 24, 1862. *[John Williams, Western Express, Jan. 1994, page 40]*

This cover was purchased from
Paper Memories, PO Box 164, Roanoke, VA on Ebay, Feb. 9, 2023

Based on the date of cancellation, this cover was carried by the Postal System from Sacramento, 100 miles south to San Francisco where it was placed on Butterfield's Overland Mail Co. eastbound stagecoach. Most likely this cover was placed on the noon Friday, March 1, 1861 stage at San Francisco and was scheduled to arrive in St. Louis on Sunday, March 24, 1861 - on one of the last trips of Butterfield's Overland Mail on the Southern Ox Bow Route. At St. Louis, Missouri this letter was transferred to a train bound for its destination in Ohio.

The town was founded in 1810 as the seat of the newly formed Clinton County. The town name was changed from Clinton to Wilmington in 1811. The village was incorporated in 1828. In 1833, Wilmington contained a brick courthouse, a jail, fourteen stores, two taverns, two groceries, four churches, and 100 residential houses. Wilmington, Ohio is home to Wilmington College, founded in 1870 by the Society of Friends. The city and the surrounding area include more than one dozen Quaker meeting houses.

Colorized photo of Main Street Wilmington, Ohio.
Image source: Pinterest page of Nicki Bennett

CHAPTER SIX

The Following Fifteen Covers Were Carried on theCentral Route by the Overland Mail Company

1861 Central Overland Mail to Elizabethtown, New York

The cover below was mailed from Marysville (Yuba County), California on Nov. 28, 1861 to Mrs. Emily Gibson, Elizabeth Town, Essex County, New York. Since the destination was over 3,000 miles, the required 10¢ postage is paid with a Scott #68 that bears a crisp black strike CDS of Marysville CAL Nov. 28 to the left and a Marysville waffle cancellation tying the stamp to this cover. This cancellation [YUB-655] was used July 4, 1858 to Dec. 20, 1869. *[John Williams, Western Express, Sept. 1994, page 64]*

From Marysville, this letter would have been carried by the postal system south 42 miles to Sacramento, then 43 miles east to Placerville to be loaded on The Overland Mail Company's daily stagecoach bound for St. Joseph, Missouri. At St. Joseph it was transferred to a train bound for New York.

This cover was purchased on Nov. 21, 2022 on HipStamps, from Doyle Tillman of Lakewood, Washington

The three page letter to his sister, Emily, (dated Nov. 27, 1861) remains inside this cover.

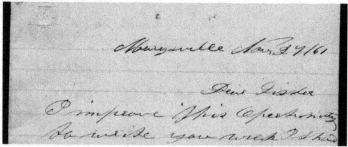

Dec. 1861 Central Overland Mail Cover to Atlanta, IL

This transcontinental cover below was mailed from Georgetown, California on Dec. 20, 1861 to Miss. J. G. Leonard, Atlanta, Illinois. This cancellation [ELD-472] was used March 3, 1857 to Sept. 5, 1864. *[John Williams, Western Express, July 1988, page 28]*

Postmarked at the Georgetown Post Office, this letter would have been carried 16 miles south to Placerville, California where it was placed on the Overland Mail Co.'s daily eastbound stagecoach to St. Joseph, Missouri. There it was transferred to a train toward Atlanta, Illinois. Since the destination was over 3,000 miles, the required 10¢ postage is paid with a Scott #68 that bears a crisp black strike CDS of GEORGETOWN Cal Dec. 20, 1861.

This cover was purchased Jan. 26, 2023 on Ebay
from Pennington of P.O. Box 87876, Vancouver, Washington 98687

W. R. Weiss, Jr. certificate reads: *"Scott #68, genuine use from Georgetown / Calif. to Illinois. Cover with faults, stamp w/light stains & faulty corner at lower left."*

Atlanta, Illinois in the early 1900's, what would later become part of Route 66.
Image source: Legends of America

April 1862 San Francisco to Portsmouth, New Hampshire

This transcontinental cover below was mailed from San Francisco, California on April 1, 1862 to Miss Lucy W. Kimball. This was written by Robert Lewis Harris back home to his girl friend and future wife Lucy W. Kimball, whom he married two years later.

Purchased on Ebay from larrysellcovers of Hornell, New York on March 6, 2023

This cancellation [SAF-330] was used Dec. 27, 1861 to June 5, 1865. *[John Williams, Western Express, March 1995, page 18]* Postmarked April 1, 1862, this letter would have been transported by steamer the 100 miles from San Francisco northeast to Sacramento. At Sacramento, this letter was transferred by the Sacramento Valley Railroad to Folsom, from there by stage to Placerville. At Placerville it caught the Overland Mail coach of Pioneer Stage Co. for the trip over the Sierra Mountains to Carson City/Virginia City, Nevada, where it was transferred to an Overland Mail Co. stagecoach to Salt Lake City. At Salt Lake City the mail was transferred to a Central Overland California & Pikes Peak Express Company (C.O.C. & P.P.Ex.Co.) stagecoach to St. Joseph, Missouri. At St. Joseph, it was transferred to a train toward its final destination in Portsmouth, New Hampshire.

Robert Lewis Harris wrote a second letter to his fiance and mailed it just 19 days later... For the evidence, see the following cover.

Robert Lewis Harris, 1834-1896 • Lucy W. Kimball Harris 1832-1924
Image source: Find a Grave

April 1862 San Francisco to Portsmouth, NH

This transcontinental cover shown below was mailed from San Francisco, California on April 20, 1862 to Miss Lucy W. Kimball. This was written by Robert Lewis Harris back home to his girl friend and future wife Lucy W. Kimball, whom he married two years later.

Postmarked April 20, 1862. This cancellation [SAF-330] was used Dec. 27, 1861 to June 5, 1865. *[John Williams, Western Express, March 1995, page 18]* This letter was transported 128 miles northeast to Placerville, California. At Placerville, the mail was transferred to an Overland Mail Co. stagecoach to Salt Lake City. At Salt Lake City the mail was transferred to a Central Overland California & Pikes Peak Express Company (C.O.C. & P.P.Ex.Co.) stagecoach to St. Joseph, Missouri. At St. Joseph, it was transferred to a train toward its final destination in Portsmouth, New Hampshire.

Since the destination was over 3,000 miles, the required 10¢ postage is paid with a Scott #68. The sender thought it was double weight so two 10¢ stamps were attached. The San Francisco Post Office however, determined that it was instead triple weight and a "10" was affixed next to the postmark to indicate that Miss. Lucy W. Kimball would need to pay 10¢ postage due upon picking up the letter at the Portsmouth, New Hampshire Post Office.

This cover is reduced at right edge where Lucy used scissors to open this letter written by her future husband. The scissors did not cut into the 10¢ stamp.

Purchased on Ebay from larrysellcovers of Hornell, New York on March 3, 2023

At the Portsmouth Athenaeum Library in Portsmouth,

New Hampshire, they have letters written by Robert Harris to his wife, Lucy W. Kimball Harris. The library records:

> **Robert Lewis Harris** (1834-1896) was born in Portsmouth, New Hampshire, and from the age of fifteen studied engineering with Ezra Lincoln in Boston. From 1852 to 1858 Harris worked on the Cleveland and St. Louis Air-Line Railway, the Delaware Railroad, Mississippi and Milwaukee Railroads, and the Interoceanic Railway in Honduras. Harris traveled west in 1860 and **from 1860-1871 worked in San Francisco**. During this time he was an engineer for the San Francisco and Oakland Railway, the California Pacific, and the Central Pacific, among others. From 1871-1872 he was superintendent of the Northern Pacific Railroad in Minnesota and worked on railroads in Canada from 1875-1876 and Texas in 1880-1882. From 1883-1891 Harris was a consulting engineer in New York City. He married **Lucy Woodward Kimball** in 1864 and died of apoplexy in New Hampshire in 1896.

May 1862 Overland Mail Auburn, CA to Windsor, Vermont

This transcontinental cover shown below was mailed from Auburn, Placer County, California on May 15, 1862 to N. E. Busbee, Windsor, Vermont. This cancellation [PLA-126] was used Aug. 2, '60 to July 24, '61. *[J. Williams, W.Express, Jan. 1991, p.60]*

This cover was purchased Feb. 23, 2023. on Ebay
from Mark Baker Enterprises, Goldrushpaper.com, Pollock Pines, California

Postmarked at the Auburn Post Office, this letter would have been carried 26 miles southeast to Placerville, California where it was placed on the Overland Mail Co.'s daily eastbound stagecoach to Salt Lake City, transferring stages on to St. Joseph, Missouri. At St. Joseph it was transferred to a train toward Windsor, Vermont.

The Constitution House, North Main Street, Windsor, Vermont
Linen postcard, by Rockwood's Pharmacy, Windsor, Vermont

Since the destination was over 3,000 miles, the required 10¢ postage is paid with a Scott #68 that is tied to this cover with a Auburn, Cal CDS May 15 1862. This "15 May 1862 AUBURN CAL" (PLA-260) cancel is over 9 months later than recorded for cancel type. Cover is reduced at left edge where recipient N. E. Busbee used scissors to open his mail.

Windsor, Vermont, 1886, Drawn and published by L. R,. Burleigh, Troy, New York

Windsor was chartered as a town on July 6, 1761, and achieved its place in Vermont history as the location where the Constitution of Vermont was adopted in 1777. This act gained it the nickname of "Birthplace of Vermont." Windsor served as the first capital of Vermont until 1805 when Montpelier became the official state capital.

July 1862 Overland Mail Tehama, CA to Freeport, Maine

The cover below was mailed from Tehama, California on July 23, 1862 to Mrs. Simeon Pratt of Freeport, Maine. This cover bears a Tehama, California 1862 blue serifed balloon CDS tying the 3¢ Washington stamp to the cover. This cancellation [TEH-1090] was used Jan. 1, 1857 to Aug. 15, 1869. *[John Williams, Western Express, Dec. 1994, page 26]*

Purchased on Hip Stamps from Jim Forte, Las Vegas, Nevada on Dec. 23, 2022

Sender wrote on left edge the sender's name and date the letter was written, *"Wm. A. Pratt, July 17, 1862"* who was the 35 year old son of Simeon Pratt.

This cover is addressed to the Simeon Pratt (1797-1875) who is buried at Freeport, Maine. He was married to Joanne E. Dennison Pratt (1814-1891). Simeon and Joanne had six children together: Robert Henry Pratt (1824-1920), George Lincoln Pratt (1825-1913), William Augustus Soule Pratt (1827-1896), John Haradon Pratt (1849-1938), Emily C. J. Pratt (1854-1933), and Alice Edwards Pratt (1860-1939).

This cover would have been carried from Tehama, south 123 miles to Sacramento, California. At Sacramento, this letter was transferred by the Sacramento Valley Railroad to Folsom, from there by stage to Placerville. At Placerville the Pioneer Stage Co. traveled over the Sierra Mountains to Carson City / Virginia City, Nevada, where it was transferred to an Overland Mail Co. stagecoach to Salt Lake City. At Salt Lake City the mail was transferred to a Central Overland California & Pikes Peak Express Company (C.O.C. & P.P.Ex.Co.) stagecoach to St. Joseph, Missouri. At St. Joseph, it was transferred to a train toward its final destination in Freeport, Maine.

Simeon Pratt, Died Aug. 26, 1875 Aged 77 yrs, 9 ms & 12 days. Source: Find a Grave

---

March 1863 Central Overland Mail to San Francisco
This letter was carried by the Overland Mail Co. over the Central Route 16 months before the end of the contract.

The cover shown below was mailed from Oswego, New York on March 10, 1863 addressed to *"Mr. Jas. L. Martel, Real Estate Broker, Court Block Clay St., Room No. 8, San Francisco, California."* There is a nice April 1863 received manuscript right below the stamp, *"Recd. April 21/63; Answered April 23/63."*

This cover was purchased Dec. 2022 on HipStamps.com,
from Rich Hemmings, 119 Shawnee Dr., Stewartstown, PA 17363

This westbound cover would have been carried by train to St. Joseph, Missouri where it was placed on the daily stage to Placerville, California. This letter was then transported 139 miles southwest to San Francisco.

Since the destination was over 3,000 miles, the required 10¢ postage is paid with a Scott #68, tied to the cover by Oswego, NY Mar 10 1863 CDS postmark. Also tied by grid cancel. The upper left corner is missing a small perforation. There are some ink spotting on face of the cover and random manuscript on reverse.

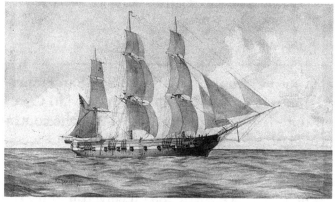

USS Sloop Dale, painted by R. G. Skerrett
James Martel served aboard the USS Dale During the Mexican American War

A short biography of the recipient, James L. Martel:
This cover's recipient, James L. Martel (1823-1893), was a real estate broker in San Francisco and a veteran of the War with Mexico having served on board the "U. S. Sloop Dale."
He was born in New Orleans, Louisiana, but lived in California since his arrival on Dec. 15, 1846.
He was a member of the Society of California Pioneers, joining on Feb. 1, 1886. Many of his papers in the collections of *The Society of California Pioneers* refer to his military service and detail the ships which he sailed on and his many different ports of call. Also in this collection are a few of his business cards, which are in English and French, his service pension declaration, an official copy of his birth certificate, and several letters regarding business transactions made with his customers concerning real estate. The files also include a newspaper clipping from 1893 about Mr. Martel and a ribbon regarding his veteran status. One of the documents is typed and dated April 19, 1906, stating that Mr. Martel has been deputized to act as a police officer in response to the 1906 earthquake. He also was appointed Inspector of Customs in San Francisco, but the years are unknown. He has a short Reminiscence written for the Pioneers, and it is digitized at the Online Archive of California. *[Source: Online Archive of California.]*

1863 Central Overland Mail - Michigan to Nevada Territory

The cover below was mailed by C & A Ives Company from Detroit, Michigan on June 16, 1863 to Butler Ives at Carson City, Nevada Territory. The ten cent overland postage rate for letters carried over 3,000 miles was paid with three 3¢ and a 1¢ postage stamp.

The senders, C & A Ives Company were bankers. The Ives family purchased a lot in 1850, with a 28 year lease for $15,916 under the condition that they would construct a brick building on the lot within one year, with one store facing Jefferson Ave., and two stores facing Griswold Street. The bank office faced Jefferson, and Albert Ives owned the grocery story facing Griswold. By 1863, S. H. had retired, and turned the bank over to Calab and Albert. Soon Butler Ives was added to the firm, and the name changed to A. Ives & sons.

This cover was purchased at the Oct. 2021 Pinpex Stamp Show in Jacksonville, AR from Kurt Harding, of Boerne, Texas,

The recipient, Butler Ives was hired by the Nevada Territorial Surveyor General on July 15, 1861. He would run a guide meridian northward, the backbone for all surveys of the Public Lands in that area.

He had been mentored by his brother William, a surveyor who had previously worked with William Austin Burt. William Ives had been Burt's compassman when Burt surveyed Michigan's Upper and Lower Peninsulas in the 1840's. At Burt's request, William was appointed a U.S. Deputy Surveyor in 1843. Butler became a Deputy Surveyor in May of 1850.

William and Butler decided to head west to explore opportunities in Oregon Territory. They traveled by boat from New York to Panama, made the crossing at the Isthmus of Panama and sailed up the Pacific coast to San Francisco. While in San Francisco they witnessed the great fire of 1851. From San Francisco they sailed north up the coast toward the Oregon Territory.

After 18 months in the Oregon Territory, William headed back to Michigan. Butler remained in the Territory until the Spring of 1855.

From Carson City, in Nov. of 1861, Butler Ives wrote to his

brother William:

"...*I have taken my present contract for subdividing 6½ townships at $12.00 per mile. About 2/3 of it is good work, the balance is in the Sierra Nevada Mountains between Carson Valley and Lake Bigler & such mountains Uncle Sam never had surveyed before. The land is worthless but the Y. Pine timber on them is very valuable, for Nevada has no timber after leaving these mountains except a few dwarf nut pines and cedars...which are worthless except for wood and taking the rags off Uncle Sam's Deputy Surveyors.*"

Butler Ives, Jr.
Jan. 31, 1830 to Dec. 27, 1871
Source: findagrave.com

Butler Ives wrote to William in the summer of 1863, "*I am tired enough to go to bed. Have 200 men at work on the road divided into four gangs and shall have 50 more this week....I have 10 to 30 miles of horseback riding every day.*"

In the mean time, confusion and unrest over the location of the boundary between the Nevada Territory and the State of California continued. Gordon Nelson writes, "*To say there was 'unrest' is mild. The Plumas County Cal. Sheriff came to Susanville with a posse of 115 to arrest the Nevada judge and sheriff. Susanville was the county seat of Roop County, Nevada. Shooting erupted with a couple of seriously wounded casualties. A plea was made for the two Governors (For Nevada Orion Clemens acting governor, Mark Twain's brother) to resolve the issues. In May 1863 a joint commission was established with Butler Ives and John P. Kidder. In the end Susanville was declared to be in California, but Aurora, County seat for Mono County, California, was declared to be in Nevada and would be county seat for Esmeralda County. An early September election was held for Nevada. Susanville voted, but in the end votes were not included. So late fall was the final solution.*" [Gordon Nelson's email to Bob Crossman, May 2, 2023]

Butler Ives died Dec. 27, 1871 while he was engaged in surveying the proposed railroad from the Summit to Sausalito, California. [Source: Wikipedia "Butler Ives"]

Oct. 1863 Overland Mail - San Francisco to Cognac, France

The letter sheet below was written by the Hellman Brothers Co. on Oct. 3, 1863, addressed to Cognac, France.

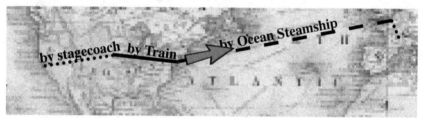

Overland to you: San Fransisco, October, 3 1863
Arbourn Maretts, Cognac
Dear Sir,
    We wrote to you 23rd ults - of which letter we enclose a duplicate...

The Overland Mail Company from San Francisco, addressed to Cognac, France

There are many historic structures in Cognac, France including: Château de Cognac, also known as Château de Valois and Château François, is a castle in Cognac, Nouvelle-Aquitaine, France. The castle has been rebuilt many times over the centuries. Fortifications have existed since Hélie de Villebois, 1st Lord of Cognac built a fort around the year 950.

This cover was purchased from A. Volle, Sant' Olcoss, Italy on Feb. 14, 2022.

The folded letter sheet shown above entered the mail at the San Francisco Post Office, and received a double circle postmark on Oct. 5, 1863. This San Francisco cancellation [SAF- 330] was used Dec. 27, 1861 to June 5, 1865. *[John Williams, Western Express, March 1995, page 18]*

It was carried 139 miles northeast to Placerville, California where it was placed on the Overland Mail Company stagecoach. Arriving at Saint Joseph, Missouri, it was transferred from stagecoach to a train. This cover arrived in New York, and received a second postmark on the front *"New York, Oct. 27."* Departing New York port by steamship, it arrived in France, at the port of Calais, receiving on the front a red double-circle postmark on Nov. 11, 1863. Then, arriving in Paris it received two double circled postmarks on the reverse side, *"Nov. 11, 1863."* From Paris is was transported to Cognac, France where it received its final double postmark on the reverse side on Nov. 12, 1863.

In Cognac it was delivered to Arbourn Marette & Co.

Nov. 1863 Overland Mail Benicia, CA to Neponsett, Mass.

The cover below was mailed from Benica, California on Nov. 25, 1863 to Miss R. M. G. Sanborn of Neponsett, Massachusetts.

This cover bears a Benicia, California postmark on a U40 embossed envelope.

This cancellation [SOL-90] began to be used Feb. 9, 1863 *[Source: John Williams, Western Express, Jan. 1994, page 54.]* The design of this envelope issued Aug. 15, 1861 and was withdrawn in 1864. Most likely this cancellation is Nov. 25, 1863.

This cover was purchased on Hip Stamps
from the APS Store, 100 Match Factory Place, Bellefonte, PA 16823

Local legends report that Benicia is the town where word of the discovery of gold at Sutter's Mill first spilled one night in 1848... spreading across the country from there.

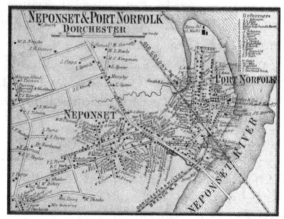

1858 Map of Neponsett, Massachusetts by H. E. Walling

The cover shown above would have been carried by the postal system from Benica, California northeast 61 miles to Sacramento, California. There mail was transferred to Pioneer Stage Co. for the journey to Placerville, California. At Placerville, the mail was transferred to an Overland Mail stagecoach to Salt Lake City. At Salt Lake City the mail was transferred to a Central Overland California & Pikes Peak Express Company (C.O.C. & P.P.Ex.Co.) stage coach to St. Joseph, Missouri. At St. Joseph, it was transferred to a train toward its final destination in Neponsett, Massachusetts.

---

ca. 1863/4 Overland Mail New York to California

The cover below was postmarked October 1 in New York, and addressed to Stephen S. Smith of San Francisco, California. It was carried by train to Saint Joseph, Missouri, where it was placed in the hands of the Overland Mail Company and its subcontractors. Arriving Placerville, California, it was transported 139 miles southwest to San Francisco.

Purchased at Chicago's 2021 APS show from Mark Reasoner of Prospect Heights, Illinois.

The postal rate for ½ ounce letters from March 3, 1863 until Sept. 31, 1883 was 3¢. This particular letter weighed 1 ounce, so the postmaster marked on the front upper left*"Due 3"* to signify that double rate needed to be charged, and 3¢ was to be collected from Stephen S. Smith when he picked up his letter in San Francisco.

Stagecoach on the Overland Trail near Laramie, Wyoming, Source Legends of America

This letter was carried by train from New York to St. Joseph, Missouri. From there a stagecoach, similar to the one shown above, carried the letter westward toward California.

The San Francisco Post Office, 1850
"A faithful representation of the crowds daily applying at that office for letters and newspapers." Lithograph by Wm. Endicott & Co.

Stephen S. Smith had to pay 3¢ to when he picked up his letter at the San Francisco Post Office in the above engraving because it was overweight and required double postage.

1863 Central Overland Stage Mail to France

Below is shown a rare surviving Butterfield carried cover from San Francisco to France. This Dec. 30, 1863 San Francisco cancellation [SAF- 330] was used Dec. 27, 1861 to June 5, 1865. *[John Williams, Western Express, March 1995, page 18]* This cover was carried 139 miles from San Francisco to Placerville, California where it was placed on the daily Overland Mail Company stagecoach bound for St. Joseph, Missouri via the Central Overland Stage Route. At St. Joseph, it was transferred to a train for New York, where it boarded the British passenger liner, Scotia for Europe on Jan. 27, 1864. It arrived at Liverpool on Feb. 5, 1864. Then on to Paris, back stamped Feb. 7, 1864. Then it arrived in Bourdoux and there received a red Calais transit stamp on front, and back stamped on Feb. 8, 1864.

H. Y. Schroder & Co. mailed this folded envelope to Veillon Frerez in Bourdoux, France. It is postmarked at San Francisco on Dec. 30, 1863. The sender paid the 15¢ unpaid treaty rate. Then a 3¢ debit was marked on the front. A hand written 8 pence debit was marked on the front at Liverpool.

Recipient wrote on reverse: *H. F. Schrider, San Francisco, 29 Dec. 1863 - Received 8 Feb. 1864 - Replied 24 Feb. 1864*

Purchased at the Pinnacle Stamp Club Show in Little Rock from Bill Burdick, owner of Bill's Stamps & Postcards of Mountain Home, Arkansas Ex, Noel, Walske 367

This cover was carried from New York to Liverpool by the

ship Scotia, shown below. The Scotia won the Blue Ribbon in 1863 for the fastest westbound transatlantic voyage. Scotia was the last oceangoing paddle steamer, and as late as 1874 she made Cunnard's second fastest voyage. Laid up on 1876, Scotia was converted to a twin-screw cable layer in 1879. She served in her new role for twenty-five years until she was wrecked off of Guam in March of 1904.

"SS Scotia" Image source: Cunard Steam Ship Co. Ltd.

1864/1865 Overland Mail - San Francisco to Washington D.C.

The cover below was mailed from San Francisco, California on April 2, addressed to Doctor Charles Sutherland, Medical Purveyor, Washington D.C. He only held this position for a portion of 1864-5, thus helping to date this cover.

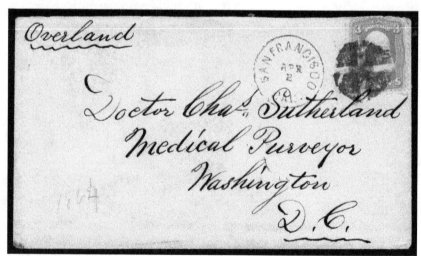

Purchased June 27, 2021 on ebay from E-Commerce Store, Charlotte, N. Carolina.

The cover above would have been carried 139 miles northeast to Placerville, California where it was transferred to the daily Overland Mail Company stagecoach to St. Joseph. At St. Joseph it was transferred to a train for the journey to the nation's capitol.

Postage at this point had been reduced to 3¢ even for mail traveling over 3,000 miles. The sender affixed a 3¢ Scott #65 stamp.

In the spring of 1864, Dr. Charles Sutherland, this cover's recipient, was appointed chief purveyor of the medical supply depot in Washington D.C., and was promoted to lieutenant colonel. He only held this position for a portion of 1864 and 1865, when he was then appointed chief purveyor of the New York City medical supply depot. He remained in that position until 1876.

In June of 1876, Sutherland was promoted to colonel and assigned as medical director of the Division of

General Charles Sutherland
Image source: Wikipedia

the Pacific. He held that position until 1884, when he was assigned as medical director for the Division of the Atlantic. Sutherland was promoted to brigadier general in Dec. of 1890 and appointed as Surgeon General of the United States Army. In 1893, he retired and was succeeded by George Miller Sternberg as Surgeon General.

1864 Central Overland Mail - San Francisco to Tennessee

The cover below was mailed from San Francisco, California on May 3, 1864 to Mr. C. W. Christy of Memphis, Tennessee. This cancellation [SAF- 330] was used Dec. 27, 1861 to June 5, 1865.

[John Williams, Western Express, March 1995, page 18]

This cover was carried to Placerville, California then by Overland Mail Co. stage to Salt Lake, then on to St. Joseph. Then, transferring to a Missouri River steamboat to St. Louis, then by steamboat down the Mississippi River to Memphis.

This cover was purchased on ebay from
Richard Quining, 3207 Peace Rose St., Bakerfield, California 93311-2990

At the time of this letter, the Sanitary Commission reports that Mr. Christy was the Superintendent and Relief Agent of "Soldier's Lodge." *(The Sanitary Commission was a predecessor of The American Red Cross.)* In a letter from Mr. Christy, printed in the 1864 issue of *The Sanitary Reporter*, he reported that in April, 1864 the Soldier's Lodge in Memphis serviced 1,420 soldiers, serving 4,802 meals, and furnished 1,324 nights lodging. They also furnished transportation to 127 soldiers, clothing to 6, added in correcting papers to 9, aided in drawing pay to 13, gave money to 5, and sent 13 to the hospital.

Soldier's Home, The Western Sanitary Commission, Memphis, (Hunt-Phelan house), historic-memphis.com

1864 Central Overland Mail - San Francisco to New York

The cover below was mailed from San Francisco on Aug. 30. This cancellation [SAF- 330] was used Dec. 27, 1861 to June 5, 1865. *[John Williams, Western Express, March 1995, page 18]*

Based on the type postmark used, the year of mailing is between Aug. of 1862 and Aug. of 1864.

If the postmark is August 30, 1864, it most likely was one of the last covers carried over the Central Route on the Overland Mail Company that John Butterfield founded before it's postal contract ended in Sept. of 1864.

Purchased on Ebay April 9, 2023 from Matt Liebson, Paper History, Solon, Ohio.

At San Francisco, the sender did not want his letter to be carried by stagecoach, and so he requested the letter be carried *"By Steamer"* as written in the lower left. However, the steamers only departed San Francisco twice a month, and this letter was posted too late to make the steamer, and so it received a *"Too Late"* oval stamp in the upper left.

Typically, in this situation the letter would be held for two weeks at the post office to wait for the next steamer. The letter would arrive two weeks later than the sender anticipated, and the *"Too Late"* oval marking would explain why to the recipient.

In this case, however since it arrived in only 29 days, most likely this letter was carried to Placerville, California and placed on the daily Overland Mail Co. stagecoach toward Salt Lake City, and the train at St. Joseph, Missouri. If it had been held for the next available ocean steamer bound for Panama, and then on to New York the transit time would have been closer to forty-five plus days.

This cover above arrived in Marcellus, New York, receiving a faint round arrival stamp in the upper left on Aug. 29th, only 29 days in transit.

Mr. W. S. Franklin, had moved from Marcellus, and so the post office crossed through the city and county, and added his new residence, *"Eaton, Madison Co., NY"* in the lower left.

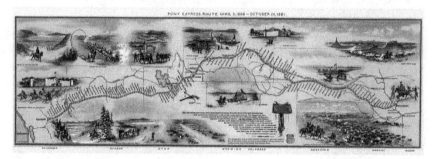

Pony Express Route with roughly 186 stations, about ten miles apart.
Image source: National Pony Express Association

The Coming and Going of the Pony Express (Oil on Canvas), by Frederic Remington

The Author's Field Trip to the Central Route, Oct. 22, 2022

Hollenberg Ranch Pony Express Station
This building constructed in 1857 by C. H. Hollenberg on his ranch here on the Oregon Trail, was a station on the Pony Express route in 1860-1861. It is believed to be the ONLY such station which has remained unaltered in its original site.

On Oct. 22, 2022, the author of this book, Bob Crossman, visited the Hollenberg Station two miles east of Hanover, Kansas.

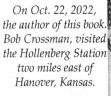

The stairs above led to the attic. Newspapers at the time mentioned that employees slept in bunks in the attic. A bill from April, 1862 shows that livestock, and three employees boarded here. They were charged 27 ⅓ cents for meals.

Overland Mail Co. Bibles on the Central Route

Copies of the American Bible Society, 1859 40th edition Bibles were apparently distributed to Butterfield Overland Mail Co. employees on the Central Route. They were a thick pocket-sized volume, bound in eights (5.5 x 3.5 inches). The covers read: *"Station Overland Mail Company. For Use of Travellers and Station Agents."*

A postcard inside this copy of the Bible states that the volume was found *"in the basement of the Episcopal Church, Placerville (Built in 1865-66)."*

This copy was sold by Heritage Auctions, Lot #45132, on Oct. 15, 2020 for $5,000.

These are different than the Bibles distributed to Pony Express employees. Those Bibles contain the additional inscription: *"Presented by Russell, Majors & Waddell 1858."*

CHAPTER SEVEN

The Central Overland Mail Route 1861 to 1869

The Central Overland Mail Route AFTER THE JULY 1, 1864 END OF The Overland Mail Company's contract

Some of the Last Mail Carried by Stagecoach Over the Central Route

1868/1869 Eastbound Overland Mail Covers to Connecticut

About five months before the end of the Central Overland Mail the six covers below, from the same sender in Alton, New Hampshire, were mailed from Oakland, California to Allyn Stanley Kellogg of Vernon, Connecticut.

The recipient of these covers was Allyn Stanley Kellogg (1824-1893), Vernon Connecticut's historian. He was born on Oct. 15, 1824 to Deacon Allyn Kellogg (1794-1873) and Eliza White (1807-1876). Deacon Allyn was the son of Ebenezer Kellogg, Jr (1764-1812) and the grandson of Rev. Ebenezer Kellogg (1737-1817), the first pastor of the Congregational Church in Vernon.

Allyn Stanley Kellogg

Allyn Stanley chose to go into ministry rather than business and graduated from Williams College in 1846 with high honors. He went on to Yale Theological Seminary and graduated in 1850 at age 26. In the late 1880's a number of articles written by Allyn Stanley were published in the new Rockville Journal. Other publishers of genealogies and town histories often credited A. Stanley Kellogg as a source.

These covers were purchased from Postal Stationary.com of Alton, New Hampshire in Feb. and June of 2021, and Nov. of 2022.

OAKLAND, CALIFORNIA TO VERNON, CONNECTICUT - 3,020 MILES

The 1st cover was mailed May 16, 1868 and was received 21 days later on June 6, 1868.
The 2nd cover was mailed Dec. 17, 1868 and was received 19 days later on Jan. 5, 1869.
The 3rd cover was mailed Jan. 6, 1869 and was received 17 days later on Jan. 23, 1869.
The 4th cover was mailed Jan. 16, 1869 and was received 17 days later on Feb. 2, 1869.
The 5th cover was mailed Feb. 6, 1869 and was received 43 days later on March 15, 1869.
The 6th cover was mailed Feb. 18, 1869 and received 25 days later on March 15, 1869.

1869 Westbound Overland Mail Covers to California

The two covers shown below were mailed at Saco, Maine and addressed to Mr. William Pierce at the firm of H & W Pierce in San Francisco, California with a 3¢ Scott #65 stamps affixed.

Pur-chased from Michael Patkin, 10 Attitash Ave., Merrimac, Massachusetts

The receiver mark on reverse: ***H & W. Pierce S.F. Mar 29 1869,*** reports the year, and reveals that delivery took 42 days to complete. The above cover is postmarked: Saco, Maine, Feb. 15. The cover shown below is postmarked: Saco, Maine, Jan. 3.

Purchased from Michael Patkin, 10 Attitash Ave., Merrimac, Massachusetts

Henry came to San Francisco in 1850 and started a bakery, and was later joined by his brothers. In *California Ranchos*, by Burgess Mc Shumway, chapter XXV San Francisco, an 1865 record is found of Wm. Pierce obtaining a 942 acre ranch.

In 1885, Henry Pierce and H & W Pierce exhibited cattle at the San Francisco Fair: Class IV Holstein Bulls, in the one year old category four bulls named Edmund 5th, Edgar S., Dugald S. and Donatus S., in the category of cows, three years old and over: Annie. Several of their cattle won "best bull of show" and "best cow of show."

Henry became a prominent investor and one of San Francisco's first millionaires before he died in 1903.

A Postage Story from 1861

In early 1861 at Fort Yuma, when soldiers wrote letter to their families back in the east, those letters were carried by the Butterfield Overland Mail Co. The soldiers would have kept a supply of 10¢ stamps to pay the postage on their letters back home. In the March 1, 1861 issue of *The Constitutional Union*, Des Arc, Arkansas the following article appears:

"Novel Use for Post Office Stamps. – A correspondent of The New York Times, writing from California gives an amusing story, the particulars of which happened at Fort Yuma, in Arizona. He says:

An officer was telling me the other day how he lost his postage stamps. He had sent up here for some twenty dollars' worth, and had left them on his table. Now, the habits, manners and customs thereabouts are considerably on the free and easy style, and the [civilians] are allowed to run around the garrison at libitum, if they behave themselves.

On this occasion a young [civilian,] who had run of the quarters, and was very much at home anywhere and every-where, happened to stray into my friend's room, and seeing the postage stamps, began to examine them with much curi-osity. She discovered that they would stick, if wet, and forth-with a happy idea struck her. Now, the fashionable dress of the ladies in that warm climate is of the briefest description. She was ambitious to dress up and excite the envy of the other [young women.]

So she put on the postal currency, and much to the aston-ishment of the garrison, made her appearance on the parade ground presently entirely covered over with postage stamps. She was stuck all over with Benjamin Franklin, and the Fa-ther of his Country was placarded all over her ladyship's glossy skin indis-criminately, regardless of dignity and decency.

The roar that greeted her, from the commander down to the drummer boy, was loud enough to be heard nearly at headquarters in San Francisco, but [...] she preserved her equanimity, and did not seem at all disconcerted, but sailed off with the step and air of a princess, while my friend rushed into his quarters to discover himself minus of his twenty dollars' worth of postage stamps, and that was intended for the mail had been appropriated to the female.

She might have been put in the Overland coach and gone through – she certainly could not have been stopped for want of being prepaid."

Note: The original language of this article, printed in
the March 1, 1861 issue of the Constitutional Union, Des Arc, Arkansas
contained disparaging references to Native American women.

CHAPTER EIGHT

Image Soure:"Pokin Around: Historic stagecoach, once at Silver Dollar City, about to embark on 100-mile journey" by Steve Pokin, May 18, 2022. Photo by Dennis Crider

U.S. Postal Service
Remembering The Butterfield

1958 Reenactment of Butterfield's Overland Mail

On the 100th Anniversary of the first trip of Butterfield's Overland Mail, many re-enactments were held across the old "oxbow" route from San Francisco to the Mississippi river towns of Memphis and St. Louis.

The cover below was postmarked at St. Louis on Sept. 16, 1958 and addressed to J. T. Green of Mountain View, California.

This Aristocrats cachet cover below received a *"First Day of Issue"* postmark at San Francisco, California at 9 am on Oct. 10, 1958 on the first day the affixed new US postage stamp was available for sale The new 4¢ stamp commemorates *"Overland Mail • 1858 • 1958"*.

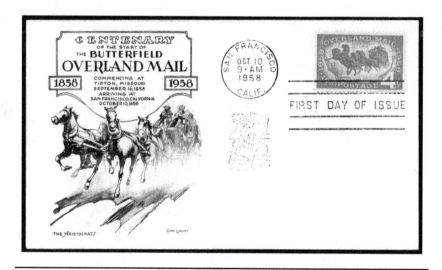

Even 35 Years After the 1958 Centennial, Butterfield Had NOT Been Forgotten by the US Postal Service

In 1994, the US Postal Service printed a sheet of postage stamps, with each stamp in the sheet commemorating a different person or "Legend of the West." One of the stamps, was a 29¢ stamp shown on this cover commemorating the Overland Mail. The stamp is affixed to a Collins Hand Painted First Day Cover.

The US Postal Service expanded the "Legends of the West" series by also printing a two sided postcard for each of the persons or events in the series. The postcard below commemorates the Overland Mail. Both sides of the postcard are shown below.

Image of front and reverse of postcard.
Purchased Aug. 2021 on ebay from Asset Auctions, Indianapolis, Indiana.

The US Postal Service has also remembered the stagecoach as an historic means of transporting the mails. In 1794, Congress authorized the postmaster general to use stagecoaches to transport the mail, because the volume had become far too great for it to be carried efficiently over long distances on horseback.

As part of the celebration for the bicentennial of the American Postal Service, a 10¢ stamp Scott #1572 was produced with the image of a stagecoach and an 18 wheel postal truck.

Below, this Fleetwood Cachet first day cover was postmarked Sept. 3, 1975 in Philadelphia, Pennsylvania.

Purchased Feb. 20, 2023 on Ebay from Richard Moti Freeman, Parkville, Missouri

In 1982 the postal administration issued this 4¢ stamp Scott #1898A with the image of a stagecoach.

This GillCraft Cachet first day cover was postmarked Aug. 14, 1982, at Milwaukee, Wisconsin.

Purchased Feb. 20, 2023 on Ebay from D. W. Stiegler, Shelton, Connecticut

In 1989 the postal administration issued this 25¢ stamp Scott #2434 with the image of a stagecoach.

Below, this Fleetwood Cachet first day cover is postmarked Nov. 19, 1989, at Washington, D. C.

Purchased Feb. 20, 2023 on Ebay
from Eduard Frelikh, 20434 Osage Ave., Unit C, Torrance, California

In 1997 the postal administration issued this 32¢ stamp Scott #3131 with the image of a stagecoach.

Below, this Fleetwood Cachet first day cover is postmarked March 13, 1997 in New York, NY.

Purchased Feb. 20, 2023 on Ebay from
Alex Bereson, 1200 E. Yuma Ave., McAllen, Texas

1860's Ben Holladay's Overland Mail and Express Company Check, Waybill, and Special Deposit Slip

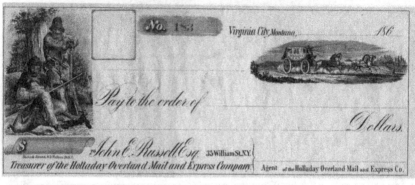

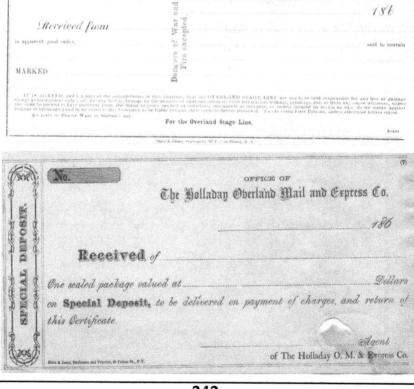

Appendix A
Postmasters General, 1857 - 1866

Aaron Brown
1857-1859

Joseph Holt
1859-1860

Horatio King
1861

Montgomery Blair
1861-1864

William Dennison, Jr.
1864-1866

Alexander W. Randall
1866 - 1869

Appendix B

Report of the Postmaster General, December 1, 1857
Pages 986 to 1011

REPORT OF THE POSTMASTER GENERAL.

POST OFFICE DEPARTMENT, *December* 1, 1857.

To the President of the United States :

OVERLAND MAIL SERVICE TO CALIFORNIA.

In order to carry into effect the act of Congress approved the third of March, 1857, relative to the overland mail to California, the department issued the following notice, and caused the same to be regularly advertised according to law:

"POST OFFICE DEPARTMENT,
"*April* 20, 1857.

"An act of Congress, approved 3d March, 1857, making appropriations for the service of the Post Office Department for the fiscal year ending 30th June, 1858, provides :

"'SEC. 10. That the Postmaster General be, and he is hereby, authorized to contract for the conveyance of the entire letter mail from such point on the Mississippi river as the contractors may select to San Francisco, in the State of California, for six years, at a cost not exceeding three hundred thousand dollars per annum for semi-monthly, four hundred and fifty thousand dollars for weekly, or six hundred thousand dollars for semi-weekly service, to be performed semi-monthly, weekly, or semi-weekly, at the option of the Postmaster General.

"'SEC. 11. That the contract shall require the service to be performed with good four-horse coaches or spring wagons, suitable for the conveyance of passengers as well as the safety and security of the mails.

"'SEC. 12. That the contractor shall have the right of pre-emption to three hundred and twenty acres of any land not then disposed of or reserved, at each point necessary for a station, not to be nearer than ten miles from each other ; and provided that no mineral land shall be thus pre-empted.

"'SEC. 13. That the said service shall be performed within twenty-five days for each trip ; and that, before entering into such contract, the Postmaster General shall be satisfied of the ability and disposition of the parties *bona fide* and in good faith to perform the said contract, and shall require good and sufficient security for the performance of the same—the service to commence within twelve months after the signing the contract.'

"Proposals will accordingly be received at the Contract Office of the Post Office Department until 3 p. m. of the 1st day of June, 1857, for conveying mails under the provisions of the above act.

"Besides the starting point on the Mississippi river, bidders will name intermediate points proposed to be embraced in the route, and otherwise designate its course as nearly as practicable.

"Separate proposals are invited for *semi-monthly*, *weekly*, and *semi-weekly* trips each way.

"The decision upon the proposals offered will be made after the Postmaster ·eneral shall be satisfied of the ability and disposition of the parties in good faith to perform the contract.

"A guarantee is to be executed, with good and sufficient sureties, that the contract shall be executed with like good security, whenever the contractor or contractors shall be required to do so by the Postmaster General, and the service must commence within twelve months after the date of such contract."

In pursuance of the said advertisement, the Postmaster General and his three assistants assembled in the Contract Office and opened the respective bids, making the following abstract of them, and causing said abstract to be copied into a separate book, and also in the route book for California.

ABSTRACT OF THE BIDS.

John Butterfield, William B. Dinsmore, William G. Fargo, James V. P. Gardner, Marcus L. Kinyon, Hamilton Spencer, and *Alexander Holland:* From St. Louis, by Springfield, and from Memphis, by Little Rock, connecting at a common point at or eastward of Albuquerque; thence west, to and along the military road to Colorado river; thence up the valley of the Mohahoc river, to and through the Tejon passes of the Sierra Nevada; and thence along the best route to San Francisco; *weekly*, $450,000; *semi-weekly*, $600,000.

John Butterfield and others: From Memphis, by Little Rock, Albuquerque, mouth of Mohahoc, on the Colorado river, and one of the Tejon passes of the Sierra Nevada, to San Francisco; *semi-monthly*, $300,000; *weekly*, $450,000; *semi-weekly*, $595,000.

John Butterfield and others: From St. Louis, by Springfield, to Albuquerque; thence, as above, to San Francisco; *semi-monthly*, $300,000; *weekly*, $450,000; *semi-weekly*, $585,000.

James E. Birch: From Memphis, by Little Rock, Washington, Fulton, Clarksville, Gainesville, Fort Chadbourne, head spring of Conche river, to Pecos river, nearly due west; thence, along Pecos river, Delaware creek, through the Guadalupe and Hueco mountains, to the Rio Grande river; thence, over the emigrant road, to Fort Yuma; thence, by San Gorgona pass, San Bernardino, Tejon, Tulare, or Salinas valleys, to San Francisco; *semi-weekly*, $600,000.

James Glover: From Memphis, by Helena, Little Rock, across Texas, to El Paso, Fort Yuma, San Bernardino, Los Angeles; thence, between the coast range and Sierra Nevada mountains, to San

988   REPORT OF THE

Francisco ; or, from Vicksburg, by Shrevesport, to El Paso, &c., &c., (as above ;) *semi-monthly*, $300,000; *weekly*, $450,000; *semi-weekly*, $600,000.

S. Howell and A. E. Pace: From Gaines' Landing, on the Mississippi, to San Francisco ; term of four years ; commence at Vicksburg, if preferred ; *weekly*, $1,000,000 for the first year, $800,000 for the second year, $700,000 for the third year, $600,000 for the fourth year.

David D. Mitchell, Samuel B. Churchill, Robert Campbell, William Gilpin, and others: From St. Louis to San Francisco ; *semi-weekly*, $600,000.

James Johnston, jr., and Joseph Clark: From St. Louis, by Fort Independence, Fort Laramie, Salt Lake City, or any other point named by the department, to San Francisco ; *semi-monthly*, $260,000; *weekly*, $390,000; *semi-weekly*, $520,000.

Irregular (after time) bid. *William Hollinshead,* president Minnesota, Nebraska, and Pacific Mail Transportation Company: From St. Paul, by Fort Ridgely, South Pass, Soda Springs, Humboldt river, Honey Lake valley, Noble's pass, Shasta City, to San Francisco ; *semi-weekly*, $550,000.

On the second day of July, 1857, the department, after full and mature consideration, made the following order in relation to the route selected and the bid accepted :

"12,578. From St. Louis, Missouri, and from Memphis, Tennessee, converging at Little Rock, Arkansas ; thence, *via* Preston, Texas, or as nearly so as may be found advisable, to the best point of crossing the Rio Grande, above El Paso, and not far from Fort Fillmore ; thence, along the new road being opened and constructed under the direction of the Secretary of the Interior, to Fort Yuma, California ; thence, through the best passes, and along the best valleys for safe and expeditious staging, to San Francisco.

"The foregoing route is selected for the overland mail service to California, as combining, in my judgment, more advantages and fewer disadvantages than any other.

"No bid having been made for this particular route, and all the bidders (whose bids were considered regular under the advertisement and the act of Congress) having consented that their bids may be held and considered as extending and applying to said route :

"Therefore, looking at the respective bidders, both as to the amount proposed and the ability, qualifications, and experience of the bidders to carry out a great mail service like this, I hereby order that the proposal of John Butterfield, of Utica, New York, William B. Dinsmore, of New York city, William G. Fargo, of Buffalo, New York, James V. P. Gardner, of Utica, New York, Marcus L. Kinyon, of Rome, New York, Alexander Holland, of New York city, and Hamilton Spencer, of Bloomington, Illinois, at the sum of $595,000 (five hundred and ninety-five thousand dollars) per annum for semi-weekly service, be accepted. The contractors, however, to have the privilege of selecting lands, under the act of Congress, on only one of the roads, or branches, between Little Rock and the Mississippi river—

the one selected by them to be made known and inserted in the contract at the time of its execution.''

Subsequently, on re-examining the proposal, the above acceptance was modified so as to fix the pay at $600,000 per annum, that being the true amount of the bid.

Under strong representations that a better junction of the two branches of said road could be made at Preston than at Little Rock, on the eleventh day of September, 1857, the following order was made :

'' That whenever the contractors and their sureties shall file in the Post Office Department a request, in writing, that they desire to make the junction of the two branches of said road at Preston, instead of Little Rock, the department will permit the same to be done by some route not further west than to Springfield, Missouri, thence by Fayetteville, Van Buren, and Fort Smith, in the State of Arkansas, to the said junction, at or near the town of Preston, in Texas ; but said new line will be adopted on the express condition that the said contractors shall not claim or demand from the department, or from Congress, any increased compensation for or on account of such change in the route from St. Louis, or of the point of junction of the two routes from Little Rock to Preston ; and on the further express condition that whilst the *amount* of lands to which the contractors may be entitled under the act of Congress may be estimated on either of said branches from Preston to St. Louis or Memphis, at their option, yet the said contractors shall take one-half of that amount on each of said branches, so that neither shall have an advantage in the way of stations and settlement over the other ; and in case said contractors, in selecting and locating their lands, shall disregard this condition, or give undue advantage to one of said branches over the other, the department reserves the power of discontinuing said new route from St. Louis to Preston, and to hold said contractors and their sureties to the original route and terms expressed and set forth in the body of this contract.''

In pursuance of the above orders and proceedings, on the 16th day of September, 1857, the following contract was entered into between the department and the contractors whose bid had been accepted :

No. 12,578.—$600,000 per annum.

This article of contract, made the sixteenth day of September, in the year one thousand eight hundred and fifty-seven, between the United States (acting in this behalf by their Postmaster General) and John Butterfield, of Utica, New York, William B. Dinsmore, of New York city, William G. Fargo, of Buffalo, New York, James V. P. Gardner, of Utica, New York, Marcus L. Kinyon, of Rome, New York, Alexander Holland, of New York city, and Hamilton Spencer, of Bloomington, Illinois, and Danford N. Barney, of the city of New York, Johnston Livingston, of Livingston, New York, David Moulton, of Floyd, New York, and Elijah P. Williams, of Buffalo, New York, witnesseth :

That whereas John Butterfield, William B. Dinsmore, William G. Fargo, James V. P. Gardner, Mascus L. Kinyon, Alexander Holland, and Hamilton Spencer, have been accepted, according to law, as contractors for transporting the entire letter mail, agreeably to the provisions of the 11th, 12th, and 13th sections of an act of Congress approved March 3, 1857, (making appropriations for the service of the Post Office Department for the fiscal year ending June 30, 1858,) from the Mississippi river to San Francisco, California, as follows, viz: from St. Louis, Missouri, and from Memphis, Tennessee, converging at Little Rock, Arkansas; thence, *via* Preston, Texas, or as near so as may be found advisable, to the best point of crossing the Rio Grande above El Paso, and not far from Fort Fillmore ; thence, along the new road being opened and constructed under the direction of the Secretary of the Interior, to or near Fort Yuma, California ; thence, through the best passes and along the best valleys for safe and expeditious staging, to San Francisco, California, and back, twice a week, in good four-horse post coaches or spring wagons suitable for the conveyance of passengers as well as the safety and security of the mails, at six hundred thousand dollars a year, for and during the term of six years, commencing the sixteenth day of September, in the year one thousand eight hundred and fifty-eight, and ending with the fifteenth day of September, in the year one thousand eight hundred and sixty-four: Now, therefore, the said John Butterfield, William B. Dinsmore, William G. Fargo, James V. P. Gardner, Marcus L. Kinyon, Alexander Holland, and Hamilton Spencer, contractors, and Danford N. Barney, Johnston Livingston, David Moulton, and Elijah P. Williams, their sureties, do jointly and severally undertake, covenant, and agree with the United States, and do bind themselves: 1st. To carry said letter mail within the time fixed by the law above referred to—that is, within twenty-five days for each trip, and according to the annexed schedule of departures and arrivals; 2d. To carry said letter mail in a safe and secure manner, free from wet or other injury, in a boot, under the driver's seat, or other secure place, and in preference to passengers, and to their entire exclusion, if its weight and bulk require it; 3d. To take the said letter mail and every part of it from, and deliver it and every part of it at, each post office on the route, or that may hereafter be established on the route, and into the post office at each end of the route, and into the post office at the place at which the carrier stops at night, if one is there kept ; and if no office is there kept, to lock it up in some secure place, at the risk of the contractors.

They also undertake, covenant, and agree with the United States, and do bind themselves, jointly and severally, as aforesaid, to be answerable for the persons to whom the said contractors shall commit the care and transportation of the mail, and accountable to the United States for any damages which may be sustained by the United States through their unfaithfulness or want of care ; and that the said contractors will discharge any carrier of said mail when required to do so by the Postmaster General; also, that they will not transmit, by themselves or their agent, or be concerned in transmitting, commercial intelligence more rapidly than by mail, other than by telegraph, and that they will not carry out of the mail letters or newspapers which should go by post; and further, the said contractors will convey, without additional charge, the special agents of the department, on the exhibition of their credentials.

They further undertake, covenant, and agree with the United States, that the said contractors will collect quarterly, if required by the Postmaster General, of postmasters on said route, the balances due from them to the General Post Office, and faithfully render an account thereof to the Postmaster General in the settlement of quarterly accounts, and will pay over to the General Post Office all balances remaining in their hands.

For which services, when performed, the said John Butterfield, William B. Dinsmore, William G. Fargo, James V. P. Gardner, Marcus L. Kinyon, Alexander Holland, and Hamilton Spencer, contractors, are to be paid by the United States the sum of six hundred thousand dollars a year, to wit, quarterly, in the months of May, August, November, and February, through the postmasters on the route, or otherwise, at the option of the Postmaster General of the United States; said pay to be subject, however, to be reduced or discontinued by the Postmaster General, as hereinafter stipulated, or to be suspended in case of delinquency.

It is hereby also stipulated and agreed by the said contractors and their sureties, that in all cases there is to be a forfeiture of the pay of a trip when the trip is not run; and of not more than three times the pay of the trip when the trip is not run and no sufficient excuse for the failure is furnished; and a forfeiture of a due proportion of it when a grade of service is rendered inferior to the mode of conveyance above stipulated; and that these forfeitures may be increased into penalties of higher amount, according to the nature or frequency of the failure and the importance of the mail; also, that fines may be imposed upon the contractors, unless the delinquency be satisfactorily explained to the Postmaster General in due time, for failing to take from or deliver at a post office the said letter mail or any part of it; for suffering it to be wet, injured, lost, or destroyed; for carrying it in a place or manner that exposes it to depredation, loss, or injury, by being wet or otherwise; for refusing, after demand, to convey a letter mail by any coach or wagon which the contractors regularly run or are concerned in running on the route beyond the number of trips above specified; or for not arriving at the time set in the schedule. And for setting up or running an express to transmit letters or commercial intelligence in advance of the mail, or for transmitting knowingly, or after being informed, any one engaged in transporting letters or mail matter in violation of the laws of the United States, a penalty may be exacted of the contractors equal to a quarter's pay; but in all other cases no fine shall exceed three times the price of the trip. And whenever it is satisfactorily shown that the contractors, their carrier or agent, have left or put aside the said letter mail, or any portion of it, for the accommodation of passengers, they shall forfeit not exceeding a quarter's pay.

And it is hereby further stipulated and agreed by the said contractors and their sureties, that the Postmaster General may annul the contract for repeated failures; for violating the post office laws; for disobeying the instructions of the department; for refusing to discharge a carrier when required by the department; for assigning the contract, or any part of it, without the consent of the Postmaster General; for setting up or running an express as aforesaid; or for transporting persons conveying mail matter out of the mail as aforesaid; or whenever either of the contractors shall become a postmaster, assistant postmaster, or member of Congress; and this contract shall in all its parts be subject to the terms and requirements of an act of Congress passed on the twenty-first day of April, in the year of our Lord one thousand eight hundred and eight, entitled "An act concerning public contracts."

And the Postmaster General may also annul the contract whenever he shall discover that the same, or any part of it, is offered for sale in the market for the purpose of speculation.

It is hereby further stipulated and agreed, that if obstacles, such as the want of water or feed, or physical obstructions, should be found between the points herein designated, so that time cannot be made, and a better line can be found between those points, the Postmaster General may vary the route to such better line.

And it is also further understood and agreed, that the contractors shall have all the rights of pre-emption, whatever they may be, secured by the 12th section of the act of Congress aforesaid, approved March 3, 1857, on either of the lines from the Mississippi river to the point of their junction with the main stem, but not on both—the election to be made by them at any time within twelve months after the date of the execution of this contract.

In witness whereof, the said Postmaster General has caused the seal of the Post Office Department to be hereto affixed, and has attested the same by his signature, and the said contractors and their sureties have hereunto set their hands and seals the day and year set opposite their names respectively.

AARON V. BROWN, [L. S.]
Postmaster General.

JOHN BUTTERFIELD,	[L. S.]	Sept. 16.
W. B. DINSMORE,	[L. S.]	"
WM. G. FARGO,	[L. S.]	"
J. V. P. GARDNER,	[L. S.]	"
M. L. KINYON,	[L. S.]	"
ALEX. HOLLAND,	[L. S.]	"
H. SPENCER,	[L. S.]	"
D. N. BARNEY,	[L. S.]	"
JOHNSTON LIVINGSTON,	[L. S.]	"
DAVID MOULTON,	[L. S.]	"
ELIJAH P. WILLIAMS.	[L. S.]	"

Signed, sealed, and delivered by the Postmaster General in the presence of—

    WM. H. DUNDAS.

And by the other parties hereto in the presence of—

    REVERDY JOHNSON.
    ISAAC V. FOWLER.

I hereby certify that I am well acquainted with Danford N. Barney,

Johnston Livingston, David Moulton, and Elijah P. Williams, and the condition of their property, and that, after full investigation and inquiry, I am well satisfied that they are good and sufficient sureties for the amount in the foregoing contract.

ISAAC V. FOWLER,
Postmaster at New York, N. Y.

[Endorsement.]

Ordered: That whenever the contractors and their securities shall file in the Post Office Department a request in writing that they desire to make the junction of the two branches of said road at Preston, instead of Little Rock, the department will permit the same to be done by some route nót further west than to Springfield, in Missouri, thence by Fayetteville, Van Buren, and Fort Smith, in the State of Arkansas to the said junction at or near the town of Preston, in Texas; but said new line will be adopted on the express condition that the said contractors shall not claim or demand from the department or from Congress any increased compensation for or on account of such change in the route from St. Louis, or of the point of junction of the two routes from Little Rock to Preston ; and on the further express condition, that whilst the *amount* of lands to which the contractors may be entitled under the act of Congress may be estimated on either of said branches from Preston to St. Louis, or Memphis, at their option, yet the said contractors shall take one-half of that amount on each of said branches, so that neither shall have an advantage in the way of stations and settlement over the other; and in case said contractors, in selecting and locating their lands, shall disregard this condition, or give undue advantage to one of said branches over the other, the department reserves the power of discontinuing said new route from St. Louis to Preston, and to hold said contractors and their securities to the original route and terms expressed and set forth in the body of this contract.

AARON V. BROWN,
Postmaster General.

SEPTEMBER 11, 1857.

Having furnished the above detail of facts, the department does not consider it improper to submit a few observations in relation to the reasons which induced a preference for the route selected.

The law of Congress not being mandatory, the department did not feel at liberty, in the exercise of a sound discretion, to select any route over which it was considered physically impossible to obtain the service within the time and by the mode of conveyance specified in the act. The trip was to be made within twenty-five days, in four-horse coaches, suitable for the conveyance of passengers as well as the safety and security of the mails. Applying these requirements to the extreme northern route proposed, from St. Louis by Fort Independence, Fort Laramie, Salt Lake, &c., the department had the recorded experience of many years against the practicability of procuring anything like a regular and certain service on that route. The United States had had a mail carried for years on that route, and the

Vol. II——63

returns in the department showed the most conclusive facts against its selection. The mails for November, December, and January, 1850-'51, did not arrive until March, 1851. The winter months of 1851-'52 were very severe. The carrier and postmaster reported that they started in time, but had to turn back. The mails of February, March, and December, of 1853, were impeded by deep snow. Those of January and February, 1854, on account of deep snow, did not arrive until the month of April. There was no improvement in the service even down to the November mail of 1856, which left Independence on the first of November, and, on account of deep snow, was obliged to winter in the mountains. The snow caused almost an entire failure for four months of the year. These actual experiments, made from the year 1850 to the present time, without referring to the concurring testimony of explorers and travellers, put this route entirely out of the question.

The next route to be considered was the one by Albuquerque—whether the same might start from Memphis or St. Louis. Is this route sufficiently level and exempt from snow, ice, and extremely cold weather, to give the promise that the required service can be performed with regularity and certainty throughout the entire year? and if it can be so performed, can it be done with reasonable safety and comfort to the passengers who are to be transported over it? The mere transmission of the "letter mail" was certainly not the sole object of the law. It looks expressly to the comfort of travellers in the stage, and doubtless to the millions of emigrants and others who, for ages, might pass to and from our Pacific States.

By an inspection of the general profile sheets accompanying the Pacific Railroad Reports, it will be seen that the mean elevation of the plateau of the Sierra Madre and Rocky mountains is about 7,000 feet above the level of the sea near the 35th parallel, (Albuquerque route,) and near the 32d parallel (El Paso route) it is about 4,000 or 4,200 feet, (Lieut. Parke,) giving a difference of 2,800 or 3,000 feet. This difference in elevation, in a climatological point of view, is very important, as will be shown by comparison of extremes of climate on these routes.

Next, with regard to the climate of winter, particularly along these routes, we present the following facts:

Albuquerque route.—At Albuquerque, according to the meteorological report of the medical department of the United States army, the maximum and minimum temperatures, respectively, were, for the winter months of 1849 and 1850: in December, 53°, 5°; January, 49°, *minus* 12°; February, 57°, 17°. For 1850 and 1851: in December, 52°, *minus* 5°; January, 57°, 8°; February, 59°, 7°. For 1852 and 1853: in December, 65°, 21°; January, 65°, 19°; February, 66°, 13°. For 1853 and 1854: in December, 66°, 20°; January, 68°, 5°; February, 67°, 15°; and in December, 1854, 58°, 19°.

At Fort Defiance, about twenty miles north of Campbell's Pass in latitude, and from 300 to 500 feet higher, the maximum and minimum temperatures, respectively, were: for the month of December, 1851, 62°, 4°; 18 inches snow. For 1852 and 1853: in December,

50°, 2°; January, 55°, 7°; February, 56°, 6°. For 1853 and 1854: in December, 57°, 6°; January, 49°, *minus* 20°; February, 54°, 2°. For 1854 and 1855: December, 65°, 10°; January, 59°, *minus* 17°; February, 61°, 13°. For 1855 and 1856: December, 56°, *minus* 25°; January, 54°, *minus* 8°; February, 51°, *minus* 3°.

At Albuquerque, December, 1856, the maximum was 65°, minimum 5°; Rio Grande frozen over, so as to be passable from 7th to 25th January, 1857; maximum 66°, minimum 4°; on the 9th, 10th and 11th the thermometer stood, respectively, *minus* 3°, *minus* 2°, *minus* 4°. February, 1857, maximum 72°, minimum 10°.

At Fort Defiance, December, 1856, the maximum was 50°, minimum *minus* 11°. On the 2d the thermometer stood, at 9 p. m., *minus* 2°; on the 3d, at 7 a. m. and 9 p. m., *minus* 2°; on the 4th, at 7 a. m., *minus* 10°; on the 5th, at 7 a. m., *minus* 6°; on the 6th, at 7 a. m., *minus* 11°; on the 7th, at 7 a. m., *minus* 7°; on the 8th, at 7 a. m., *minus* 1°; on the 10th, at 7 a. m., *zero*; on the 13th, at 7 a. m., *minus* 9°, and at 9 p. m., *minus* 7°.

For January, maximum 54°, minimum *minus* 11°. On the 9th, 10th, and 11th, the thermometer stood, at 7 a. m., respectively, *minus* 7°, *minus* 11°, *minus* 11°; on the 10th, at 9 p. m., *minus* 4°.

For February, maximum was 60°, minimum *minus* 12°.

"On December 25, 1855, the thermometer at the hospital at Fort Defiance gave a reading of thirty-two degrees (32°) below zero, at 6½ a. m. The hospital is not by any means in the coldest portion of the garrison. Two hundred yards distant the mercury, in January, 1856, ranged from four to eight degrees below that at the hospital, and there is not the slightest doubt of the freezing of the mercury had the instrument been placed in the more exposed situation on the morning of December 25, 1855. *A number of men on detached service had their hands and feet frozen, and some badly.* The mercury was below zero four mornings in December, 1855; six mornings in January, 1856; three mornings in February, and on the mornings of the 1st and 2d of March, it was below zero.

"The table above will give a fair idea of the climate of the country. The winter of 1855 and 1856 was more severe than any one known for many years. The wintry weather commenced on the 1st of November, 1855, and has continued up to the present time, March 14, 1856. The Rio Grande, at Albuquerque, was frozen over, and with ice sufficiently strong to bear a horse and carreta. Those Indians who live habitually to the north of Fort Defiance were obliged to abandon that portion of the country and move south, with their flocks and herds, in quest of grazing, on account of the depth of snow, which, in the mountains, at whose base the fort is situated, was over two feet in depth in March, 1856."—(*Correspondence, J. Letherman, Assistant Surgeon, U. S. A.; Smithsonian Report, 1855, page 287.*)

On the 24th of December, 1853, Captain Whipple experienced snow storms and weather sufficiently cold to contract the mercury 3½ degrees below zero, near the San Francisco mountains, and still further west, in the Aztec Pass, to 2½ degrees below zero, when he experienced another severe snow storm. So much for the climate of winter on the Albuquerque route.

Let us compare this account of the climate, extracted from undoubted sources, with that along the more southern route selected.

At Fort Fillmore, on the El Paso route, the meteorological report above referred to shows the minimum temperature at this place, up to 1854, to be but 10 degrees.

At Tucson, February, 1854, Lieutenant Parke reports the minimum temperature 32 degrees, and on one occasion, on the San Pedro, to be 12 degrees at sunrise. We have searched in vain every source of information, and have yet to learn that snow ever lies upon the plains near the El Paso route, or that the thermometer ever descended below zero. The mean temperature of winter at Fort Fillmore is about 46.6 degrees. The mean temperature of winter at Fort Webster, (Copper Mines,) north of *Ojo de la Vaca*, and 6,350 feet above the sea level, is but 41.3 degrees, while at Fort Defiance, a corresponding position, with reference to the Albuquerque route, it is 28.7 degrees, and at Albuquerque it is 37 degrees. At Fort Yuma, (mouth of the Gila,) on the El Paso route, the mean temperature of winter is 56.8 degrees.

Although this superiority of climate on the El Paso route must be admitted, still it has been and may be argued that the degree of cold on the Albuquerque route is not greater than on many of the stage routes of the Atlantic States—not greater, perhaps, than between Philadelphia and Pittsburg, or between Baltimore and Wheeling. Without admitting the fact, at all events so far as the latter route is concerned, it requires but little effort to remember how uncertain during the winter season was the transportation of the mails when the roads were in their natural state, and with what extreme suffering from the cold staging used to be performed between those cities, with all the advantages of short and well-appointed stations for recruiting the energies of the benumbed and exhausted passengers.

But would Congress or the public be content with a route to California no better in point of climate than those by Harrisburg and Cumberland, when a more mild and favorable one could be easily procured? Imagine four stages to start out from St. Louis on the Albuquerque route with eight passengers in each, thirty-two in number. At the starting point the snow is eight or ten inches deep, which it often is for weeks together. They are to go *day and night*, the thermometer ten or fifteen degrees *above*, not below zero. They progress westward, ascending every mile higher and higher, the cold increasing with every mile, for an entire week. At last they reach Albuquerque, an elevation of 6,000 feet, the mercury standing four or five degrees below zero. Benumbed by the cold for more than a week, overcome by the loss of sleep, they begin another ascent to Campbell's Pass, the best on the route, about 7,000 feet in height, in the vicinity of which the thermometer is standing, by authentic and undoubted observations, from 2° to 32° below zero.

How can thirty-odd passengers, men, women, and children, some feeble in health or delicate in constitution, be otherwise than in almost a dying condition? This is no picture of the imagination; it is one of those practical views which common sense will always suggest as to the sufferings and exposures of stage travelling under circumstances so inauspicious. But a truer picture of more intense suffering may be found in the groups of emigrants camped out amid the snows, or struggling to get on, when the mercury, as it very often happens, is down at or below zero—whether a few degrees above or below makes no difference, for a long continued stage or emigrant travel, under circumstances of so much severe exposure, would, in a few years, mark every station with the fresh graves of its victims. Most emigrants are compelled to be *en route* in some portion of the winter months. Most families cannot well start from the Atlantic to the Pacific or interior States until they have first finished and disposed of the crop of the preceding season ; at all events, it must be so far matured before they start that something approaching its value can be realized from it, in order to help in defraying the expenses of removal. Nor can emigrants linger too long on the way. They must go on, however much exposed to hardships, in order to reach their new homes in time to make a crop the next season. The poor cannot lose two crops in succession without being ruined. The southern or El Paso route is eminently comfortable and desirable for winter emigration, which the Albuquerque one cannot be, whatever might be said in its favor as a route in the summer season. The department supposed Congress to be in search of a route that could be found safe, comfortable, and certain during every season of the year, as well for the transportation of the mails as for the accommodation of emigrants and the future location of a railroad to the Pacific.

In relation to the relative facility with which four-horse stage coaches can be run over the Albuquerque and the El Paso routes, it must be remembered that this service was to commence within twelve months. The distance was more than two thousand miles, over many ranges of mountains, and nearly the whole distance uninhabited. There were no roads yet opened, and even the foot of the white man had not yet trodden many portions of the way which might finally be selected. Still, the stages must be running within twelve months. To do so it was evident that some route must be selected which was *naturally a good one*—such a one that, by cutting down some trees and blazing others, as mere guide posts, digging down occasional hillsides, and building slight and temporary bridges, the work of transportation might begin within the brief period required by the law. It was not enough that, by great labor of years and by large expenditure of money, a graded turnpike *could* be made, or a railway constructed, at the end of some half dozen years, or even a longer period, but it must be over a surface of country naturally so favorable that stage coaches, with their mails and passengers, could be running within twelve months with a rapidity scarcely equalled on the best routes of the older States. To make the trip in twenty-five days they must go day and night, averaging about eighty miles each day. Now, which of these two routes presented the greatest probability of affording such a service? Captain Marcy explored both routes as far as the Rio Grande, and, after having examined both, he gave a decided preference to the southern or El Paso route. He says, on page 228 of his report, after a favorable description of the route from the Rio Grande to the Pecos :

" Our road from here runs across the Llano Estacado for seventy-eight miles, upon a perfectly level prairie as firm and smooth as marble. It then descends from the high table land, about fifty feet, into a rolling prairie country, where the Colorado of Texas has its source. Thus far there is but little timber or water on our route, except at certain points noted upon the map ; but these points can be made from day to day with loaded teams. As if, however, in compensation for the absence of other favors, nature, in her wise economy, has adorned the entire face of the country with a luxuriant verdure of different kinds of grama grass, affording the most nutritious sustenance for animals, and rendering it one of the best countries for grazing large flocks and herds that can be conceived of.

" Immediately after we descended from the high table lands, we struck upon an entirely different country from the one we had been passing over before. By a reference to the map it will be seen we kept near the plain upon the head branches of the Colorado and the Clear Fork of the Brazos. Here we found a smooth road over a gently undulating country of prairies and timber, and abounding with numerous clear spring branches for two hundred miles, and in many places covered with large groves of mezquite timber, which makes the very best of fuel. The soil cannot be surpassed for fertility. The grass remains green during the entire winter, and the climate is salubrious and healthy. Indeed, it possesses all the requisites that can be desired for making a fine agricultural country ; and I venture to predict that at no very distant period it will contain a very dense population. It is only necessary for our practical farmers to see it, and have protection from the incursions of the Indians, to settle it at once.

" Soon after crossing the Rio Brazos, our road strikes out upon the high ridge lying between the waters of the Trinity and Red rivers ; and it appears as if nature had formed this expressly for a road, as it runs for a hundred miles through a country which is frequently much broken up on each side with hills and deep ravines, and the only place where wagons can pass is directly upon the crest of this natural defile. It is as firm and smooth as a turnpike, with no streams of magnitude or other obstruction through the entire distance to near Preston, where we left it and crossed the Red river—from Preston o Fort Washita, and thence to our outward route upon Gaines' creek, the road passing through the Chickasaw country, which is rolling, and in many places covered with a great variety of large timber and well watered, with no mountains or high hills to pass over. Hence you will perceive that from Doña Ana to Fort Smith, a distance of 994 miles, our road passes over smooth and very uniformly level ground, crossing no mountains or deep valleys, and for five hundred miles, upon the eastern extremity, runs through the heart of a country possessing great natural advantages. I conceive this to be decidedly the best overland wagon route to California, for several reasons."

We will now call attention to the evidence of Captain John Pope, Topographical Engineers, who has been stationed a long time in New Mexico, and has seen a great portion of the plains between the 32d and 39th parallels. In chapter XI, Pacific Railroad Reports, vol. 2, speaking of the general character of the country along the 32d parallel route, he says:

"In glancing at the topographical features of the immense plains which extend westward from the frontiers of Arkansas and Missouri, the first great peculiarity which strikes the attention is the remarkable interruption to their vast monotony presented by the belt of country between the 32d and 34th parallels of latitude. The great deserts, commencing about the 97th meridian, extend over a distance of six hundred miles to the eastern base of the Rocky mountains. In this whole extent they are badly watered by a few sluggish streams which intersect them, many of which disappear altogether in the dry season, and are destitute absolutely of timber, except a sparse growth of dwarf cotton along the streams. From the northern part of the United States, at the parallel of 49°, this immense region of desert country extends without interruption as far to the south as the parallel of 34°. At this parallel its continuity is suddenly and remarkably interrupted. Between the 32d and 34th parallels of latitude a broad belt of well-watered, well-timbered country, adapted in a high degree to agricultural purposes, projects for three hundred and twelve miles, like a vast peninsula, into the parched and treeless waste of the plains, and at its western limit approaches to within less than three hundred miles of the Rio Grande at El Paso."

The same distinctive preference to the El Paso route (the one selected) over the Albuquerque route is given by Commissioners Emory and Bartlett, Lieutenant Parke, and A. H. Campbell, at the head of the Pacific Wagon Road Office, Interior Department, who accompaned Captain Whipple over the Albuquerque route, and Lieutenant Parke over the El Paso, as principal engineer, in 1853, '54, and '55. The comparison of the two routes west of the Rio Grande the department considered equally favorable to the one selected. Beside the fact of its being over a country about 3,000 feet lower than the Albuquerque route, Congress had appropriated $200,000 on this route to be expended in the construction of a wagon road between the Rio Grande and Fort Yuma, on the Colorado. So large a sum expended on a surface so favorable by nature will, doubtless, prove of an immense advantage in expediting the proposed service, both as to regularity and speed. Before this appropriation was made by Congress, Mr. Secretary Davis, who collected a larger amount of reliable information on this subject than any other person, reported to Congress that the most practicable and economical route for a railroad from the Mississippi river to the Pacific ocean was the one which the department has selected. Lieut. Mowry, writing on this subject, since the route was established, says: "For years, a mail has been regularly carried from San Antonio to El Paso without difficulty or danger, except from Indians. At present a monthly mail is carried from El Paso to Tucson, 340 miles west, by government express, for the benefit of the troops in Arizona. This express has a military escort. Fort Yuma and San Diego, California, have for five years been connected by a semi-monthly mail, (government express,) which, during my two years' service at Fort Yuma, was as regular in its arrival as the steamer from the east at San Francisco.

"The only part of the newly selected route not now opened by a mail is that from Fort Yuma to Tucson, 260 miles ; and this is almost daily travelled by the people of the Territory, by emigrants, and by Mexicans. Tucson is a growing town, and will afford all the grain needed for the road to El Paso. The Pimas villages, on the Gila river, will supply grain for the route to Fort Yuma, besides any quantity to transport to any desired point, or a depot of supply.

"At Fort Yuma, last year, a large quantity of corn was allowed to rot for want of a market, and there is grazing for ten thousand animals on the river banks. A few military posts, which would be necessary on either of the other routes, will make the southern route perfectly safe ; and the immense mineral wealth, in silver and copper, will at once draw to Arizona a large population. *It is the only available route at all seasons of the year.* The route through the South Pass is as much closed by snow from four to six months in the year as if barred by a gate of adamant. During the winter of 1854-'55, I was in the Salt Lake valley, and no mail from the east reached us from November to April. The mail was at that time transported on pack mules, and was in the charge of experienced men, who had spent their lives on the plains.

"If they could not get the mail through either way, how much less the chance is there for Concord coaches? The central route is no better. I refer to Colonel Frémont or Lieutenant Beale to state, upon their reputation as travellers and 'mountain men,' how much dependence can be placed upon the regular transmission of a semi-weekly mail through the Cocheetopee Pass in December, January, February, or March. The route by El Paso and Fort Yuma is open the entire year. On both the other routes artesian wells are necessary to get water at convenient distances, and this necessity upon the southern route is therefore no extraordinary argument against it. I may be allowed to remark that the impression so generally diffused in the eastern States, that Arizona Territory is a desert and a God-forsaken country, is entirely erroneous. It will be recollected that California, now celebrated as an agricultural State, was stigmatized with the same epithets, and said to produce nothing but gold. Arizona promises to convince the world that she is able to produce silver enough to supply all the demands of commerce, and to show to the emigrant in search of a quiet and fruitful homestead beautiful valleys and clear running streams, where he may cultivate his crops with a fullness of fruition only known to the virgin soil of our western possessions."

The scarcity of water has been often urged against the southern or El Paso route. There is no route between the Mississippi river and California against which the same objection may not be made. After much examination, we believe that the route selected is freer from this objection than almost any other. The statements of Lieutenant Mowry and Mr. Campbell are fully sustained by other authorities. The former, in a published statement, says :

"The country from El Paso to Tucson, three hundred and forty miles, is susceptible of early settlement, and is, moreover, one of the finest routes ever opened towards our western possessions. In no part of it is there a distance of over thirty miles without water, and it is often found at distances of ten and fifteen, with plenty of good grazing throughout the entire distance.

"From Tucson, the principal town of the Territory of Arizona, (throughout the whole length of which the route runs,) to the Gila river, ninety miles, there is no water in the dry season, and two artesian wells will be necessary. In the wet season there is plenty of water. This distance is travelled at all seasons with mule teams and oxen, without difficulty. Down the Gila to Fort Yuma, one hundred and seventy-five miles, there is plenty of water and grass. From Fort Yuma, on the Colorado river, to Carissa creek and San Diego county, California, about one hundred miles, the route is heavy with sand, and water is found in but three places at all seasons of the year. In the wet season water is found every few miles. Twenty-four miles from Fort Yuma, or Colorado City, are Cook's wells, which, at an expense of $1,000, can be made to furnish an ample supply. Twenty-six miles beyond are the Alamo Mucho wells, which can be enlarged, at the same cost, to any quantity desired. Thirty miles further on are the Indian wells, which will also yield an ample supply. Twenty miles further are the Sackett's wells, which are fed by a subterranean stream, and can also be made to supply any quantity of water.

"These two distances, from Tucson to the Gila and from Fort Yuma to Carissa, present the only difficulties on the route. United, the distance is but one hundred and ninety miles, and it is travelled at all seasons of the year by heavily loaded teams.

"From Carissa creek into San Diego the route is well watered and affords excellent grazing. The distance is one hundred and twenty-five miles; but the supervisors of San Diego county are now engaged in laying out a new road, which will much shorten the distance."

Mr. Campbell, who, as we have before stated, travelled over both routes, has borne the most ample testimony "that between the Rio Grande and the San Pedro river there are thirteen permanent water stations in about two hundred and twenty-four miles, giving an average of one in seventeen miles, and eighteen, including several fine rain-water stations, where water can be preserved, which will give an average of one in twelve miles."

We have submitted this letter of Lieutenant Mowry to Mr. Campbell. He confirms the statements of Lieutenant Mowry in every important particular, and further informs us "that the ninety miles *jornada* from the Tucson to the Gila is avoided entirely by following down the San Pedro and Gila rivers to the Pimas villages. The distance from the San Pedro, by either route, to the Gila, is about the same; and it is probable that, by following down the Aravaypa, a tributary of the Gila, discovered by Lieutenant Parke's party, a distance of many miles can be saved; and in the Calitro mountains, along this route, there is an abundance of pure water in living streams, fine grazing, and oak, ash, walnut, and some pine timber. Deer, antelope, bear, and grouse abound there also, and many indications of gold were observed, and gold was found near the San Pedro river."

1002 REPORT OF THE

Captain Humphreys, in his report to the Secretary of War, and Lieutenant Parke, both testify that a sufficient supply of water can be had on the route for either a railroad or stage line.

In relation to the relative distance on the two routes, an examination of the map will exhibit the fact that the distance from Boston, New York, Philadelphia, Baltimore, and Washington, to San Francisco, is about the same upon both routes.

Albuquerque route.

Distance from San Francisco to Fort Smith, on the Albuquerque route, (see Captain Whipple's report, vol. 2, p. 76)	1,952	miles.
From Fort Smith to New York, (Captain Humphreys' report, Pacific Railroad Report, vol. 1, p. 108)	1,345	"
Total	3,297	"

El Paso route.

From San Francisco Bay (San José) to Fulton, (Lieut. Parke's report, 1855, unpublished,)	1,972	miles.
From San Francisco Bay (San José) to San Francisco	44	"
From Fulton to New York, (Humphreys' report, in Pacific Railroad Report, vol. 1, p. 108)	1,335	"
Total	3,351	"

Making a difference of only fifty-four miles in favor of the Albuquerqe route, as shown by the Pacific railroad surveys—a difference too small to be a matter of grave objection. These and other estimates of distance cannot be expected to be entirely correct; but they approximate the precise distances as nearly as published surveys and explorations will allow of. The above difference of fifty-four miles, however, is reduced to four miles, if we estimate the distance from San Bernardino to San Francisco, via the Cajon Pass, Cañada de los Uvas, and Estero Plain,* as in the following table, thereby avoiding the detour of Lieutenant Parke's route via Santa Barbara and the Gaviote Pass.

From the latest authorities, for the respective routes from the Mississippi river, at St. Louis, via Albuquerque, and at Memphis, via El Paso and Fort Yuma, to San Francisco, California, I find the most direct distances over which the mail should travel as follows:

* See Birch's proposal.

Route from Memphis, via El Paso, &c.

From Memphis to Preston (a)...........................	375	miles.
From Preston to Waco Tanks (b).........................	615	"
From Waco Tanks to Fort Fillmore (c)...........	40	"
From Fort Fillmore to Pimas villages (d)................	306	"
From Pimas villages to Fort Yuma (e)...................	167	"
From Fort Yuma to San Bernardino (f).	180	"
From San Bernardino to San Francisco, via Cajon Pass, Cañada de los Uvas, and Estero Plain (g)..............	420	"
	2,103	

Route from St. Louis, via Springfield, Antelope Hills, or Canadian river, Albuquerque, &c., to San Francisco.

From St. Louis to head of Pajarito creek (h)............	860	miles.
From head of Pajarito creek to San Francisco (via Cañon Carnuel or San Antonio, New Mexico,) and via Tah-ee-chay-pah Pass, California...................	1,246	"
	2,106	"
From St. Louis to Campbell's Pass, via Galisteo (i)...	1,080	"
From Campbell's Pass to San Francisco, as above (j).	1,085	"
	2,165	"

NOTE.—As an interesting comparison between these two routes, take Captain Whipple's modified distance—1,952 miles—from Fort Smith to San Francisco, and add 250 miles in a direct line from Fort Smith to Memphis, from the General Railroad Map above referred to, and we have from the same initial point—Memphis—a distance to San Francisco of 2,202 miles.

Thus the difference in the distances of the two routes between the Mississippi river and San Francisco is too inconsiderable to become material.

(a) See General Pacific Railroad Map, in hands of engraver.
(b) See Captain J. Pope's report, 1854, Ho. Doc. 129, page 61.
(c) General Pacific Railroad Map
(d) Lieut. Parke's report, unpublished.
(e) Major Emory's reconnaissance, 1846, and Pacific Railroad profile, 32d parallel route.
(f) Lieut. Williamson's surveys. Ho. Doc. 129, &c. &c.
(g) Lieut. Williamson, 1853–'54, and Lieut. Parke, '54–'55, unpublished map and report.
(h) General Pacific Railroad Map, &c.
(i) General Pacific Railroad Map and Captain Whipple's undistributed report.
(j) Captain Whipple's report and General Pacific Railroad Map, &c., &c.

As a pioneer route for the first great railroad that may be constructed to the Pacific, the Postmaster General has bestowed upon it all the labor and examination which the multiplied business of his department would allow of. If all or a greater portion of the railroads from the large cities and the States east of the Mississippi had concentrated at any one point on that river, such point would have been selected for the overland route to California. But such is not the fact. They concentrate chiefly at St. Louis, Cairo, and Memphis. Cairo is mentioned in this connexion because, through the Illinois Central, nearly all the railroads constructed for St. Louis may be said also to connect with the Mississippi at Cairo. Finding, therefore, no common centre *on* the Mississippi, the next desirable object was to find some common point *west* of that river from which a main stem could be projected passing westward to California. If you started out from St. Louis west you must lose all the connexions with the Cairo and Memphis railroads; but by starting out from St. Louis, and diverging south with her railroad now making to her Iron Mountain, you will presently receive the great railroad coming out from Cairo, so richly endowed that it is sure to be made at no distant day. Still bearing southwestward, we presently receive, at Little Rock, the other branch of the road from Memphis, connecting the line with all the great railroads of Virginia, South Carolina, Georgia, Alabama, Tennessee, and Kentucky. Not far from Little Rock the Vicksburg and New Orleans and Texas railroads fall in, bringing in, from almost every portion of the great river, all the connexions which all the Atlantic States north and south can make to that great highway which we are trying to establish. Thus it is that we have found *west* of the Mississippi what we could not obtain *on it*—a common concentration of railroads to a single point from which the future railroad may commence, swollen and enlarged in its common stem by the contributions of the railways coming in from nearly every State of the Union.

This diversion of the route to a southern direction by Little Rock or Preston has, however, other advantages than any to which we have as yet adverted.

"By starting from St. Louis, the great western mart, and connecting at Little Rock or Preston with the line from Memphis, the two great sections of the country are accommodated.

"Instead of projecting this mail, and its attendant benefits, into the wilderness, from the frontier of Missouri, to buffet with north winds and snows upon the plains of Kansas in winter, and drag over monotonous, waterless, treeless wastes in summer, it was located through the centre of Missouri, of Arkansas, and throughout the western frontier of Texas. It will thus develop hitherto unknown resources in those States. It will open a vast agricultural and mineral region in Missouri; lend a helping hand to the young, growing, and unappreciated State of Arkansas; and conduct the hardy pioneer to the delightful woodlands and prairies of Texas. For nearly a thousand miles the traveller will be traversing a country abounding in beauty and in healthfulness, possessing a salubrious climate and a fruitful soil."

Nor should it be forgotten that the southern location of the route, especially if it shall be followed by the construction of a railroad, may serve a valuable purpose in reference to the neighboring republic of Mexico. In time of peace it will shed its blessings on both nations, whilst in time of war it will furnish a highway for troops and munitions of war, which might enable us to vindicate our rights, and preserve untarnished our national honor.

I have the honor to be, very respectfully, your obedient servant,
AARON V. BROWN.

———

NOTE.—Since the action of the department on this important subject, a publication has appeared in the public journals, from the pen of Mr. Bartlett, late of the Boundary Commission, so full of valuable and reliable information, that the Postmaster General respectfully begs leave to subjoin it to this report, as follows:

THE OVERLAND MAIL TO CALIFORNIA.

[From the Providence Journal of August 18.]

Communication from Mr. John R. Bartlett.

The recent decision of the Postmaster General, in adopting the southern route as the one over which the United States mail shall be carried between the valley of the Mississippi river and San Francisco, in California, having attracted much attention, I have deemed it a duty to submit a few remarks on the subject. In doing this, I do not propose to discuss the geographical question of a northern, a central, or a southern route, or the advantages or disadvantages which may accrue to any particular section of the country from the selection of a route, but simply to speak of the advantages which I believe the route adopted to possess, and of the facility with which a wagon road may be constructed over it. My conclusions are based, not upon the reports or explorations of others, but from my own observations while employed upon the survey of the Mexican boundary line.

The government has doubtless made its choice from the reports of the examinations made by the several parties which crossed the country with a view to collect such facts as would enable it to decide upon a route for a railroad to connect the Atlantic with the Pacific ocean.

It is well known that the surveys and explorations of the United States Boundary Commission, with which I was connected from the year 1850 to 1853, were near the parallel of 32 degrees, both east and west of the Rio Grande. Our journeys in Texas commenced near the 97th meridian of longitude, whence we passed to the table lands at the north, and traversed the country a distance of nearly six hundred miles between the 31st and 32d parallels. From the woodless nature of the country here, one is enabled from any hill or eminence to cast his eye over a vast surface, as though looking at a map, and notice all mountains, elevations, and depressions; the rivers and small watercourses, the water-sheds, and the timbered lands; in fact, over so open a district as here exists, an observer may obtain a most exact idea of the face of the country for fifty or a hundred miles from his point of observation, particularly if that point is on the summit of an isolated hill, of which there are many in the district in question.

For a large portion of this journey we travelled, with seven loaded wagons, where no travellers had been before, following no track and directed by no guide. Water was found in the various tributaries of the Colorado, which river was in sight at the north, and until we reached the sources of the Concho. Here came the first desert, and here begins the vast desert region which extends to the Rio Grande. This line of desert reaches far to the north, and includes the well known Llåno Estacado, which was crossed by our party at its shortest angle, about sixty-five miles across. This plain is level and hard the entire distance, and would require no labor to make a road across it available. It is without wood and water, yet in several depressions water is often found, and there is little doubt that by sinking wells it might be procured at all times. In the passes of Castle mountain, ten miles east of the Pecos, there were traces of water, where it might be found by digging. We followed the Pecos and its tributary, Delaware creek, for more than a hundred miles, the country being quite level the entire distance to the Guadalupe mountains and pass. From this the country is comparatively level to the Rio Grande. There are no mountains to cross, except the Hueco range, twenty-eight miles from El Paso, and these are attended with trifling difficulties. In water there is the greatest deficiency, there been no running streams between the Guadalupe mountains and El Paso, a distance of about one hundred and ten miles. The first water is a spring called Ojo del Cuerpo, about fifteen miles northwest of the pass, and ten miles further a pond where there is water and grass at all times; next, at the Cornudos del Alamo, and again at the Sierra Hueco, where there are springs and natural water tanks or basins. These, by being dug out and properly opened, could be made to furnish the necessary water for the stations. This district, between the Guadalupe mountains and the Rio Grande, is the longest and most difficult to cross of any east of that river, on account of the deficiency of water; yet, reckoning two springs at the Cornudos del Alamo, ten miles apart, and there are five watering-places in the one hundred and ten miles. Of this distance, eighty-two miles is over a hard rolling country, where we ran our teems without danger; the remaining twenty-eight miles, from the Hueco mountains, is sandy. At the several watering-places there is an abundance of grama grass.

The route thus far described lies a little to the south of that selected by the Postmaster General for the California mail, though the western portion of it for nearly three hundred miles (presuming that of Captain Marcy to be followed) will be the same. From this point, on the Pecos, to the 99th meridian, the character of the country is much the same. The Llano Estacado is crossed further north, after which the route is intersected by the northern tributaries of the Colorado, while the Boundary Commission crossed the southern ones. Thence he follows the Brazos and Washita rivers. The country here, from the Pecos to the Red river, except across the plain referred to, is well watered, with timber bordering most of the streams, many of which have valleys or bottoms well adapted for cultivation. This belt of country, which is watered by the Colorado, the upper Brazos, and the Red river, projects three hundred miles or more beyond the generally acknowledged limit of population west of the Mississippi, thereby lessening the distance of desert to be crossed in order to reach the Rio Grande. For this reason, therefore, the southern route along the line traced has advantages over the central one in having a much narrower belt of woodless and waterless country to pass over, while the whole distance is about the same.

The next advantage of the southern line, and a most important one, is, that the summit level at El Paso is from 3,800 to 4,000 feet above the level of the sea, while that of the central or Albuquerque route, near the 35th parallel, is, according to the Pacific Railroad Reports, not far from 7,000 feet. The temperature at these two points corresponds with the difference in elevation. At Albuquerque the mercury sinks below zero, and the Rio Grande is sometimes frozen over so that persons may cross on the ice. At El Paso it has never been known to sink as low as zero. The Boundary Commission wintered there in 1850-'51, which was pronounced the coldest ever known there. Snow fell once or twice at night, but disappeared the day following before noon, and the mercury sank on a single occasion to 10°.

These conclusions are not new, as the same opinion was expressed in my "Personal Narrative"—a report of explorations connected with the Boundary Commission, published immediately on the return of that body from the survey of the line. In volume one of that work, page 139, in speaking of the district east of the Rio Grande, it is stated that—

"The country is well adapted for a wagon road, and equally so for a railway. From Fredericksburg, in Texas, all the way to the Rio Grande, *there is a natural road,* which, as a whole, is better than one-half the roads in the United States west of the Mississippi. Very little has been done to this road of nearly 600 miles to render it what it is; and a little labor where the streams are crossed, with a bridge across the Pecos, which could be constructed with ease and at a small expense, would make the whole of it equal to our best turnpikes."

In continuation of my remarks on the practicability of constructing a great wagon road near the parallel of 32°, I suggested the necessity of sinking wells at certain places, and further stated as my belief, from what I had heard from Mexicans who had travelled the country between the Pecos and the Rio Grande, that water could be found in other places not then known to travellers, thereby removing one of the greatest obstacles in crossing this arid region.

The district of country bordering on the Rio Grande at El Paso is the widest and richest portion of the bottom lands along that stream, and hence capable of sustaining a larger population than at any other point. The strip of bottom land known as the "Mesilla Valley," though not one-half the extent of that south of El Paso, is also valuable; and at Doña Ana, as well as a few miles to the north, the bottom lands again expand into a broad plain, admirably adapted to artificial irrigation and agriculture, and consequently to the sustaining of a larger population than is elsewhere to be found in that vicinity. Indeed, it may with truth be asserted that the richest portion of the valley of the Rio Grande lies between the parallels of 31° 30' and 33 degrees. El Paso lies in 31° 45'. Of the extent of the culturable valley near the parallel of 35° I am not prepared to speak with confidence.

I will now speak of the country west of the Rio Grande near the parallel of 32 degrees, near which the contemplated mail route is to run. This district was frequently crossed and recrossed by myself personally, as well as by various engineering parties of the Boundary Commission. To avail ourselves of the few watering-places then known, we followed the Rio Grande to Santa Barbara, thence westwardly to Cooke's spring. Our surveying parties, which followed the line of 32° 22', found springs at several places between Doña Ana and Cooke's spring, and in their various reconnaissances discovered water in many places not marked on the maps or known to travellers. Proceeding west, the Rio Mimbres and a copious spring called Ojo de Vaca followed at intervals of ten and twelve miles.

Westward from Ojo de Vaca the vast region extending to Tucson was entirely unknown, and I am not aware was ever traversed by any party of white men previous to 1851, when it became necessary that our Commission should penetrate it. When Col. Cooke was here in 1847 with his battalion, on his march to California, his guide, Leroux, was afraid to cross it, not knowing of the existence of water there. He therefore advised the Colonel to take a southwesterly course to the Guadalupe Pass, in Sonora, thence to San Pedro river, Tucson, and the Gila. Col. Cooke took this route and opened a way, which has since been laid down on the maps as Cooke's road, while the district avoided by him is designated "as an open prairie and a good route, if water can be found." Such was simply the "*belief*" of Leroux. In entering upon this unknown district we had many fears; yet, with a train of both heavily laden wagons and pack mules, we took a course due west from Ojo de Vaca, and found in the Burro mountains, fifteen miles distant, an abundance of water and a small stream, which I think extended to the Gila. We had followed a ravine for five miles through the mountains, and supposed we should be obliged to retrace our steps; yet, after searching an hour or two, we found a passage through the mountains for our wagons without using a spade or encountering any steep ascent or descent.

Thus the whole party for the survey of the line to its western extremity, and that for the survey of the Gila, as well as one of the Rio Grande divisions, with their loaded wagons, pack mules, a herd of twenty-five oxen and one hundred and fifty sheep, traversed this unknown region, crossing mountains, ridges, open plains, and desert wastes, without losing or crippling a wagon; without suffering for the want of water, which was always found at convenient distances until the rivers San Pedro and Gila were reached. In some cases where no water was seen we dug for it, and in every instance found it near the surface. In every mountain range defiles easy of access, with gradual ascents and descents, were everywhere found by diverging a little to the right or left. Grass, too, for our large train of mules, horses, cattle, and sheep, was always found in abundance. When encamping on the woodless plains there was a deficiency in fire-wood, but when near the mountains or streams there was plenty. Sometimes we were put to a little inconvenience to find wood, water, and grass at once; but I saw enough to satisfy me that a party exploring for the purpose, and not confined to a particular line, could find all these necessaries in abundance and at convenient distances from the Rio Grande to the valley of the Santa Cruz.

The valley of the Santa Cruz is the richest, and, though quite limited in breadth, contains more land suitable for agricultural purposes than any between the Rio Grande and the Pacific within the belt between the 31st parallel and the Gila. Here, too, near Santa Cruz, Tubac, Tumacacovi and Tucson, are forests of mesquit, and the only considerable tracts of woodland (the mountains excepted) in this large district. In this valley are some of the oldest missionary establishments in America, Marco de Niza and Coronado having traversed this valley and made known its advantages before the year 1550. Such is the superior excellence of this valley, as compared with the other portions of the so-called "Gadsden Purchase," lying west of the Rio Grande valley, that it should be made available for as many stations as possible on the contemplated mail route. It contains the chief population of the district; is traversed by an excellent road; it opens the most direct and best route to Sonora, and is bounded on the east by the Santa Rita and other mountains known to abound in iron as well as the precious metals. The valley of San Pedro is admirably adapted for grazing, but not for agricultural purposes.

That my ideas with regard to this route are not now stated for the first time, but were made known to the government six years ago, I will quote from my despatch from Santa Cruz to the Hon. Alexander H. H. Stuart, Secretary of the Interior, dated September 27, 1851:

"Being the first party of which we have knowledge which has crossed the unknown region lying east of the San Pedro and south of the Gila, * * * I am now enabled to state, with great satisfaction, that the direct route travelled by the commission, nearly west from Ojo de Vaca, is a route far more practicable for a road or railway than Cooke's route; that the distance from water to water is less; that the hills and mountains to be crossed are infinitely less in height and easier to pass; and, lastly, that there is a saving in the distance, between this and Cooke's, of more than 100 miles."

A more extended view was given by me of the adaptation of this route for a wagon road or railway in a communication to the president of the Atlantic and Pacific Railway Company, in reply to a note from him asking my opinion on the subject. My letter was dated December 21, 1853, and appeared in several New York and other papers. I make a few extracts:

"Until recently, the maps of the interior portions of our continent have exhibited a great chain, known as the Rocky mountains, as continuous from a high northern latitude to the Isthmus of Panama, thereby presenting a barrier to the construction of a great public highway; but such does not convey an accurate idea of the geographical features of this region. * * * * * * *

"About the parallel of 32° 32' the Rocky mountains suddenly drop off, eight miles south of Fort Webster, and, with the exception of a few

Vol. ii——64

spurs, seem to disappear entirely for about 100 miles. Here we emerge into the great plateau, elevated from 4,000 to 5,000 feet above the level of the sea, which is crossed by no continuous range of mountains for the distance stated. Short, isolated mountains and conical hills alone appear at intervals, and these are sometimes separated by fifty miles of plain. Through the State of Chihuahua this plateau is limited on the west by the Sierra Madre, but on the east it crosses the Rio Grande and extends across the northern portion of Texas.   *   *   *

"The belt of country here noted may safely be set down at from 80 to 100 miles in width, and extends from the Rio Grande to the Coast range of mountains on the Pacific. The mountains present no barrier to the construction of a railway, being in short ridges from five to ten miles in length, overlapping each other, with broad defiles or open spaces between, affording easy passages through.   *   *   *   We travelled, with loaded wagons, more than thirty miles a day across this district, without once locking their wheels, and this too where there was no road. Every mountain range was passed through without difficulty; and, in some instances, so gradual was the ascent and descent as to be scarcely perceptible."

It will thus appear that this entire district, from the Rio Grande to the Colorado, with its broad, open, gravelly plains, is admirably adapted for either a great wagon road or a railway. From Tucson to the Gila is a desert of ninety miles without water. This desert is as hard as marble and perfectly level. Midway, at the Picacho, is a depression where water is often found, and where it would be advisable to sink wells. Twelve miles south of the Gila are similar cavities.

At the Pimo villages, on the Gila, is a fine agricultural district, consisting of a plain more than twenty miles in length by four in width, which for ages has been cultivated by the semi-civilized Indians. Immediately to the north of this is another large and excellent agricultural district, bordering on the Salinas, which enters the Gila seven miles below the Pimo villages. This river is much larger than the Gila. I traced its course for about forty miles, and found its bottom lands intersected in all directions by ancient irrigating canals; while the numerous tumuli, mounds, and crumbling edifices of a race now passed away show that it once sustained a large population.

The Gila would be followed by a road for about one hundred and eighty miles to Fort Yuma, at the junction with the Colorado, chiefly on the adjacent plateau, which is hard and level. The bottom varies in width, and in many places bears a heavy growth of cotton-wood. The Colorado, which is crossed by ferries, might easily be bridged. Here, again, is a wide valley or bottom susceptible of a high degree of cultivation. This, too, is marked by the remains of irrigating canals, first dug by the aboriginal tribes, and subsequently by the old Spaniards, who had a mission here.

We now reach the California desert, about one hundred miles across. This is very hard and level, with occasional spots of sand. It is entirely destitute of wood, and nearly so of grass. Water in the dry season is only to be obtained by digging. This is found at Cooke's wells, Alamo Mucho, and Sackett's wells. By sinking large wells it could doubtless be found in any quantity desirable. In seasons when the Colorado overflows its banks, its waters fill large basins in the desert, where it sometimes remains two or three years before it is entirely absorbed by the sands or evaporated by the sun. Carissa creek, a small stream, which, after flowing a few miles, is lost in the sands, furnished water in the driest seasons. From this point to San Diego there is not only water at convenient distances, but an abundance of grass.

The route here described from eastern Texas is taken by numbers of emigrant trains, except that portion of it from the Rio Grande to the Santa Cruz valley, which, until the Boundary Commission followed it, was unknown. The emigrants took Cooke's road, which was a hundred miles longer. On my return from California we met emigrant parties every day after leaving the Gila, and in one instance a drove of 17,000 sheep, all bound for San Francisco.

As these remarks have already been too much extended, I forbear mentioning other and more minute particulars of the advantages which may be claimed for the southern route. From what has been stated, it is evident that the region over which it is to pass is not the paradise which some have claimed for it ; but, poor as it is in many respects, it is infinitely better and presents more advantages for a great national highway than any yet discovered to California.

—————————End Appendix B—————————

The Honorable Aaron V. Brown
Postmaster General • Former Governor of Tennessee
Engraving by H. B. Hall

– 269 –

Appendix C

A digital scan of the original document below was provided compliments of The Huntington Library of San Marino, California.

The 15 page booklet transcribed below was published by R. C. Root, Anthony & Co., Stationers and Printers, No. 16 Nassau Street, Corner of Pine, New York, 1860.

ARTICLES OF ASSOCIATION OF THE OVERLAND MAIL COMPANY, 1857. New York

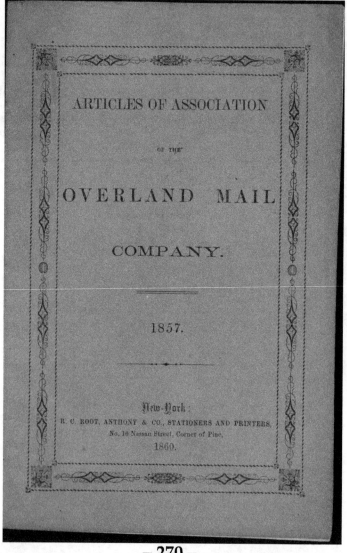

Articles of Association and Agreement, made and concluded this 23rd day of October, A.D. 1857, by and between JOHN BUTTERFIELD, WILLIAM B. DINSMORE, WILLIAM G. FARGO, JAMES V. P. GARDNER, MARQUIS L. KINYON, ALEXANDER HOLLAND, HAMILTON SPENCER, DANFORD N. BARNEY, JOHNSTON LIVINGSTON, DAVID MOULTON, AND ELIJAH P. WILLIAMS, for themselves, their assigns and associates, WITNESSETH:

Parties Contracting

That the persons above-named, parties to these presents, have severally mutually, promised covenanted and agreed, and do hereby severally, mutually promise, covenant and agree to and with each other, and each for himself and his legal representatives with all the others, to form a Joint Stock Company, with the intent and for the purpose of prosecuting, transacting, carrying on, and executing the following named objects, undertakings, business and affairs, to wit:

Statement of Mutual Contract,

The transportation of the United States mails, from the Mississippi River, overland, to San Francisco, in the State of California, in conformity with the provisions of a contract made on the 16th day of September, 1857, by and between the above JOHN BUTTERFIELD, WILLIAM B. DINSMORE, WILLIAM G. FARGO, JAMES V. P. GARDNER, MARQUIS L. KINYON, ALEXANDER HOLLAND, HAMILTON SPENCER, of the one part, and the UNITED STATES POST-MASTER GENERAL of the other:

Objects of Contract,

To transport U.S. Mails, under Contract of Sept. 16th, 1857,

For the transportation of the United States mails and passengers on any other mail routes that now are or that may hereafter be established:

To transport other mails and Passengers,

For the transportation of persons, property, merchandise, gold and silver coin, bank bills, or other values on any of said mail routes west of the Mississippi River:

To transport Persons and Property,

For the transaction of a general express forwarding, commission, exchange and agency business, at and between such points or places west of the Mississippi River, as may hereafter, from time to time, be designated by the Directors hereinafter named, or their successors.

To do Express Business.

And for the construction, purchase, and working, in whole or in part, of any and all telegraph lines that may in like manner be designated by said Directors.

To construct Telegraph Lines.

For the construction, improvement or purchase, in whole or in part, of all roads, bridges, steamboats, vessels, railroads, cars, carriages, houses, storehouses, or other erections, appurtenant to, or requisite to carry into effect the objects and undertakings above mentioned.

To do other things as appertaining.

All of which said affairs, undertakings and business

shall be carried on, transacted and done in pursuant to, and in conformity with the stipulations, covenants and agreements in the following articles of association and agreement contained.

ARTICLE I.

The name of this Association and Joint Stock Company shall be, "THE OVERLAND MAIL COMPANY," and said Association and this agreement shall continue in full force and virtue for and during the term of twenty years, from the first day of January, A.D. 1858, unless sooner dissolved by law, or a vote of the Directors as is hereinafter provided.

Name and Duration of Company.

ARTICLE II.

The capital, property and interests of said Joint Stock Company, shall be divided into and held in shares, valued for the purpose of this contract at one hundred dollars each; the number of said shares being hereby for present purposes, limited and fixed at twenty thousand. It being, however, hereby expressly understood and agreed, that the number of said shares, so representing the capital, property and interests of said Company, may, from time to time, be increased or decreased by a resolution of the Boar of Directors; provided, however, that the said resolution shall be offered for consideration at a regular meeting, and shall be adopted by a vote of at least two-thirds of all the members thereof, at a subsequent regular meeting. And provided also, that such increase or decrease shall not be made or disposed of, as to lessen the intrinsic value of the shared already issued.

Number and Value of Shares.

How Increased.

The interest of the Shareholders in said Company shall be represented by proper certificates or scrip, in which shall be specified the number of shares to which the holder is entitled, that each shall is liable to the payment of twenty-five dollars, and also subject to such assessments as may from time to time, be required and made by the Directors, to pay any losses, damages, expenses or other liabilities which may accrue in the prosecution of the legitimate business of said Company. It shall also contain a stipulation, constituting each and every owner and holder thereof a member of said Company, entitled to all the rights and benefits, and subject to all the liabilities thereto appertaining. Said script shall be signed by the President and Secretary of said Company, and counter-signed by the Treasurer.

Scrip, and what it shall Contain.

ARTICLE III.

The shares in said Company shall be assignable in the

Scrip, how Transferred.

usual form, either in person or by attorney, but no transfer shall be valid so as to discharge the assignor from subsequent liability as a member of said Company until entered on the transfer book, to be kept by the Treasurer thereof, and assigned script surrendered. Nor shall any assignment or transfer be made while any call or assessment remains unpaid thereon, nor where for any reason the Board of Directors may deem it injurious to the best interests of said Company; provided however, that in such case, said Board, on request of the owner, shall be bound to purchase for and on account of said Company the shares proposed to be transferred, at their true value, which said value shall be determined by the appraisement of one or more disinterested persons, to be mutually chosen by said Board and the holder of said shares. Nor shall an assignment by any member of said Company, of his whole interest therein, discharge him from any liability arising previous to the date of such transfer upon the books of the Company.

Conditions of Transfer.

Transfer not to discharge liability for previous acts.

ARTICLE IV.
And the Joint associates, parties to these presents, do hereby mutually covenant, promise and agree, to and with each other, and each for himself and his legal representatives, to and with all the others, doth hereby covenant, promise and agree to pay twenty-five dollars per share for whatever number of shares in said Company he may subscribe, or of which he may otherwise become the owner or holder, three dollars per share on subscribing, and the balance in such installments, and at such times as the Directors of said Company may call for, in accordance with the provisions hereinafter contained, and also to pay and fully discharge any and all assessments which said Directors may so make. And further, that in case of the refusal or neglect of any Shareholder to pay and fully discharge any installment or assessment, made as above mentioned by the Board of Directors, at such time and place as said Board by direct, the whole, or so many of his said shares, and the property and values thereby represented, as may be requisite to pay such installment or assessment, or any part thereof, may be taken and sold by said Board of Directors at public or private sale. And said Board of Directors are hereby expressly authorized and empowered, by each and every of the Shareholders in said Company, to take and sell his said shares as above mentioned. It being, however, hereby further expressly understood and agreed, that said Board of Directors may at their option prosecute for, and

Agreement to pay Installments as Called.

And Assessments.

Directors Authorized to sell Stock of delinquent Stockholders.

To prosecute for.

recover by a suit at law, any and every such installment or installments, assessment or assessments. Such suit to be brought in the name of the President.

ARTICLE V.

Scope and object of Company.

The scope and business of the Joint Stock Company hereby constituted, shall embrace and include the various objects, affairs, business and undertakings hereinbefore specified, together with whatever other lawful acts or transactions may be therewith connected or thereto incident. And with the intent and for the purpose of carrying on, doing and transacting said business, objects, undertakings and affairs, said Company shall have power, and is hereby authorized to take, purchase, hire, own, hold, rent, hypothecate, assign, mortgage and convey all such personal and real estate, property, express, telegraph and stage lines, mail, express or other contracts, actions, advantages, conveniences and things, which in the judgment of the Directors may be necessary or proper to the transaction of its business, or otherwise for the advancement of its best interests, and for these purposes to enter into, make, execute and deliver, or cause to be made, executed and delivered, all contracts, agreements, deeds, bonds, or other legal instruments that may be required therefor.

Power of Company to carry out objects.

ARTICLE VI.

Directors to Manage and Control.

Pursuant to an act of the Legislature of the State of New-York, passed April 15th, 1854, the capital, property, business and affairs of said Joint Stock Company, shall be conducted, managed and controlled by a Board of not less than seven, or more than eleven, Directors, each of whom shall be the owner of at least one hundred shares therein, to be chosen by the Shareholders, as is herein provided, to hold their offices for one year, and until others shall be elected in their stead. And JOHN BUTTERFIELD, WILLIAM B. DINSMORE, WILLIAM G. FARGO, JAMES V. P. GARDNER, MARQUIS L. KINYON, ALEXANDER HOLLAND, HAMILTON SPENCER, DANFORD N. BARNEY, JOHNSTON LIVINGSTON, DAVID MOULTON, AND ELIJAH P. WILLIAMS, shall constitute the first Board of Directors, and they are hereby chosen, each and every of them, such Directors. It being further hereby expressly understood and agreed, that in case a vacancy should occur in said Board, by death, resignation or otherwise, prior to, or in the interval of any election by the Stockholders, such vacancy may be filled by said Board of Directors, who may elect by ballot any Stockholder eligible under the provisions herein contained.

Power to fill Vacancies.

Said Board of Directors shall elect by ballot from their own body, a President, Vice-President and Secretary, who shall hold their offices for one year, and until others shall be chosen in their stead.

President, Vice-President and Secretary how chosen.

ARTICLE VII.

Whenever any number of Shareholders, owning and holding a majority of the shares in said Company, shall unite in presenting to the Secretary a written request for an election of Directors, it shall be the duty of said Secretary to call a meeting of the Stockholders for that purpose, by a notice of at least sixty days - stating therein the time, place and purpose of said meeting. The manner of serving said notices shall be prescribed by the Board of Directors, who shall also appoint the proper inspectors, and make all other needful rules and regulations thereto appertaining. Said election shall be by ballot, and each Shareholder shall be entitled to as many votes as he owns shares in said Company, either in person or by proxy.

Provisions for Elections of Directors.

Provided, however, and it is hereby expressly understood and agreed, that but one election shall be holden in any one year.

ARTICLE VIII.

The Directors of said Joint Stock Company, or a majority of them, shall, and they are hereby authorized and empowered to direct, manage, and control the capital, property, business and affairs thereof; to do, or cause to be done and executed, the objects, undertakings and business, specified, contemplated or intended in article sixth of these presents, and further to do and execute all and every authority, power and thing within the general scope and purpose of this Association, which might or could, legally, be done by all the Joint Associates or Co-partners if present and acting, except as is herein provided. And with this intent and meaning said Board of Directors shall have power to make all necessary rules, regulations, and by-laws for their own government, and for the regulation and government of the business of said Company, and for the safe keeping and disposal of its property and effects. They shall especially provide in said by-laws for the taking, holding and conveying of any and all real estate, lands and tenements, in, or to which said Company may at any time become entitled, interested or concerned. It being, however hereby expressly understood and provided, that no Director shall use or employ the money, credit or name of said Company, otherwise than in its legitimate business, under

Powers conferred on Directors.

To Manage and control.

To do whatever the Joint Associates could if present.

No Director to use name or funds of Company.

the penalty of a forfeiture of his whole interest therein, and subjecting himself to a suit at law for such conversion, to be prosecuted by the Board of Directors, in the name of the President. Nor shall any Director, Shareholder or other person, except such as are duly authorized by the Board of Directors, use or sign the associate or firm name of said Company under a like forfeiture and penalty.

Penalty therefor.

Said Board of Directors shall also have power, and they are hereby authorized to call in, demand and collect, by suit or otherwise, the balance of the capital of said Company as specified in the scrip, herein before mentioned, in installments, and at such times as may be deemed best, provided however that no installment of over five dollars per share shall be called for at any one time, nor at a less notice, or at a shorter interval, than thirty days.

To call for Installments due on scrip.

And said Board of Directors are hereby authorized and empowered to make demand and collect, as above mentioned, any and all assessments that may be requisite, to pay any and all losses, damages, expenses, or other liabilities that may be incurred or accrue in the prosecution of the legitimate business and objects of said Company.

And Assessments.

Said Board of Directors shall appoint a Treasurer of said Company, and all such other officers, agents and servants as they may deep requisite, prescribe their occupations, powers, duties and compensation, and at their discretion remove and discharge the same. It shall also prescribe the duties and services of any one or all of its own members, to be rendered in and about the business of said Company, and determine and fix the compensation to be paid therefor.

To appoint Treasurer and other officers, agents, & c.

To prescribe their own duties and fix compensation.

Said Directors shall meet together for consultation relative to the business and affairs of said Company, at which meetings a majority of the whole number shall constitute a quorum. They shall keep a record of their proceedings, and in all cases of a difference of opinion a majority of those present shall decide and control, except as is herein provided.

Majority to constitute quorum.

They shall cause to be kept all proper stock and transfer books, books of account, contracts and other important records.

To keep Records, Stock and Transfer Books & c.

They shall cause semi-annual reports to be made and filed with the Treasurer or Secretary, containing a clear and simple statement of the business and affairs of said Company, showing its capital, earnings and expenses, profits and losses, cash in hand, property, debts and in-

Semi-annual Reports.

Report and books to be open to

debtedness. Which said report, together with all books of account and other records, shall, at all reasonable times, be open to the inspection of any of the Shareholders.

inspection of Stockholders.

Said Board of Directors shall also have power, and they are hereby authorized, from time to time, to declare and pay dividends out of the net earnings of said Company, or out of the proceeds of the sale of any of its property and effects or both.

To declare Dividends.

Said Directors may call meetings of the Shareholders at their discretion, and it shall be their duty to call any such meetings whenever requested so to do by a majority in interest of the Shareholders.

Stockholder's Meetings.

Said Board of Directors shall also have power, and is hereby expressly authorized, at any time after the termination of the mail contract hereinbefore mentioned, whenever it may be deemed for the best interests of said Company, by a resolution passed by a unanimous vote of all the members thereof, to dissolve said Joint Stock Company, and by themselves, or by their attorney or attorneys, to adjust, settle up, and liquidate the business and affairs thereof.

Power to dissolve and close up Company.

ARTICLE IX.

The principal office of said Company shall be located in the City of New-York, in which shall be kept its stock and transfer books, and principal books of account and other records, and all meetings of the Board of Directors shall be there held, unless otherwise ordered by said Board. Meetings of the Board of Directors may be called at any time by the President of said Company, and it shall be his duty to call such meetings whenever requested so to do by any two members of said Board of Directors, said meetings may likewise be called by any two members of said Board, by a notice to be signed by themselves.

Principal Office in City of New-York.

Where and how Meetings of Directors called.

Adequate and reasonable notice shall be given of all such meetings to every member of said Board.

ARTICLE X.

All bonds, powers of Attorney, or other sealed instruments, except deeds of real estate and leases, shall be signed by the President and Secretary, and countersigned by the Treasurer of said Company.

Execution of Sealed Instruments

ARTICLE XI.

It is hereby further agreed and declared as a condition precedent to any claim to be made by any Shareholder, or by any one claiming any right or interest in any shares, or in the joint property of this Association, or in any gains,

As to claim to withdraw capital, & c.

profits or losses thereof, that no claim shall be made to withdraw any part of the capital, or of the increase of profits, or to demand any account in relation thereto, or to make any claim whatever on the Association or its property otherwise than according to these articles, except in case of manifest assumption of authority to do what is not herein authorized, or of intentional fraud, in the Directors. And, if any such claim shall be made, this article shall be deemed an absolute bar to any such claim or demand.

ARTICLE XII.

And it is hereby further understood, covenanted and agreed by and between the parties to these presents, and they severally each for himself and his legal representatives, to and with each and all the others, promise, covenant and agree, that in case of the death or legal incapacity of any or either of them, or any number less than a majority in interest of the whole prior to the termination of this Company as fixed in these articles, such death or other legal incapacity shall not operate as a dissolution of said Joint Stock Company, nor shall its business be thereby suspended or affected. The surviving Shareholders, or those of them legally capable, being hereby expressly authorized and empowered by each and every of the parties hereto, to prosecute and transact the business of said Company in the same manner, and under the same associate name and style as if no such death or incapacity had occurred. And it is further hereby mutually understood and agreed by and between the parties hereto, and each for himself and his legal representatives, covenants and agrees, to and with each and all the others, that in case of the death of any Shareholder in said Company the survivors may and shall have the right to purchase and take the interest and shares of said deceased Shareholder by paying to his legal representatives the actual value thereof at the time of his decease, to be determined by three disinterested persons to be mutually chosen by the parties interested, unless the heirs of such deceased Shareholder shall be of age and legally competent to act, and shall elect to retain and hold such share or shares in conformity with these articles.

In witness whereof, we, the Joint Associates, have hereunto set our hand and seals the day and year first above written.

Company not dissolved by death of other disability of Shareholders.

Test.

————————End Appendix C————————

Appendix D

Report of the Postmaster General, Dec. 4, 1858
Selections from pages 718

REPORT OF THE POSTMASTER GENERAL.

POST OFFICE DEPARTMENT, *December* 4, 1858.

TO THE PRESIDENT OF THE UNITED STATES:

Page 718

OVERLAND MAIL ROUTE.

At the last session of Congress I reported fully the steps that had been taken to carry into execution the act of Congress, approved 3d March, 1857, authorizing the Postmaster General to contract for the conveyance of the entire letter mail between the Mississippi river and San Francisco.

The contract was executed on the 16th September, 1857, and service commenced within the twelve months, namely, on 15th September, 1858, agreeably to the provisions of said act.

The department is happy to announce its conclusive and triumphant success. Its departure and arrival were announced with unbounded demonstrations of joy and exultation. I submit a detailed report of Mr. Bailey, the agent of this department, who came over in the first line of stages which left San Francisco for St. Louis. It will be an important document, not less instructive at the present time than it may be interesting and curious to those who, in after times, may be desirous to know by what energy, skill, and perseverance the vast wilderness was first penetrated by the mail stages of the United States, and the two great oceans united by the longest and most important land route ever established in any country.

————— **End of Appendix D** —————

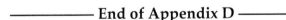

NOTE: For information about the San Antonio / San Diego "Jack Ass" Route, refer to pages 739-752 in the original Dec. 4, 1858 *Report of the Postmaster General*. It contains a 15 page detailed observation written during a trip on the San Antonio / San Diego "Jack Ass" Route.

Appendix E
Handwritten Journal of the Postmaster General, 1858 & 1864
Images located by Russell Hill, National Archives and Records Administration, Washington DC, from Record Group 28, "Records of the Post Office Depart, Office of the Postmaster General, Journal," dated Aug. 17, 1858, and August 19, 1864.

Transcription by Bob Crossman

August 17, 1858
(Overland Mails)
Route 12578 Cal St Louis and Memphis to San Francisco: John Butterfield No $600,000.
Ordered Change route so as to run from St. Louis by way of Springfield, Mo, Fayetteville, Ark., Fort Smith, Fort Belknap, Franklin, and Fort Yuma, Cal to San Francisco;
Also, from Memphis via Little Rock, to San Francisco. Contractor's to include such other offices as may be designated from time to time by the Department without change of pay.

231

August 19, 1864 page 231
Route Nᵒ. 14260 Kansas, Atchison, or St Joseph to Salt Lake City.
Ordered. John A. Heistand declining and being considered released by the action of Congress.
Contract with Ben Holladay of New York City for the conveyance of the mails daily with certainty, celerity and security from Atchison, Kansas or St. Joseph, Missouri to Salt Lake City, Utah from 1st October 1864 to 30 September 1868 agreeably to the schedule contained in the Advertisement of the 22 March 1864 supplying all intermediate offices on the route and also supplying Denver City, Colorado by side mail in due connection with mainline daily at $365,000 per anm.

Route Nᵒ 14626 Utah Salt Lake City to Virginia City.
Ordered. Contract with William B. Dinsmore of New York City (President of the Overland Mail Company) for the conveyance of the mails daily, with certainty, celerity and security from Salt Lake City, Utah to Folsom City in California from 1 October 1864 to 30 September 1868 agreeably to the schedule contained in the advertisement of 22 March 1864 on this and route No 15761 in Nevada Territory and supplying all intermediate offices on the route at $385,000 per annum.

Appendix F

*The following original document in the author's collection was purchased from
Robert Dalton Harris, agathering, P.O. Box 477, West Sand Lake, NY 12196*

35TH CONGRESS, }	SENATE.	{ Ex. Doc.
2d Session. }		{ No. 48.

REPORT

OF

THE POSTMASTER GENERAL,

COMMUNICATING,

*In compliance with a resolution of the Senate, a copy of the contract with
J. Butterfield and his associates for carrying the mail from the Mississippi river to the Pacific ocean.*

MARCH 3, 1859.—Ordered to lie on the table and be printed.

POST OFFICE DEPARTMENT,
March 3, 1859.

SIR: Agreeably to the resolution of the Senate of the 17th ultimo, I have the honor to furnish herewith, marked A, a copy of the contract with John Butterfield and his associates for carrying the mail from the Mississippi river to the Pacific ocean, or from or to any intermediate points, and also a copy of the act of Congress approved March 3, 1857, under which the contract was made.

No other contract or agreement has been made and no other securities given, except those named in the copy herewith sent.

Payments have been made as follows:

November 1, 1858, to John Butterfield, assignee............$24,456 52
February 4, 1859, to John Butterfield, assignee............. 50,000 00
February 7, 1859, to H. F. Vail, cashier, assignee.......... 50,000 00
February 12, 1859, to H. F. Vail, cashier, assignee......... 50,000 00

174,456 52

all on account of services for the quarter ending December 31, 1858.

I also transmit herewith a statement, marked B, showing the time made each trip between San Francisco and the Mississippi river.

It is impossible at this time to state *fully* "what letters, packages, and despatches, or other matter, have been carried or transported by said company" and the amount of postages thereon, or the number of passengers conveyed and for what compensation.

On the 18th instant the postmasters at St. Louis and Memphis were instructed, by telegraph, to report as far as possible on these points, and their answers are as follows:

2   CONTRACT WITH J. BUTTERFIELD AND CO.

The postmaster at St. Louis, under date of the 24th ultimo, sends copies of his accounts of mails received and sent, and says:

"The total receipts, as shown by these returns, is $2,723 27. The free letters number 1,835. I have no certain data as to the number of letters or packages, but doubtless most of these letters passed for three cents, assuming half each 3 and 10 the number would be 59,000 exclusive of those free say, over 1,800.

"It is proper I should state, also, that since November last newspaper publishers at both ends have sent and received printed slips of news items free, as exchanges, which are not included as letters. The last mail, received since your order, was found to contain *twenty-three* through and *seventy-one* way packages. It is proper I should state, also, that the postmaster at San Francisco was, until lately, in the habit of making up packages direct for many distributing post offices on the Atlantic seaboard, and even some of the interior offices, east and north of here, and he still makes up direct for the New York office, thus making the value of mail matter which I communicate much smaller than it is in fact. These letters, also, all pay 10 cents.

"There are several points in this connexion to which I wish to ask your attention.

"First. When this mail went into operation I did not feel willing to transmit letters over the route unless the parties sending them requested this route to be used, and placed on the letter ' via overland.'

"Second. The country tributary to this distributing post office had directed so long their packages ' via New York,' that the habit continued until recently, thus, in fact, cutting a supply from this route.

"Third. The 'way stations,' for a long time continued to be supplied by the old, although less direct routes; and hence our ' way mails' continued small.

"But all these difficulties are fast fading away, and the through and way mails are constantly increasing. The line is so regular that many offices (especially within the week after the departures of the steamers) send their through matter this way and thus always anticipate the next steamer, while the way offices are by this route supplied, not only days, but often weeks, in advance of former methods. As the route becomes more known, its transit being so regular, the business greatly increases.

"I am as yet unable to answer the last part of your inquiry relative to passengers."

The postmaster at Memphis also sends copies of his accounts, showing postages to the amount of $247 74, but attempts no enumeration of the letters.

Assuming that there were an equal number of three and ten cents letters, (as done by the postmaster at St. Louis,) the number would be 5,367
Number of free letters... 189
Whole number at St. Louis, including free letters................ 60,800

Total to February 24... 66,356

CONTRACT WITH J. BUTTERFIELD AND CO. 3

The report of the postmaster at St. Louis affords probably a near approximation to the number of letters conveyed between that point and San Francisco and intermediate points, namely, 60,800.

His accounts show the actual postage......................		$2,723 27
Estimate of number of letters at Memphis............	5,556	247 74
Total to February 24........................	66,356	2,971 01

Postmasters having had no instructions to keep separate accounts of letters sent and received by the route in question, it is now next to impossible, by any means, to make a correct enumeration as to the past. The nearest approach to it would be by examining all the post bills received at the several post offices on the route and the bills shown by the accounts to have been sent from those offices to offices on other routes, involving an amount of labor which could not be accomplished by the regular clerical force in addition to the current duties of this department.

The post bills to San Francisco (and California generally) are not returned to this department, on account of their great bulk, but retained in that office. The postmaster was written to on 19th instant, and instructed to furnish all possible information in answer to the inquiries as to the number of letters and passengers conveyed; but, of course, his answer cannot be received in time to be laid before the present Congress.

In future monthly reports will be made to this department of the actual number of letters, &c., conveyed, with the amount of postages, so that a more full and satisfactory answer to the inquiries of the Senate can be submitted at the meeting of the next Congress.

In reference to the number of passengers conveyed and the compensation made for the same over the said route, inquiries have been addressed to the general office of the company, New York, and whatever reply is received will be laid before the Senate at the earliest possible moment.

I have the honor to be, very respectfully, &c.,

HORATIO KING,
Acting Postmaster General.

PRESIDENT OF THE SENATE.

OVERLAND MAIL SERVICE TO CALIFORNIA.

In order to carry into effect the act of Congress approved the third of March, 1857, relative to the overland mail to California, the department issued the following notice, and caused the same to be regularly advertised according to law:

"POST OFFICE DEPARTMENT, *April* 20, 1857.

"An act of Congress, approved March 3, 1857, making appropriations for the service of the Post Office Department for the fiscal year ending June 30, 1858, provides:

4   CONTRACT WITH J. BUTTERFIELD AND CO.

" 'SEC. 10. That the Postmaster General be, and he is hereby, authorized to contract for the conveyance of the entire letter mail from such point on the Mississippi river as the contractors may select to San Francisco, in the State of California, for six years, at a cost not exceeding three hundred thousand dollars per annum for semi-monthly, four hundred and fifty thousand dollars for weekly, or six hundred thousand dollars for semi-weekly service, to be performed semi-monthly, weekly, or semi-weekly, at the option of the Postmaster General.

" 'SEC. 11. That the contract shall require the service to be performed with good four-horse coaches or spring wagons, suitable for the conveyance of passengers as well as the safety and security of the mails.

" 'SEC. 12. That the contractor shall have the right of pre-emption to three hundred and twenty acres of any land not then disposed of or reserved, at each point necesssary for a station, not to be nearer than ten miles from each other; and provided that no mineral land shall be thus pre-empted.

" 'SEC. 13. That the said service shall be performed within twenty-five days for each trip ; and that, before entering into such contract, the Postmaster General shall be satisfied of the ability and disposition of the parties *bona fide* and in good faith to perform the said contract, and shall require good and sufficient security for the performance of the same—the service to commence within twelve months after the signing the contract.'

" Proposals will accordingly be received at the Contract Office of the Post Office Department until 3 p. m. of the 1st day of June, 1857, for conveying mails under the provisions of the above act.

" Besides the starting point on the Mississippi river, bidders will name intermediate points proposed to be embraced in the route, and otherwise designate its course as nearly as practicable.

" Separate proposals are invited for *semi-monthly, weekly,* and *semi-weekly* trips each way.

" The decision upon the proposals offered will be made after the Postmaster General shall be satisfied of the ability and disposition of the parties in good faith to perform the contract.

" A guarantee is to be executed, with good and sufficient sureties, that the contract shall be executed, with like good security, whenever the contractor or contractors shall be required to do so by the Postmaster General, and the service must commence within twelve months after the date of such contract."

In pursuance of the said advertisement, the Postmaster General and his three assistants assembled in the Contract Office and opened the respective bids, making the following abstract of them, and causing said abstract to be copied into a separate book, and also in the route book for California.

ABSTRACT OF THE BIDS.

John Butterfield, William B. Dinsmore, William G. Fargo, James V. P. Gardner, Marcus L. Kinyon, Hamilton Spencer, and *Alexander Holland :* From St. Louis, by Springfield, and from Memphis, by Little

CONTRACT WITH J. BUTTERFIELD AND CO. 5

Rock, connecting at a common point at or eastward of Albuquerque; thence west, to and along the military road to Colorado river; thence up the valley of the Mohahoc river, to and through the Tejon passes of the Sierra Nevada ; and thence along the best route to San Francisco ; *weekly*, $450,000; *semi-weekly*, $600,000.

John Butterfield and others: From Memphis, by Little Rock, Albuquerque, mouth of Mohahoc, on the Colorado river, and one of the Tejon passes of the Sierra Nevada, to San Francisco ; *semi-monthly*, $300,000 ; *weekly*, $450,000; *semi-weekly*, $595,000.

John Butterfield and others: From St. Louis, by Springfield, to Albuquerque ; thence, as above, to SanFrancisco ; *semi-monthly*, $300,000 ; *weekly*, $450,000 ; *semi-weekly*, $585,000.

James E. Birch: From Memphis, by Little Rock, Washington, Fulton, Clarksville, Gainesville, Fort Chadbourne, head spring of Conche river, to Pecos river, nearly due west; thence, along said Pecos river, Delaware creek, through the Guadalupe and Hueco mountains, to the Rio Grande; thence, over the emigrant road, to Fort Yuma; thence, by San Gorgona Pass, San Bernardino, Tejon, Tulare, or Salinas valleys, to San Francisco ; *semi-weekly*, $600,000.

James Glover: From Memphis, by Helena, Little Rock, across Texas, to El Paso, Fort Yuma, San Bernardino, Los Angeles; thence, between the Coast Range and Siera Nevada mountains, to San Francisco ; or, from Vicksburg, by Shrevesport, to El Paso, &c., &c., (as above ;) *semi-monthly*, $300,000 ; *weekly*, $450,000 ; *semi-weekly*, $600,000.

S. Howell and A. E. Pace: From Gaines' Landing, on the Mississippi, to San Francisco ; term of four years ; commence at Vicksburg, if preferred ; *weekly*, $1,000,000 for the first year, $800,000 for the second year, $700,000 for the third year, $600,000 for the fourth year.

David D. Mitchell, Samuel B. Churchill, Robert Campbell, William Gilpin, and others : From St. Louis to San Francisco; *semi-weekly*, $600,000.

James Johnston, jr., and Joseph Clark: From St. Louis, by Fort Independence, Fort Laramie, Salt Lake City, or any other point named by the department, to San Francisco; *semi-monthly*, $260,000; *weekly*, $390,000 ; *semi-weekly*, $520,000.

Irregular (after time) bid. *William Hollingshead*, president of Minnesota, Nebraska, and Pacific Mail Transportation Company : From St. Paul, by Fort Ridgeley, South Pass, Soda Springs, Humboldt river, Honey Lake valley, Noble's Pass, Shasta City, to Francisco; *semi-weekly*, $550,000.

On the second day of July, 1857, the department, after full and mature consideration, made the following order in relation to the route selected and the bid accepted:

" 12,578. From St. Louis, Missouri, and from Memphis, Tennessee, converging at Little Rock, Arkansas; thence, *via* Preston, Texas, or as nearly so as may be found advisable, to the best point of crossing the Rio Grande, above El Paso, and not far from Fort Fillmore; thence, along the new road being opened and constructed under the direction of the Secretary of the Interior, to Fort Yuma, California ;

thence, through the best passes, and along the best valleys for safe and expeditious staging, to San Francisco.

" The foregoing route is selected for the overland mail service to California, as combining, in my judgment, more advantages and fewer disadvantages than any other.

" No bid having been made for this particular route, and all the bidders (whose bids were considered regular under the advertisement and the act of Congress) having consented that their bids may be held and considered as extending and applying to said route:

" Therefore, looking at the respective bidders, both as to the amount proposed and the ability, qualifications, and experience of the bidders to carry out a great mail service like this, I hereby order that the proposal of John Butterfield, of Utica, New York ; William B. Dinsmore, of New York city; William G. Fargo, of Buffalo, New York ; James V. P. Gardner, of Utica, New York ; Marcus L. Kinyan, of Rome, New York ; Alexander Holland, of New York city, and Hamilton Spencer, of Bloomington, Illinois, at the sum of $595,000 (five hundred and ninety-five thousand dollars) per annum for semi-weekly service, be accepted; the contractors, however, to have the privilege of selecting lands, under the act of Congress, on only one of the roads, or branches, between Little Rock and the Mississippi river—the one selected by them to be made known and inserted in the contract at the time of its execution."

Subsequently, on re-examining the proposal, the above acceptance was modified so as to fix the pay at $600,000 per annum, that being the true amount of the bid.

Under strong representations that a better junction of the two branches of said road could be made at Preston than at Little Rock, on the eleventh day of September, 1857, the following order was made :

" That whenever the contractors and their sureties shall file in the Post Office Department a request, in writing, that they desire to make the junction of the two branches of said road at Preston, instead of Little Rock, the department will permit the same to be done by some route not further west than to Springfield, Missouri, thence by Fayetteville, Van Buren, and Fort Smith, in the State of Arkansas, to the said junction, at or near the town of Preston, in Texas ; but said new line will be adopted on the express condition that the said contractors shall not claim or demand from the department, or from Congress, any increased compensation for or on account of such change in the route from St. Louis, or of the point of junction of the two routes from Little Rock to Preston ; and on the further express condition that whilst the *amount* of lands to which the contractors may be entitled under the act of Congress may be estimated on either of said branches from Preston to St. Louis or Memphis, at their option, yet the said contractors shall take one-half of that amount on each of said branches, so that neither shall have an advantage in the way of stations and settlement over the other ; and in case said contractors, in selecting and locating their lands, shall disregard this condition, or give undue advantage to one of said branches over the other, the department reserves the power of discontinuing said new route from

St. Louis to Preston, and to hold said contractors and their sureties to the original route and terms expressed and set forth in the body of this contract.''

In pursuance of the above orders and proceedings, on the 16th day of September, 1857, the following contract was entered into between the department and the contractors whose bid has been accepted :

A.

No. 12,578.—$600,000 per annum.

This article of contract, made the sixteenth day of September, in the year one thousand eight hundred and fifty-seven, between the United States (acting in this behalf by their Postmaster General) and John Butterfield, of Utica, New York, William B. Dinsmore, of New York city, William G. Fargo, of Buffalo, New York, James V. P. Gardner, of Utica, New York, Marcus L. Kinyon, of Rome, New York, Alexander Holland, of New York city, and Hamilton Spencer, of Bloomington, Illinois, and Danford N. Barney, of the city of New York, Johnston Livingston, of Livingston, New York, David Moulton, of Floyd, New York, and Elijah P. Williams, of Buffalo, New York, witnesseth :

That whereas John Butterfield, William B. Dinsmore, William G. Fargo, James V. P. Gardner, Marcus L. Kinyon, Alexander Holland, and Hamilton Spencer, have been accepted, according to law, as contractors for transporting the entire letter mail, agreeably to the provisions of the 11th, 12th, and 13th sections of an act of Congress, approved March 3, 1857, (making appropriations for the service of the Post Office Department for the fiscal year ending June 30, 1858,) from the Mississippi river to San Francisco, California, as follows, viz: from St. Louis, Missouri, and from Memphis, Tennessee, converging at Little Rock, Arkansas; thence, *via* Preston, Texas, or as near so as may be found advisable, to the best point of crossing the Rio Grande above El Paso, and not far from Fort Fillmore ; thence, along the new road being opened and constructed under the direction of the Secretary of the Interior, to or near Fort Yuma, California ; thence, through the best passes and along the best valleys for safe and expeditious staging, to San Francisco, California, and back, twice a week, in good four-horse post coaches or spring wagons suitable for the conveyance of passengers as well as the safety and security of the mails, at six hundred thousand dollars a year, for and during the term of six years, commencing the sixteenth day of September, in the year one thousand eight hundred and fifty-eight, and ending with the fifteenth day of September, in the year one thousand eight hundred and sixty-four : Now, therefore, the said John Butterfield, William B. Dinsmore, William G. Fargo, James V. P. Gardner, Marcus L. Kinyon, Alexander Holland, and Hamilton Spencer, contractors, and Danford N. Barney, Johnston Livingston, David Moulton, and Elijah P. Williams, their sureties, do jointly and severally undertake, covenant, and agree with the United States, and do bind themselves : 1st. To carry said letter mail within the time fixed by the law above referred to—that is, within twenty-five days for each trip, and according to the annexed schedule of departures and arrivals; 2d. To carry said letter mail in a safe and secure manner, free from wet or other injury, in a boot, under the driver's seat, or other secure place, and in preference to passengers, and to their entire exclusion, if its weight and bulk require it; 3d. To take the said letter mail and every part of it from, and deliver it and every part of it at, each post office on the route, or that may hereafter be established on the route, and into the post office at each end of the route, and into the post office at the place at which the carrier stops at night, if one is there kept; and if no office is there kept, to lock it up in some secure place, at the risk of the contractors.

They also undertake, covenant, and agree with the United States, and do bind themselves, jointly and severally, as aforesaid, to be answerable for the persons to whom the said contractors shall commit the care and transportation of the mail, and accountable to the United States for any damages which may be sustained by the United States through their unfaithfulness or want of care; and that the said contractors will discharge any carrier of said mail when required to do so by the Postmaster General; also, that they will not transmit, by themselves or their agent, or be concerned in transmitting, commercial intelligence more rapidly than by mail, other than by telegraph, and that they will not carry out of the mail letters or newspapers which should go by post; and further, the said contractors will convey, without additional charge, the special agents of the department, on the exhibition of their credentials.

They further undertake, covenant, and agree with the United States, that the said contractors will collect quarterly, if required by the Postmaster General, of postmasters on said route, the balances due from them to the General Post Office, and faithfully render an account thereof to the Postmaster General in the settlement of quarterly accounts, and will pay over to the General Post Office all balances remaining in their hands.

For which services, when performed, the said John Butterfield, William B. Dinsmore, William G. Fargo, James V. P. Gardner, Marcus L. Kinyon, Alexander Holland, and Hamilton Spencer, contractors, are to be paid by the United States the sum of six hundred thousand dollars a year, to wit: quarterly, in the months of May, August, November, and February, through the postmasters on the route, or otherwise, at the option of the Postmaster General of the United States; said pay to be subject, however, to be reduced or discontinued by the Postmaster General, as hereinafter stipulated, or to be suspended in case of delinquency.

It is hereby also stipulated and agreed by the said contractors and their sureties, that in all cases there is to be a forfeiture of the pay of a trip when the trip is not run; and of not more than three times the pay of the trip when the trip is not run and no sufficient excuse for the failure is furnished; and a forfeiture of a due proportion of it when a grade of service is rendered inferior to the mode of conveyance above stipulated; and that these forfeitures may be increased into penalties of higher amount, according to the nature or frequency of the failure and the importance of the mail; also, that fines may be

CONTRACT WITH J. BUTTERFIELD AND CO.   9

imposed upon the contractors, unless the delinquency be satisfactorily explained to the Postmaster General in due time, for failing to take from or deliver at a post office the said letter mail or any part of it ; for suffering it to be wet, injured, lost or destroyed ; for carrying it in a place or manner that exposes it to depredation, loss, or injury, by being wet or otherwise; for refusing, after demand, to convey a letter mail by any coach or wagon which the contractors regularly run or are concerned in running on the route beyond the number of trips above specified ; or for not arriving at the time set in the schedule. And for setting up or running an express to transmit letters or commercial intelligence in advance of the mail, or for transmitting knowingly, or after being informed, any one engaged in transporting letters or mail matter in violation of the laws of the United States, a penalty may be exacted of the contractors equal to a quarter's pay ; but in all other cases no fine shall exceed three times the price of the trip. And whenever it is satisfactorily shown that the contractors, their carrier or agent, have left or put aside the said letter mail, or any portion of it, for the accommodation of passengers, they shall forfeit not exceeding a quarter's pay.

And it is hereby further stipulated and agreed by the said contractors and their sureties that the Postmaster General may annul the contract for repeated failures ; for violating the post office laws ; for disobeying the instructions of the department ; for refusing to discharge a carrier when required by the department ; for assigning the contract, or any part of it, without the consent of the Postmaster General ; for setting up or running an express as aforesaid ; or for transporting persons conveying mail matter out of the mail as aforesaid ; or whenever either of the contractors shall become a postmaster, assistant postmaster, or member of Congress : and this contract shall in all its parts be subject to the terms and requirements of an act of Congress passed on the twenty-first day of April, in the year of our Lord one thousand eight hundred and eight, entitled ''An act concerning public contracts.''

And the Postmaster General may also annul the contract whenever he shall discover that the same, or any part of it, is offered for sale in the market for the purpose of speculation.

It is hereby further stipulated and agreed, that if obstacles, such as the want of water or feed, or physical obstructions, should be found between the points herein designated, so that time cannot be made, and a better line can be found between those points, the Postmaster General may vary the route to such better line.

And it is also further understood and agreed, that the contractors shall have all the rights of pre-emption, whatever they may be, secured by the 12th section of the act of Congress aforesaid, approved March 3, 1857, on either of the lines from the Mississippi river to the point of their junction with the main stem, but not on both—the election to be made by them at any time within twelve months after the date of the execution of this contract.

In witness whereof, the said Postmaster General has caused the seal of the Post Office Department to be hereto affixed, and has attested the same by his signature, and the said contractors and their sureties

Ex. Doc. 48——2

10 CONTRACT WITH J. BUTTERFIELD AND CO.

have hereunto set their hands and seals the day and year set opposite their names respectively.

AARON V. BROWN, [L. s.]
Postmaster General.

JOHN BUTTERFIELD. [L. s.] Sept. 16.
W. B. DINSMORE. [L. s.] "
WM. G. FARGO. [L. s.] "
J. V. P. GARDNER. [L. s.] "
M. L. KINYON. [L. s.] "
ALEX. HOLLAND. [L. s.] "
H. SPENCER. [L. s.] "
D. N. BARNEY. [L. s.] "
JOHNSTON LIVINGSTON. [L. s.] "
DAViD MOULTON. [L. s.] "
ELIJAH P. WILLIAMS. [L. s.] "

Signed, sealed, and delivered by the Postmaster General in the presence of—

WM. H. DUNDAS.

And by the other parties hereto in the presence of—

REVERDY JOHNSON.
ISAAC V. FOWLER.

I hereby certify that I am well acquainted with Danford N. Barney, Johnston Livingston, David Moulton, and Elijah P. Williams, and the condition of their property, and that, after full investigation and inquiry, I am well satisfied that they are good and sufficient sureties for the amount in the foregoing contract.

ISAAC V. FOWLER,
Postmaster at New York, N. Y.

[Endorsement.]

Ordered.: That whenever the contractors and their securities shall file in the Post Office Department a request in writing that they desire to make the junction of the two branches of said road at Preston, instead of Little Rock, the department will permit the same to be done by some route not further west than to Springfield, in Missouri, thence by Fayetteville, Van Buren, and Fort Smith, in the State of Arkansas, to the said junction at or near the town of Preston, in Texas; but said new line will be adopted on the express condition that the said contractors shall not claim or demand from the department or from Congress any increased compensation for or on account of such change in the route from St. Louis, or of the point of junction of the two routes from Little Rock to Preston; and on the further express condition, that whilst the *amount* of lands to which the contractors may be entitled under the act of Congress may be estimated on either of said branches from Preston to St. Louis, or Memphis, at their option, yet the said contractors shall take one-half of that amount on each of said branches, so that neither shall have an advantage in the way of stations and settlement over the other; and in case said

CONTRACT WITH J. BUTTERFIELD AND CO.   11

contractors, in selecting and locating their lands, shall disregard this condition, or give undue advantage to one of said branches over the cther, the department reserves the power of discontinuing said new route from St. Louis to Preston, and to hold said contractors and their securities to the original route and terms expressed and set forth in the body of this contract.

AARON V. BROWN,
Postmaster General.

SEPTEMBER 11, 1857.

B.

A table showing the time in carrying the great overland mail between St. Louis and Memphis and San Francisco, route No. 12578, from September 16, 1858, to December 31, 1858.

Date of departure from St. Louis and Memphis.	Date of arrival at San Francisco.	Number of days in making trip.
September 16, 1858	October 10, 1858	24
September 20, 1858	October 15, 1858	25
September 23, 1858	October 17, 1858	24
September 27, 1858	October 23, 1858	26
September 30, 1858	October 26, 1858	26
October 4, 1858	October 30, 1858	26
October 7, 1858	November 1, 1858	25
October 11, 1858	November 5, 1858	25
October 14, 1858	November 7, 1858	24
October 18, 1858	November 12, 1858	25
October 21, 1858	November 15, 1858	25
October 25, 1858	November 19, 1858	25
October 28, 1858	November 22, 1858	25
November 1, 1858	November 27, 1858	26
November 4, 1858	November 29, 1858	25
November 8, 1858	December 2, 1858	24
November 11, 1858	December 6, 1858	25
November 15, 1858	December 11, 1858	26
November 18, 1858	December 16, 1858	28
November 22, 1858	December 18, 1858	26
November 25, 1858	December 20, 1858	25
November 29, 1858	December 25, 1858	26
December 2, 1858, St. Louis	December 25, 1858	23
December 2, 1858, Memphis	December 29, 1858	27
December 6, 1858, St. Louis	December 29, 1858	23
December 6, 1858, Memphis	January 3, 1859	28

B—Continued.

Date of departure from San Francisco.	Date of arrival at St. Louis.	Number of days in making trip.
September 16, 1858	October 9, 1858	23
September 20, 1858	October 16, 1858	26
September 24, 1858	October 18, 1858	24
September 27, 1858	October 23, 1858	26
October 1, 1858	October 26, 1858	25
October 4, 1858	October 30, 1858	26
October 8, 1858	November 3, 1858	26
October 11, 1858	November 6, 1858	26
October 15, 1858	November 9, 1858	25
October 18, 1858	November 14, 1858	27
October 22, 1858	November 16, 1858	25
October 25, 1858	November 20, 1858	26
October 29, 1858	November 24, 1858	26
November 1, 1858	November 28, 1858	27
November 5, 1858	December 2, 1858	27
November 8, 1858	December 4, 1858	26
November 12, 1858	December 9, 1858	27
November 15, 1858	December 11, 1858	26
November 19, 1858	December 15, 1858	26
November 22, 1858	December 17, 1858	25
November 26, 1858	December 22, 1858	26
November 29, 1858	December 25, 1858	26
December 3, 1858	December 30, 1858	27
December 6, 1858	January 1, 1859	26

Date of departure from San Francisco.	Date of arrival at Memphis.	Number of days in making trip.
September 16, 1858	October 13, 1858	27
September 20, 1858	October 18, 1858	28
September 24, 1858	October 21, 1858	27
September 27, 1858	October 28, 1858	31
October 1, 1858	October 29, 1858	28
October 4, 1858	November 1, 1858	28
October 8, 1858	November 7, 1858	30
October 11, 1858	November 9, 1858	29
October 15, 1858	November 12, 1858	28
October 18, 1858	November 18, 1858	31
October 22, 1858	January 6, 1859, returned back to San Francisco by mistake.	
October 25, 1858	November 23, 1858	29
October 29, 1858	November 25, 1858	27
November 1, 1858	December 1, 1858	30
November 5, 1858	December 5, 1858	30
November 8, 1858	December 6, 1858	28
November 12, 1858	December 11, 1858	29
November 15, 1858	December 11, 1858	26
November 19, 1858	December 17, 1858	28
November 22, 1858	December 28, 1858	36
November 26, 1858	December 28, 1858	32
November 29, 1958	December 28, 1858	29
December 3, 1858	January 3, 1859	31
December 6, 1858	January 6, 1859	31

————— **End Appendix F** —————

Appendix G

Report of the Postmaster General, Dec. 3, 1859
Selections from pages 1410-1412

REPORT

OF THE

POSTMASTER GENERAL,

DECEMBER, 1859.

POST OFFICE DEPARTMENT, *December* 3, 1859.

SAN ANTONIO AND SAN DIEGO MAILS.

**Page
1410**

This semi-monthly was, on the 29th day of October, 1858, improved to a weekly service between San Antonio and El Paso and El Paso and Fort Yuma, and the compensation was fixed at $196,000. The product of the route during the past year, as already shown, was but $601—loss to the department at the rate of $195,399 per annum.

With this conclusive indication of its want of importance and value for postal purposes, I directed that the service should, on the 1st of July last, be put on its original footing of a semi-monthly mail, and reduced the allowance to the contractors to $120,000. Whatever objects, political or otherwise, may have been contemplated by the government in establishing this route through an almost unbroken wilderness and desert, it is clear that its continuance at the present rate of compensation is an injustice to the department. It may be convenient for the very few passengers that pass between Texas and San Diego; but as a mail accommodation it is not required in the direction of the Pacific since the people of Texas have already secured to them a regular postal communication with that coast through New Orleans, and also by the great overland mail. But it would be better that this mail—one of the lightest known to the department—should be sent even by the way of New York to California, than that the correspondence of the whole country should be oppressed by this enormous exaction for the benefit of a few contractors.

The service upon this extended route has been performed with great regularity, and generally within schedule time; but the contract has proved one of the heaviest burdens to which the department has ever been subjected. With an expenditure at the rate of $600,000 per annum, the postages received in return have not amounted to more than $27,229 94; so that, after making allowances for such increase as may be anticipated, the department, at the expiration of the six years for which the contract was entered into, will have lost from this route alone more than three millions of dollars. Feeling anxious to relieve, in some degree, the postal revenues from this exhausting drain, I proposed a reduction of the semi-weekly to a weekly service, which would have resulted in an annual saving, as compared with the present outlay, of $150,000. On referring the question, however, to the Attorney General, he determined that in consequence of the customary clause giving the Postmaster General revisory power over all mail contracts having been omitted in this, the desired curtailment could not be legally made. The whole matter being thus placed beyond the control of the department, the action of Congress alone is capable of furnishing the remedy desired; and I cannot too earnestly recommend its early and decided interposition. If no compromise can be effected with the parties upon terms deemed reasonable, then I would urge, as an act of simple justice, that this gigantic service, which was established at the instance of Congress, and in furtherance of great national objects, shall be at once charged upon the public treasury. Until a railroad shall have been constructed across the continent, the conveyance of the Pacific mails overland must be regarded as wholly impracticable. These mails, as dispatched semi-monthly, average ten tons in weight, which, if divided into semi-weekly departures, would give two and a half tons for each—thus requiring, in view of the condition of the road, ten coaches, instead of the single one now employed, and

Page 1412

costing, at the present rate of compensation, six million of dollars per annum for transportation alone, with a product of $327,202 63.

The route has now been opened, and its availability for a light mail demonstrated; so that, should war occur with any maritime power, threatening embarrassment to our ocean mails for the Pacific, the service could, without delay, be reëstablished on its present basis. Were it otherwise, that contingency is deemed too remote to justify the continuance of so enormous a tax upon the correspondence of the country. Such morbid caution and apprehension could not but be recognized as illustrating in miniature the folly of that policy which would keep our army and navy perpetually on a war footing, merely because once or twice in a century the amicable relations of the republic with other nations are liable to be disturbed.

———————— End of Appendix K ————————

NOTE: Pages 1426-30, not reproduced here, contain the Postmaster's request for US Treasury to pay for the Overland Mail routes.

Appendix H

Butterfield Employee Record Book/Notebook/Handbook
Smithsonian Object Number: 1990.0564.1
Size: 6 1/2 " high, 3 5/8 wide; 1"thick
Source: Manda Kowalczyk, Accessions Officer, National Postal History Museum
Baasil Wilder, Librarian, National Postal History Museum

Appearing here, for the FIRST TIME in print, are images of the handwritten notes within the handbook at the Smithsonian National Postal Museum. This is the ONLY known surviving copy of the Overland Mail notebook.

A leather flap clasps this notebook printed by Hellier and Company Publishers, New York. Issued by the Overland Mail Company to conductors, agents, drivers, and station managers working on the express stagecoach route, the notebook was designed for record keeping. Its accordion pocket and multiple sections hold a fold-out map of the mail route; instructions for employees of the Overland Mail Company; schedules for the stagecoach; rates of postage; and spaces to record a daily log for the calendar year 1859 and to track accounts.

Closed, Front   *Closed, Top*   *Left Spine*   *Right Spine*

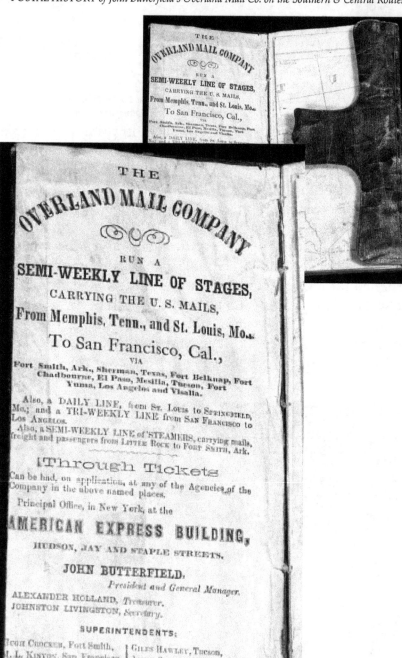

Inside front cover page 1, folded map page 2, and flap closure

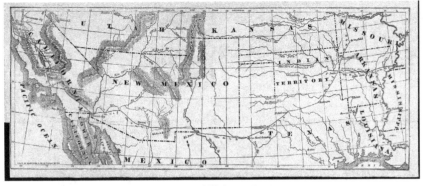

Map unfolded, page 2

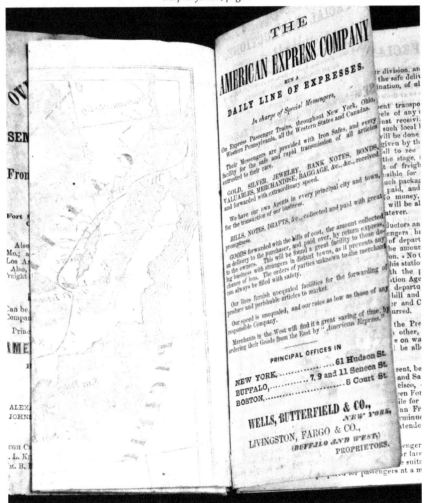

Folded map (page 2) and page 3

SPECIAL INSTRUCTIONS.

In order to carry out this undertaking, it is necessary that the following Instructions be strictly observed by all Employes of the Company.

To Conductors, Agents, Drivers and Employes.

1.—It is expected that all employes of the Company will be at their posts at all times, in order to guard and protect the property of the Company. Have teams harnessed in ample time, and ready to proceed without delay or confusion. Where the coaches are changed, have the teams hitched to them in time. Teams should be hitched together and led to or from the stable to the coach, so that no delay can occur by their running away. All employes will assist the Driver in watering and changing teams, in all cases, to save time.

2.—When a stage is seriously detained, by accident or otherwise, the Conductor or Driver will have the same noted on way bill and note book, and report fully to the Superintendent at first station, the nature and cause of such delay. Note hours of departure and arrival of all stages at stations, and keep a record of same.

3.—Conductors should never lose sight of the mails for a moment, or leave them, except in charge of the Driver or some other employe of the Company, who will guard them till his return. This rule must not be deviated from under any *circumstances*. They will also report to the Superintendent, in all cases, if Drivers abuse or mis-manage their teams, or in any way neglect or refuse to do their duty.

4.—The time of all employes is expected to be at the disposal of the Company's Agents, in all cases, at stations where they may be laying over. Their time belongs exclusively to the Company; they will therefore be always ready for duty.

5.—None but the Company's Superintendents or Agents, who have written permission, are authorized to make or contract debts, give notes, due bills, or any obligations on account of the Company.

6.—Conductors and Drivers will be very particular, and not allow the Company's property to be abused, or neglect to report to the proper parties the repairs required.

7.—Be particular to see that the mails are protected from the wet, and kept safe from injury of every

5

kind while in your possession, on your division, and you will be held personally responsible for the safe delivery at the end of your route, or point of destination, of all mails and other property in your charge.

8.—The Company will not at present transport any *through* extra baggage, freights, or parcels of any description. All employes are cautioned against receiving such matter in any shape or manner, except such local business of this nature, from place to place, as will be done according to the instructions and prices to be given by the different Superintendents. You will not fail to see that all parcels, boxes or bundles carried on the stage, shall be entered on the way bill, with amount of freight to be charged, and you will be held responsible for the safe delivery, at point of destination, of all such packages. The Agent will see that the charges are paid, and articles receipted for at time of delivery. No money, jewelry, bank notes, or valuables of any nature, will be allowed to be carried under any circumstances whatever.

9.—All Superintendents, Agents, Conductors and Drivers will see particularly that all passengers have their names entered on the way-bill, at point of departure; that their fares be paid in advance, and the amount entered on way-bill as paid to point of destination. No Conductor or Agent must allow any stage to leave his station without personally comparing the way-bill with the passengers, and knowing that they agree. Each Station Agent will be required to note the time of arrival and departure of each stage at his station, both on the way-bill and on a book kept for that purpose, giving the Driver and Conductor's name and cause of delay, if any has occurred.

10.—Superintendents will report to the President and Treasurer of the Company, and to each other, the names of the persons authorized to receipt fare on way-bill. No others than those named by them will be allowed to receipt fare.

11.—The rates of fare will, for the present, be as follows: between the Pacific Railroad terminus and San Francisco, and between Memphis and San Francisco, either way, through tickets, $200. Local fares between Fort Smith and Fort Yuma, not less than 10 cents per mile for the distance traveled. Between Fort Yuma and San Francisco, and between Fort Smith and the Railroad terminus, the rate of fare will be published by the Superintendents of those divisions.

12.—The meals and provisions for passengers are at their own expense, over and above the regular fare. The Company intend, as soon as possible, to have suitable meals at proper places, prepared for passengers at a moderate cost

Page 5

6

13.—Each passenger will be allowed baggage not exceeding 40 lbs. in any case.

14.—Passengers stopping from one stage to another, can only do so at their own risk as to the Company being able to carry them on a following stage. In cases of this nature, the Conductor or Agent at the place where they leave the stage, will endorse on the way-bill opposite their name, "Stopped over at ————." And on the way-bill of the stage in which the passenger continues his journey, the entry of his name will be made with the remark, "Stopped over from stage of the —— (giving the date). Fare paid to —— on way-bill of —— (date) from —— (name the place)."

15.—All employes are expected to show proper respect to and treat passengers and the public with civility, as well as to use every exertion to promote the comfort and convenience of passengers.

16.—Agents, Conductors, Drivers and all employes, will follow strictly all instructions that may be received, from time to time, from the Superintendents of their respective divisions.

17.—Any transactions of a disreputable nature will be sufficient cause for the discharge of any person from the employ of the Company.

18.—INDIANS. A good look-out should be kept for Indians. No intercourse should be had with them, but let them alone; by no means annoy or wrong them. At all times an efficient guard should be kept, and such guard should always be *ready* for any emergency.

19.—It is expected of every employe, that he will further the interests of the Company by every means in his power, more especially by living on good terms with all his fellow-employes, by avoiding quarrels and disagreements of every kind and nature, with all parties, and by the strictest attention of each and every one to his duties.

JOHN BUTTERFIELD, President.

M. L. KINYON, *San Francisco, Cal.*
HUGH CROCKER, *Fort Smith, Ark.*
JAMES GLOVER, *El Paso, Texas.*
WM. BUCKLEY, *Fort Yuma, Cal.*
GILES HAWLEY, *Tucson, Arizona.*
HENRY BATES, *Ft. Chadbourne, Texas.*

} *Superintendents.*

OVER

Throu

(IN

St. Louis, Mo

FORT SMIT

IN

This Sched
Employes of
not intend, by
public, to run
to conform as
of the Route, t
sity, cause var

HEL

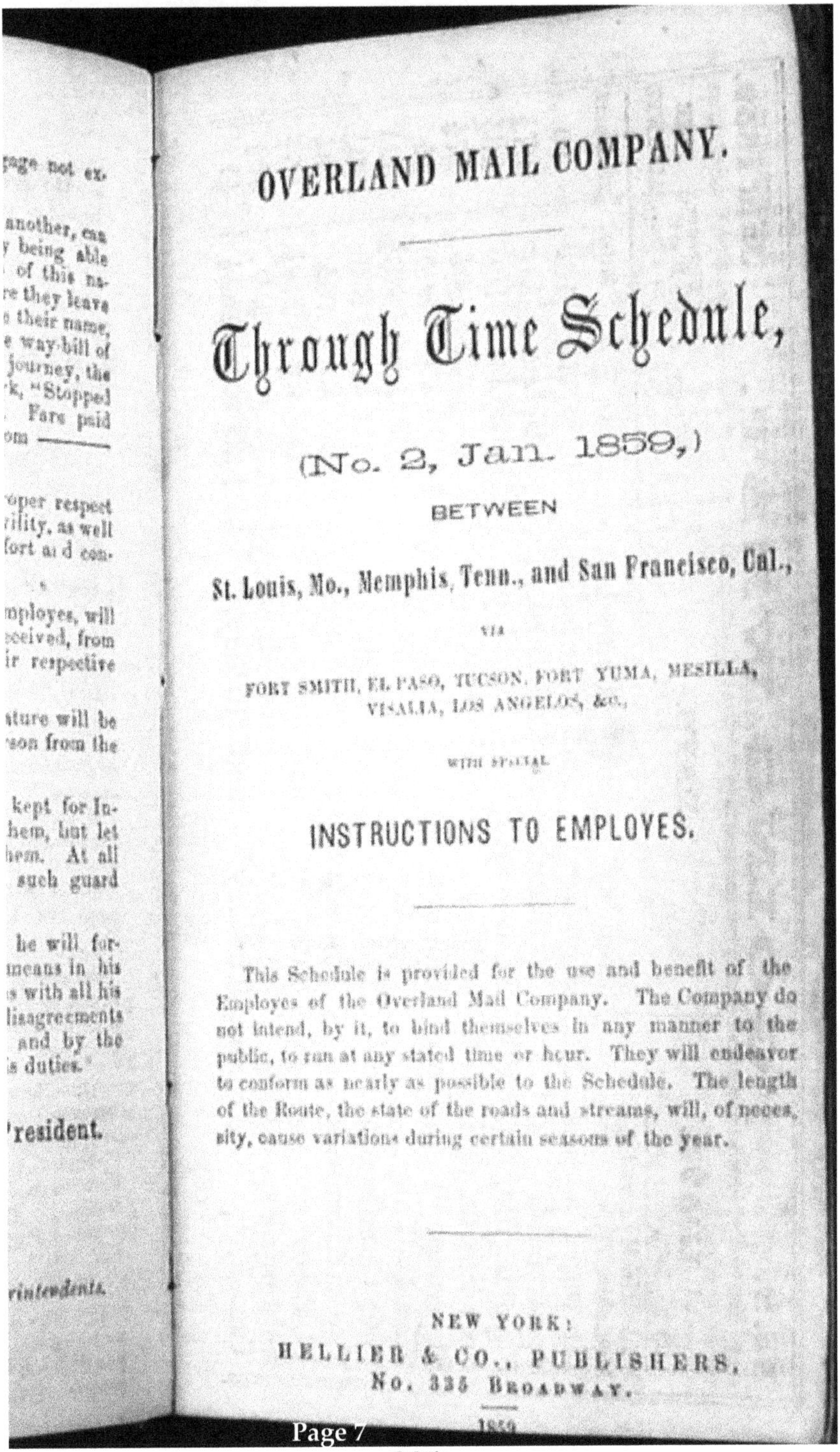

(left page, partially visible)

page not ex-

another, can
y being able
of this na-
re they leave
o their name,
e way-bill of
journey, the
k, "Stopped
Fare paid
om ——

oper respect
rility, as well
fort and con-

mployes, will
ceived, from
ir respective

ature will be
son from the

kept for In-
hem, but let
hem. At all
such guard

he will for-
means in his
s with all his
lisagreements
and by the
s duties.

'resident.

rintendents.

OVERLAND MAIL COMPANY.

Through Time Schedule,

(No. 2, Jan. 1859,)

BETWEEN

St. Louis, Mo., Memphis, Tenn., and San Francisco, Cal.,

VIA

FORT SMITH, EL PASO, TUCSON, FORT YUMA, MESILLA,
VISALIA, LOS ANGELOS, &c.,

WITH SPECIAL

INSTRUCTIONS TO EMPLOYES.

This Schedule is provided for the use and benefit of the
Employes of the Overland Mail Company. The Company do
not intend, by it, to bind themselves in any manner to the
public, to run at any stated time or hour. They will endeavor
to conform as nearly as possible to the Schedule. The length
of the Route, the state of the roads and streams, will, of necessity, cause variations during certain seasons of the year.

NEW YORK:
HELLIER & CO., PUBLISHERS,
No. 335 BROADWAY.

1859

Page 7

No. 2.	GOING WEST.			Jan. 1859.		
LEAVE.	**DAYS.**			**Hour.**	Distance, Place to Place.	TIME ALLOWED
St. Louis, Mo., and Memphis, Tenn.,	Monday	and	Thursday,	8.00 A.M	Miles.	No. Hours.
Tipton, Mo.	Monday	and	Thursday,	6.00 P.M	160	10
Springfield, "	Wednesday	and	Saturday,	7.45 A.M	143	37¾
Fayetteville, Ark.	Thursday	and	Sunday,	10.15 A.M	100	26½
Fort Smith, "	Friday	and	Monday,	3.30 A.M	65	17¼
Sherman, Texas.	Sunday	and	Wednesday,	12.30 A.M	205	45
Fort Belknap, "	Monday	and	Thursday,	9.00 A.M	146½	32½
Fort Chadbourne, "	Tuesday	and	Friday,	3.15 P.M	136	30½
Pecos River Crossing,	Thursday	and	Sunday,	3.45 A.M	165	36½
El Paso,	Saturday	and	Tuesday,	11.00 A.M	248½	55½
Soldier's Farewell,	Sunday	and	Wednesday,	8.30 P.M	150	33½
Tucson, Arizona	Tuesday	and	Friday,	1.30 P.M	184½	41

Page 8

Gila River,* "	Wednesday	and	Saturday,	9.00 P.M	141	31½
Fort Yuma, Cal.	Friday	and	Monday,	3.00 A.M	135	30
Los Angelos, "	Sunday	and	Wednesday,	8.30 A.M	254	53½
Fort Tejon, "	Monday	and	Thursday,	7.30 A.M	96	23
Visalia, "	Tuesday	and	Friday,	11.30 A.M	127	28
Firebaugh's Ferry, "	Wednesday	and	Saturday,	5.30 A.M	82	18
(Arrive) San Francisco,	Thursday	and	Sunday,	8.30 A.M	163	27

* The Station referred to on the Gila River is 40 miles west of the Maricopa Wells.

This Schedule may not be exact—all employes are directed to use every possible exertion to get the Stage through in quick time, even though ahead of this time.

No allowance is made in the time for ferries, changing teams, &c. It is necessary that each driver increase his speed over the average per hour enough to gain time for meals, changing teams, crossing ferries, &c.

Every person in the Company's employ will remember that each minute is of importance. If each driver on the route loses 15 minutes, it would make a total loss of time, on the entire route, of 25 hours, or, more than one day. If each one loses 10 minutes, it would make a loss of 16½ hours, or the best part of a day.

If each driver gains that time, it leaves a margin against accidents and extra delays.

All will see the necessity of promptness; every minute of time is valuable, as the Company are under heavy forfeit if the mail is behind time.

JOHN BUTTERFIELD, President.

Page 9

No. 2.	GOING EAST.			Jan. 1859.		
LEAVE.	**DAYS.**			**Hour.**	Distance, Place to Place.	TIME ALLOWED
San Francisco, Cal.	Monday	and	Friday,	12.00 M	Miles.	No. Hours.
Firebaugh's Ferry, "	Tuesday	and	Saturday,	3.00 P.M	163	27
Visalia, "	Wednesday	and	Sunday,	9.00 A.M	82	18
Fort Tejon, "	Thursday	and	Monday,	1.00 P.M	127	28
Los Angelos, "	Friday	and	Tuesday,	12.00 M	96	23
Fort Yuma, "	Sunday	and	Thursday,	5.30 P.M	254	53½
Gila River,* Arizona	Monday	and	Friday,	11.30 P.M	135	30
Tucson, "	Wednesday	and	Sunday,	7.00 A.M	141	31½
Soldier's Farewell, "	Friday	and	Tuesday,	12.00 M	184½	41
El Paso, Texas.	Saturday	and	Wednesday,	9.30 A.M	150	33½
Pecos River Crossing, "	Monday	and	Friday,	4.45 P.M	248½	55½
Fort Chadbourne, "	Wednesday	and	Sunday,	5.15 A.M	165	36¾
Fort Belknap, "	Thursday	and	Monday,	11.30 A.M	136	30½
Sherman, Ark.	Friday	and	Tuesday,	5.00 P.M	205	45
	Sunday	and	Thursday,	10.15 A.M	65	17¼
			Friday,		100	26

Page 10

						5.15 A.M	165	
		ednesday	and	Sunday,		5.15 A.M	165	
Fort Belknap,	"	Thursday	and	Monday,	11.30 A.M		136	30¼
Sherman,	"	Friday	and	Tuesday,	8.00 P.M		146½	32½
Fort Smith,	Ark.	Sunday	and	Thursday,	5.00 P.M		205	45
Fayetteville,	"	Monday	and	Friday,	10.15 A.M		65	17¼
Springfield,	Mo.	Tuesday	and	Saturday,	12.45 P.M		100	26½
Tipton,	"	Thursday	and	Monday,	2.30 A.M		143	37¾
(Arrive) ST. LOUIS, Mo., and MEMPHIS, Tenn. }		Thursday	and	Monday,			160	10

* The Station referred to on the Gila River, is 40 miles west of the Maricopa Wells.

This Schedule may not be exact—all employees are directed to use every possible exertion to get the Stages through in quick time, even though ahead of this time.

No allowance is made in the time for ferries, changing teams, &c. It is necessary that each driver increase his speed over the average per hour enough to gain time for meals, changing teams, crossing ferries, &c.

Every person in the Company's employ will remember that each minute is of importance. If each driver on the route loses 15 minutes, it would make a total loss of time, on the entire route, of 25 hours, or, more than one day. If each one loses 10 minutes it would make a loss of 16½ hours, or the best part of a day.

If each driver gains that time, it leaves a margin against accidents and extra delays.

All will see the necessity of promptness; every minute of time is valuable, as the Company are under heavy forfeit if the mail is behind time. **JOHN BUTTERFIELD, Pres.**

WAGES TABLE.

Daily Wages. 8 cts.	¼ $cts	½ $cts	¾ $cts	1 $cts	2 $cts	3 $cts	4 $cts	5 $cts	6 $cts	7 $cts	8 $cts	9 $cts	10 $cts	11 $cts	12 $cts
50	12	25	37	50	1 00	1 50	2 00	2 50	3 00	3 50	4 00	4 50	5 00	5 50	6 00
56	14	28	42	56	1 12	1 69	2 25	2 81	3 37	3 94	4 50	5 06	5 62	6 19	6 75
62	16	31	47	62	1 25	1 87	2 50	3 12	3 75	4 37	5 00	5 62	6 25	6 87	7 50
69	17	34	52	69	1 37	2 06	2 75	3 44	4 12	4 81	5 50	6 19	6 87	7 56	8 25
75	19	37	56	75	1 50	2 25	3 00	3 75	4 50	5 25	6 00	6 75	7 50	8 25	9 00
81	20	40	60	81	1 62	2 44	3 25	4 06	4 87	5 69	6 50	7 31	8 12	8 94	9 75
87	22	44	65	87	1 75	2 62	3 50	4 37	5 25	6 12	7 00	7 87	8 75	9 62	10 50
94	23	47	70	94	1 87	2 81	3 75	4 69	5 62	6 56	7 50	8 44	9 37	10 31	11 25
1 00	25	50	75	1 00	2 00	3 00	4 00	5 00	6 00	7 00	8 00	9 00	10 00	11 00	12 00
1 06	26	53	79	1 06	2 12	3 19	4 25	5 31	6 37	7 44	8 50	9 56	10 62	11 69	12 75
1 12	28	56	84	1 12	2 25	3 37	4 50	5 62	6 75	7 87	9 00	10 12	11 25	12 37	13 50
1 19	29	59	89	1 19	2 37	3 56	4 75	5 94	7 12	8 81	9 50	10 69	11 87	13 06	14 25
1 25	31	62	94	1 25	2 50	3 75	5 00	6 25	7 50	8 75	10 00	11 25	12 50	13 75	15 00
1 31	33	66	99	1 31	2 62	3 94	5 25	6 56	7 87	9 19	10 50	11 81	13 12	14 44	15 75

Daily Wages.	¼	½	¾	1	2	3	4	5	6	7	8	9	10	11	12
1 37	34	69	1 03	1 37	2 75	4 12	5 50	6 87	8 25	9 62	11 00	12 37	13 75	15 12	16 50
1 44	36	72	1 08	1 44	2 87	4 31	5 75	7 19	8 62	10 06	11 50	12 94	14 37	15 81	17 25
1 50	37	75	1 12	1 50	3 00	4 50	6 00	7 50	9 00	10 50	12 00	13 50	15 00	16 50	18 00
1 56	39	78	1 17	1 56	3 12	4 69	6 25	7 81	9 37	10 94	12 50	14 06	15 62	17 19	18 75
1 62	41	81	1 22	1 62	3 25	4 87	6 50	8 12	9 75	11 37	13 00	14 62	16 25	17 87	19 50
1 69	42	84	1 26	1 69	3 37	5 06	6 75	8 44	10 12	11 81	13 50	15 19	16 87	18 56	20 25
1 75	44	87	1 31	1 75	3 50	5 25	7 00	8 75	10 50	12 25	14 00	15 75	17 50	19 25	21 00
1 81	45	91	1 36	1 81	3 62	5 44	7 25	9 06	10 87	12 69	14 50	16 31	18 12	19 94	21 75
1 87	47	94	1 41	1 87	3 75	5 62	7 50	9 37	11 25	13 12	15 00	16 87	18 75	20 62	22 50
1 94	48	97	1 45	1 94	3 87	5 81	7 75	9 69	11 62	13 56	15 50	17 44	19 37	21 31	23 25
2 00	50	1 00	1 50	2 00	4 00	6 00	8 00	10 00	12 00	14 00	16 00	18 00	20 00	22 00	24 00
2 06	51	1 03	1 54	2 06	4 12	6 19	8 25	10 31	12 37	14 44	16 50	18 56	20 62	22 69	24 75
2 12	53	1 06	1 59	2 12	4 25	6 37	8 50	10 62	12 75	14 87	17 00	19 12	21 25	23 37	25 50
2 19	54	1 09	1 62	2 19	4 37	6 56	8 75	10 94	13 12	15 31	17 50	19 69	21 87	24 06	26 25
2 25	56	1 12	1 69	2 25	4 50	6 75	9 00	11 25	13 50	15 75	18 00	20 25	22 50	24 75	27 00
2 30	58	1 16	1 74	2 31	4 62	6 94	9 25	11 56	13 87	16 19	18 50	20 81	23 12	25 44	27 75
2 37	59	1 19	1 78	2 37	4 75	7 12	9 50	11 87	14 25	16 62	19 00	21 37	23 75	26 12	28 50
2 44	61	1 22	1 83	2 44	4 87	7 31	9 75	12 19	14 62	17 06	19 50	21 94	24 37	26 81	29 25
2 50	62	1 25	1 87	2 50	5 00	7 50	10 00	12 50	15 00	17 50	20 00	22 50	25 00	27 50	30 00

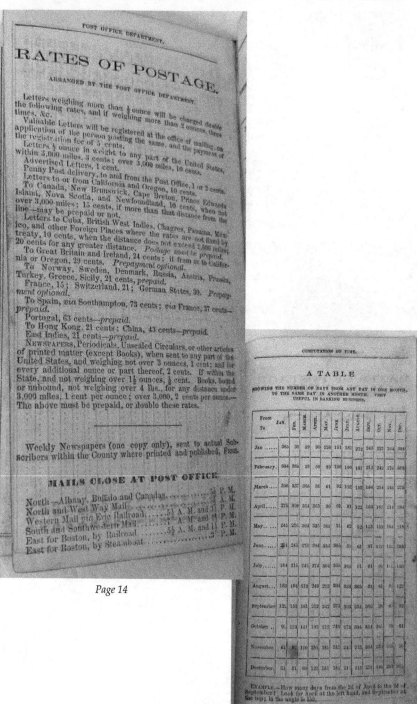

POST OFFICE DEPARTMENT.

RATES OF POSTAGE.

ARRANGED BY THE POST OFFICE DEPARTMENT.

Letters weighing more than ½ ounce will be charged double the following rates, and if weighing more than 2 ounces, three times, &c.

Valuable Letters will be registered at the office of mailing, on application of the person posting the same, and the payment of the registration fee of 5 cents.

Letters ½ ounce in weight to any part of the United States, within 3,000 miles, 3 cents; over 3,000 miles, 10 cents.

Advertised Letters, 1 cent.

Penny Post delivery, to and from the Post Office, 1 or 2 cents.

Letters to or from California and Oregon, 10 cents.

To Canada, New Brunswick, Cape Breton, Prince Edwards Island, Nova Scotia, and Newfoundland, 10 cents, when not over 3,000 miles; 15 cents, if more than that distance from the line—may be prepaid or not.

Letters to Cuba, British West Indies, Chagres, Panama, Mexico, and other Foreign Places where the rates are not fixed by treaty, 10 cents, when the distance does not exceed 2,500 miles; 20 cents for any greater distance. *Postage must be prepaid.*

To Great Britain and Ireland, 24 cents; if from or to California or Oregon, 29 cents. *Prepayment optional.*

To Norway, Sweden, Denmark, Russia, Austria, Prussia, Turkey, Greece, Sicily, 21 cents, *prepaid.*

France, 15; Switzerland, 21; German States, 30. *Prepayment optional.*

To Spain, *via* Southampton, 73 cents; *via* France, 37 cents—*prepaid.*

Portugal, 63 cents—*prepaid.*

To Hong Kong, 21 cents; China, 43 cents—*prepaid.*

East Indies, 21 cents—*prepaid.*

NEWSPAPERS, Periodicals, Unsealed Circulars, or other articles of printed matter (except Books), when sent to any part of the United States, and weighing not over 3 ounces, 1 cent; and for every additional ounce or part thereof, 2 cents. If within the State, and not weighing over 1½ ounces, ½ cent. Books, bound or unbound, not weighing over 4 lbs., for any distance under 3,000 miles, 1 cent per ounce; over 3,000, 2 cents per ounce.— The above must be prepaid, or double these rates.

Weekly Newspapers (one copy only), sent to actual Subscribers within the County where printed and published, Free.

MAILS CLOSE AT POST OFFICE.

North—Albany, Buffalo and Canadas.................3¼ P. M.
North and West Way Mail........................8 A. M.
Western Mail *via* Erie Railroad......5½ A. M. and 3½ P. M.
South and Southwestern Mail......7 A. M. and 4½ P. M.
East for Boston, by Railroad......5½ A. M. and 1 P. M.
East for Boston, by Steamboat......................3 P. M.

Page 14

COMPUTATION OF TIME.

A TABLE

SHOWING THE NUMBER OF DAYS FROM ANY DAY IN ONE MONTH,
TO THE SAME DAY IN ANOTHER MONTH. VERY
USEFUL IN BANKING BUSINESS.

From To	JAN.	FEB.	MARCH	APRIL	MAY.	JUNE	JULY.	AUGUST.	SEPT.	OCT.	NOV.	DEC.
Jan	365	31	59	90	120	151	181	212	243	273	304	334
February .	334	365	28	59	89	120	150	181	212	242	273	303
March	306	337	365	31	61	92	122	153	184	214	245	275
April.....	275	306	334	365	30	61	91	122	153	183	214	244
May.....	245	276	304	335	365	31	61	92	123	153	184	214
June	214	245	273	304	334	365	31	61	92	122	153	183
July......	184	215	243	274	304	335	365	31	61	91	122	152
August...	153	184	212	243	273	304	334	365	31	61	92	122
September	122	153	181	212	242	273	303	334	365	30	61	91
October ..	92	123	151	182	212	243	273	304	334	365	31	61
November .	61	92	120	151	181	212	242	273	304	334	365	30
December .	31	61	90	121	151	182	212	243	273	304	334	365

EXAMPLE—How many days from the 2d of April to the 2d of September? Look for April at the left hand, and September at the top; in the angle is 153.

Page 15

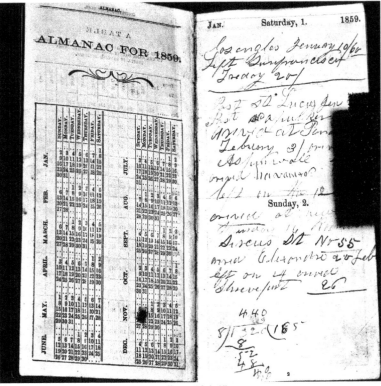

Pages 16 & 17

Editor Note: Based on the content of pages 17 to 27, these notes describe a January 10, 1860 trip out of Los Angeles to Cuba. Possibly a passenger disembarking the Butterfield stage at Los Angeles was given an 'out of date' 1859 handbook to use as a travel journal before he boarded the S. S. Senator to San Francisco; then the S.S. Cortes to Aspinwall; the S.S. North Star to Havana; where he boarded the S.S. Daniel Webster to New Orleans; then on to Alexandria and Shreveport, Louisiana. Pages 28 & 29, may have been written by a different hand 21 years later - on those pages the year 1859' is crossed out and '1881' is written in its place.

Jan. Saturday, 1. 1859.
 "*Los Angeles January 10/60 Left San Francisco on Tuesday 20/*
Past St Lucus Jan __ Past Acapulco Arrived at Panama February 3/ arrived
Aspinwall 4 arrived Havana 8 left on the 12
Sunday, 2. *arrived at New Orleans Tuesday 16 Roomed Circus St No 55*

arrived Alexandria 20 Feb left on 24 arrived Shreveport 26

Jan. Wednesday, 5, 1859
D B Jackson
San Fransisco
Bar Keepe Cortes

Page 18 is blank   Page 19

Steamships Mentioned in the Handbook
on the January 1860 Journey from San Francisco to New Orleans

"Vanderbilt's Private Steamship, The North Star"

S. S. Senator

This is an oil painting of the steamer Senator by artist James Bard. It was likely painted shortly after the ship was launched in 1848 in New York. Senator was a wooden, side-wheel steamship built in New York in 1848. She was one of the first steamships on the California coast and arguably one of the most commercially successful, arriving in San Francisco at the height of the California gold rush. Senator began a 26-year long career sailing between San Francisco and Southern California ports. Source: Wikipedia

The North Star was the name of 252-foot steamship launched for the Cornelius Vanderbilt's family's first Grand Tour of Europe in 1852. From 1854 to 1855, and 1859 to 1865 she ran from Aspinwlll to Havana to New York. She was scrapped in 1866. Source:: Frank Leslie's Popular Monthly, and exhibitions.library.vanderbilt.edu

Uessels Advertised.

NEW YORK AND SAN FRANCISCO STEAMSHIP LINE.

FOR PANAMA.

The new and magnificent double-engine Steamship
CORTES,
Thomas R. Cropper, Commander,
Will leave Central Wharf for PANAMA, (touching only at Acapulco.)
On WEDNESDAY, Dec. 1st, at 8 o'clock. A. M., connecting at Aspinwall (Navy Bay) with the splendid steamship UNITED STATES, to leave immediately on arrival of passengers and treasure, for New York, direct.

Arrangements having been perfected for the conveyance of passengers and guarding of treasure by this line, it is expected that they will reach New York in less than 25 days from this port.

The sailing qualities and comfortable accommodations of this boat are unsurpassed.

TREASURE for shipment will be received at the office of the Line until 4 o'clock, P. M. on Tuesday, 30th November.

Passengers are requested to be on board before 7 o'clock, A. M. of day of sailing.

For freight or passage apply to
WM. F. BABCOCK & CO.,
no25-7   Iron Building, Clay St., 2 doors from Niantic Hotel

Advertisement for the S.S. Cortes.

The double-engine Steamship Cortes made frequent trips from San Francisco to Panama. On one occasion, in ___ she made the run from San Francisco to Acapulco in 7 days and 6 hours, then from Acapulco to Panama in 6 days, 1 hour. Source: www.maritimeheritage.org

S.S. Daniel Webster

The S. S. Daniel Webster was 1035 tons, length 223.3ft x beam 31ft, wooden hull, side paddle wheels, with three masts. Built with 31 staterooms and accommodation for 116 passengers. Launched by William H. Brown, in New York on 20th September 1851 for Cornelius Vanderbilt and sailed from New York on her first voyage to San Juan de Nicaragua on November 22, 1851. She continued to operate from New York and New Orleans to San Juan and later Aspinwall for Vanderbilt, and later Charles Morgan until 1859. Chartered to the War Department 1861-1865 and sank on 3rd Oct.1866 on passage to Mobile. Passengers were saved by the Steamship George Cromwell. *Source:: wikimedia.org and www.theshipslist.com*

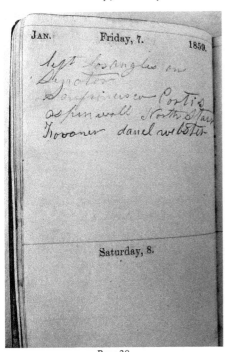

Page 20

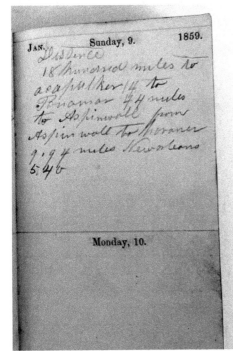

Page 21

Jan. Friday, 7. 1859
left Los Angeles on
Senator
San Francisco Cortes
Aspinwall North Star
Havana daniel webster

Editor's Note:
Apparently this is a list of his ships and destinations, perhaps meaning: 'I left Los Angeles on the S.S. Senator bound for San Francisco, then boarded the S.S. Cortes for the Isthmus of Panama. After crossing the Isthmus by railway, I departed the city of Aspinwall on the S.S. North Star bound for Havana, where I boarded the S.S. Daniel Webster for New Orleans.'

[Editors's Note: Aspinwall known today as Colón, was founded in 1850 by Americans working on the Isthmus of Panama railroad that linked the east and west coasts of that country. The U.S. Postal System had a contract for eastbound mail to pass through Aspinwall on the journey between San Francisco and New Orleans or New York.]

Jan. Sunday, 9. 1859.

Distance
18 hundred miles to
Acapulco 14 to
Panamas 44 miles
to Aspinwall from
Aspinwall to Havana
9.94 miles New Orleans
5.40

[Editor's Note: It is not clear what "9.94" and "5.4" were referring to. The notes on this page 21 for Jan. 9th, may be a record of the estimated "1,800" miles sailed on the trip listed on the adjoining page for Jan. 7th (see above).]

Jan.
Thursday, Jan.
13 1859.
*"Left Los Angeles
Jan 10/60"*

Page 22 blank   Page 23

Page 24   Page 25

Jan. Saturday, 15. 1859.

Cotton	62.45	
20 bu corn	10.00	
	2/72.45	
	36.22	½
	20.22	
to be divided	2/16.02	¼
	8.02	¼
henry's hogs	7.00	
the mair	17.50	
hogs	3.50	
	5.00	
	41.00	

Jan. Monday, 17. 1859.

Amt of Cotton raised		
1 Bale 55.45		55.45
last Cotton		7.00
half mine		2/ 62.45
		2/31.22 ½
half to devide		15.61 ¼
Cash paid on debts		
to Blake & Co		11.45
to Miss Jenette Ashbrooks		2.00
for hauling		3.74
to the Seveyor		1.50
Black Smithing		1.50
total debts		20.20

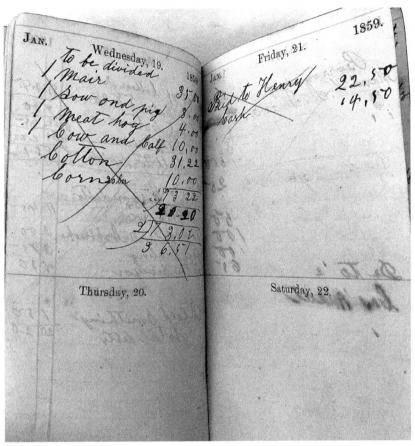

Page 26   Page 27

Jan. Wednesday, 19. 1859.

to be divided	
1 Mair	35.00
1 Sow and pig	3.00
1 meat hog	4.00
1 Cow and Calf	10.00
Cotton	31.22
Corn	10.00
	93.22
	/20.20
	2/73.02
	36.51

Jan. Friday, 21. 1859.

Paid to Henry	22.50
Cash	14.50

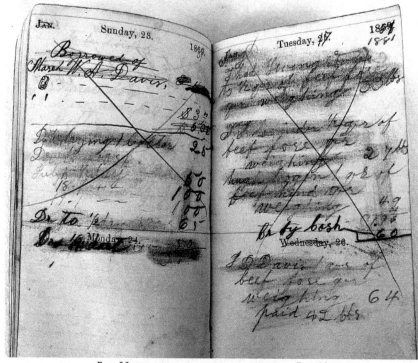

Page 28

Page 29

Jan. Sunday, 23.. ~~1859.~~

> 81

Borrowed of
Mesrs W. A. Davis

	$ 3.00
	6.00
Date buying / Cotton	25.00
Dr to --iosh	
July 15 --osh	50.00
18 - *first*	100.00
19 - - -	100.00
Dr to 1/2	65.00
Dr 1/2 - - rual	50.00
	54.00

The balance of the calendar pages, January 27 to December 31 pages are completely blank.

Jan. Sunday, 25.. ~~1859.~~

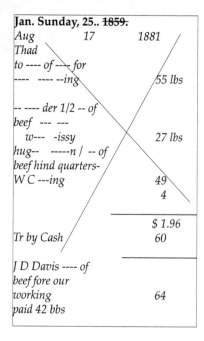

Aug 17	1881
Thad	
to ---- of ---- for	
---- ---- --ing	55 lbs
-- ---- der 1/2 -- of	
beef --- ---	
w--- -issy	27 lbs
hug-- -----n / -- of	
beef hind quarters-	
W C ---ing	49
	4
	$ 1.96
Tr by Cash	60
J D Davis ---- of	
beef fore our	
working	64
paid 42 bbs	

After the 1859 Calendar pages there are 16 blank Memoranda pages.

Then there are 24 "Cash Account" pages.
The first two January pages have entries in blue Ink, the rest are blank.

Then there is 1 blank "Summary of Cash Account" page,
followed by 10 blank "Bills Payable/Receivable" pages.

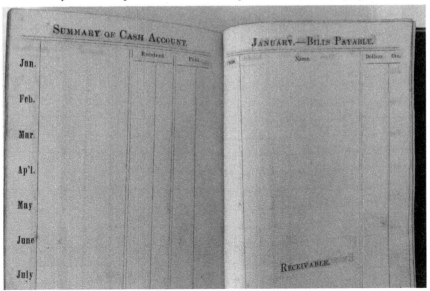

RAY BROTHERS,

8 DEY ST., NEW YORK,

Wholesale Dealers in

HARDWARE.

EVERY DESCRIPTION OF

AMERICAN HARDWARE,

Axes, Hammers, Saws, Anvils, Planes, Tools,

CUTLERY,

SCREWS, BUTTS, LOCKS,

Ames' and all other Shovels, Spades, Hoes,

Farmers' and Planters' Tools,

ROPE, SLATE, SAND-PAPER,

Tacks, Nails,

EVERY DESCRIPTION OF

Builders' and Carpenters' Hardware,

PICTURE NAILS, CURTAIN FIXTURES,

Upholsterers' Hardware,

Brass Kettles, Pails, Buckets, Chains, &c.

Orders from the Trade Respectfully Solicited. All Orders by Mail will receive prompt and faithful attention.

Last Page

*I am so grateful to
Manda Kowalczyk,
Accessions Officer, and to
Baasil Wilder, Librarian,
National Postal History Museum
for making these pages
of the handbook available.*

ADVERTISEMENTS.

AMERICAN EXPRESS BUILDINGS,

Cor. Hudson, Jay and Staple Sts., N. Y.

DAILY EXPRESSES

TO AND FROM

NEW YORK, THE WESTERN STATES

And Canadas,

Goods, Packages, Money, Jewelry, &c., &c. forwarded on Express Trains, in charge of Special Messengers.

BILLS, NOTES, AND DRAFTS COLLECTED AND PAID.

Time unsurpassed, and rates as low as by any other route.

AGENCY AND OFFICE OF THE

OVERLAND MAIL CO.

Semi-Weekly Stages through to

SAN FRANCISCO, CALIFORNIA,

By way of Fort Smith, El Paso, Tucson, Fort Yuma, and Los Angeles.

AGENCY OF THE ATLANTIC ROYAL MAIL CO'S

New York & Galway Steamships,

THE SHORTEST SEA VOYAGE BETWEEN AMERICA AND EUROPE.

By FIRST CLASS STEAMSHIPS. The fare and accommodations by this Line are unsurpassed. Through Tickets from New York to any of the principal Cities on the Railway Lines of Great Britain, giving the passenger an opportunity to visit Ireland and see the best portion of Great Britain, in less time, in a more pleasant manner, and at less expense than by any other route.

First Class Passage, ... $80
Second " " 50
Third " " 30

Return Tickets can also be procured, upon application to the

AMERICAN EXPRESS CO.

No. 61 Hudson St, cor. Jay.

*This may be the
FIRST TIME
several of these three
dozen pages have
appeared in print.*

——— End Appendix H ———
– 312 –

Inside Back Cover

Appendix I

Report of the Postmaster General, Dec. 1, 1860
Selections from pages 433 - 437

REPORT OF THE POSTMASTER GENERAL.

POST OFFICE DEPARTMENT,
December 1, 1860.

PACIFIC MAILS.   Page 433

By the terms of the act of June 15, 1860, the compensation for the ocean service between our Atlantic and Pacific coasts was limited to the postages received on the mails conveyed. Immediately after the passage of this law, a correspondence was opened with the owners of the steamships engaged in the trade between New York and San Francisco, and the mails were offered to them on the conditions of the act referred to, but they were peremptorily declined, on the ground that

Page 434

in consequence of the diversion of a large part of the letter mail to the overland route, the postages would afford a wholly inadequate remuneration. This fact the President of the United States at once communicated to Congress, and urged that the act of June 15 should be so modified as to authorize the department to contract for the continuance of the then existing transportation of the mails between New York and San Francisco, on such terms as might be deemed reasonable and just. Congress, however, adjourned without taking any further action upon the subject. In view of the importance of these mails and of the impracticability, from their great weight and bulk, of forwarding them over land, a renewed effort was made for their transmission by sea, and finally Cornelius Vanderbilt agreed to convey them until the 4th of March next, upon the terms of the act of June 15, but upon the express assurance that the President would recommend to Congress to make to him such further allowance, over and above the postages, as would constitute a fair and adequate compensation for the service. But for this assurance, all the endeavors of the department to maintain an ocean postal communication between our Atlantic and Pacific ports would, it is confidently believed, have proved unavailing.

The subjoined table exhibits the postages received from the ocean and Isthmus route to California, as well as from the overland service, for three quarters of the present year, ending September 30:

March quarter, 1860.

Ocean and Isthmus postages..... ....$39,773 97
Overland postages.. 30,772 49

June quarter, 1860.

Ocean and Isthmus postages.....................................$33,607 62
Overland postages 34,509 73

September quarter, 1860.

Ocean and Isthmus postages.....................................$25,644 70
Overland postages.. 37,010 75

It will be seen that the revenue from the ocean service has constantly diminished, while that from the overland route has constantly increased, though not in the same proportion. The diminution and increase are alike due to the order of this department under date of 17th of December, 1859, directing letter mails, which had previously gone by the steamers, to be made up and forwarded overland. During the last quarter, which was the first under the existing contract, the falling off in the receipts from the ocean service was very rapid, having declined to $25,644 70. This is probably below the quarterly average for the year. Assuming, however, the receipts for the preceding quarter

Page 435

to be the average, this would give at the rate of $134,430 48 per annum. That this sum, should it even be realized, is not a full compensation for the service as actually performed, is undeniable, but what further allowance should be made to the contractor, is a question which belongs to the discretion of Congress to determine. Prior to the 30th of June, 1860, the transmission of these mails, including a direct service from New Orleans, cost the government at the rate of $350,000 per annum. The present contract does not embrace the New Orleans mails, but it provides for an additional monthly trip between New York and San Francisco, making the service tri-mouthly instead of semi-monthly from New Orleans, cost the government at the rate of $350,000 per annum. The present contract does not embrace the New Orleans mails, but it provides for an additional monthly trip between New York and San Francisco, making the service tri-mouthly instead of semi-monthly as heretofore. It is due to the contractor to say that he has thus far faithfully fulfilled his engagement with the department, and as he came to its relief in a conjuncture of great embarrassment, his claim for remuneration should be frankly and liberally met. I should not regard the government as honorably acquitted of its obligations to him, without a full redemption of the pledge implied in the assurance which the President, from high considerations of the public interest, felt justified in giving him.

In addition to this tri-monthly mail by the ocean, there exist at present the following overland postal connections with the Pacific, viz:

1. A semi-monthly mail from St. Joseph, Missouri, via Salt Lake City, to Placerville, California. The expenditure upon this route was reduced $47,000, on the 6th day of June, 1860, by the establishment of a "star" in lieu of the preëxisting coach service between Salt Lake City and Placerville, and it has been increased at the rate of $24,381 per annum, by the improvement of the service to a weekly mail between Placerville and Carson City, and between St. Joseph and Fort Kearney, for the purpose of supplying the large and increasing populations in the regions of the Pike's Peak and Washoe mines.

2. A weekly mail from New Orleans, via San Antonio, Camp Stockton and El Paso, to San Francisco.

3. A semi-weekly letter mail from St. Louis and Memphis, via Fort Smith and El Paso and Fort Yuma, to San Francisco.

The annual cost of these routes, as now modified—estimating that by the ocean at $350,000—is $1,202,381. The receipts from them, per annum, as shown by the tables accompanying this report, do not exceed $296,469 7i. In view of this extremely limited revenue, as compared with the outlay, and of the fact that these routes were established and are maintained mainly for the advancement of certain national objects not at all postal in their character, I respectfully but earnestly renew the recommendation contained in my last annual report, that they shall be at once put upon the public treasury. Page 436

The following table of postages received from and expenditures made upon these several routes will indicate the postal value of each during the last year:

	Expenditure.	Receipts.
1. From New York to San Francisco	$350,000 00	$170,825 4
2. Overland, via El Paso, &c.	600,000 00	119,766 7
3. St. Joseph to Salt Lake City	125,000 00	4,305 6
4. Salt Lake City to Placerville	83,241 00	978 5
5. San Antonio to Camp Stockton	70,000 00	593 4

It thus appears that the revenue accruing from the service between St. Joseph and Placerville, via Salt Lake City, amounted to but $5,284 14

It thus appears that the revenue accruing from the service between St. Joseph and Placerville, via Salt Lake City, amounted to but $5,284 14; yet upon this route—adding thereto the short distances between St. Louis and St. Joseph and San Francisco and Placerville—a bill now pending before Congress proposes the establishment of a daily service, under the delusive expectation of carrying through this vast desert, and over mountains for several months of the year covered with snow, and impassable, the mails, weighing tons, which are now safely, rapidly, and regularly transported by other routes that are open and unobstructed throughout the year. The enterprise in its practical operation would, no doubt, result in a complete failure, owing to the character of the road, the rigors of the winter, and the bulk and weight of the mails. It could not be maintained at a less cost than $600,000 per annum, and while disastrous to the last degree to the postal interests, this lavish outlay would prove beneficial only to the contractors. If their importunities and the importunities of their friends cannot be withstood by the government, it would be far better that they and their descendants, for an indefinite period, should be pensioned from the treasury, than that this unparalleled waste of the public money should be allowed.

The act of Congress of 21st June, last, directed me to contract with the California Stage Company for daily service in stages, betwen Sacramento City, in California, and Portland, in Oregon, running through in seven days, from April 1 to December 1, and in twelve days the balance of the year, at $90,000 per annum. This line went into operation on the 15th of September, under my order, when the service previously existing on the road, costing $25,883 per annum, was withdrawn. The act also directed the organization of a six-times-a-week line, in steamboats and stages, between Portland, Oregon, and Olympia, in Washington Territory, at a rate of cost not exceeding that prescribed for the former route. The contractors for the semi-weekly mail already in operation between the latter points were directed to improve accordingly, making the trips in thirty-six hours, as required by the act, at $12,346 additional pay, per annum. They have not yet been heard from. The act further directed that the ocean service, performed semi-monthly since October, 1857, between San Francisco and Olympia, at $122,500 per annum, should be withdrawn, when the routes referred to were put in operation. The Pacific Mail Steamship Company, who held the

Page 437

contract therefor, have been instructed to discontinue service accordingly. As there has existed for some years a six-times-a-week steamboat service, between San Francisco and Sacramento City, 120 miles, through in eleven hours, and as the net expense of the new interior route, as arranged, is but $76,463 a year, it will be perceived that the effect of the arrangements will be to make the service between San Francisco and Olympia, (nearly one thousand miles,) much more frequent than heretofore, and at a considerable saving in expenditure; an increase of mail facilities, which will, doubtless, afford great satisfaction as well as accommodation to the numerous important towns lying between said points.

SAN ANTONIO AND SAN DIEGO.

It was stated in the last annual report that the cost of this service had been reduced from $196,000 to $120,000 per annum, by restoring it to its original footing as a semi-monthly mail. Within the past year that portion of the route between San Diego and Fort Yuma was discontinued as entirely useless, which resulted in a saving of $28,695. Between El Paso and Camp Stockton, a "star" has been substituted for the coach service, and the semi-monthly improved to a weekly mail, with a reduction of the expenditure of $12,579. The service has also been increased to a weekly mail between San Antonio and Camp Stockton. This has involved an additional annual outlay of $16,274, which, however, was necessary in order to complete the postal connection between New Orleans and San Francisco. It thus appears that the aggregate of the retrenchments made in the expenditures on this route since March, 1859, amount to $101,000. As thus modified, the route meets every postal want, and the service upon it is believed to be entirely satisfactory to the public.

—————— End of Appendix I ——————

HON. JOSEPH HOLT, SECRETARY OF WAR.—[PHOTOGRAPHED BY BRADY.]

Joseph Holt, Postmaster General, 1859-1860
Harpers Weekly, Feb. 16, 1861

Appendix J

Official March 22, 1860 List of Various Postal Routes to the West

On March 22, 1860 the Contract Office of the Post Office Department produced the following summary document that listed the various postal contracts to the west coast of the United States. The following letter was first published in *The Pony Express: A Postal History* by Richard C. Frajola, George J. Kramer, and Steven C. Walske, pages 147-149.

Post Office Department
Contract Office
March 22d 1860

Sir:

The over-land mail supposed to be referred to by your letter of this date, were let and have been curtailed as follows:

Route: 12.578

St. Louis, Missouri and Memphis, Tennessee converging at Fort Smith, Arkansas - To San Francisco twice a week: let to John Butterfield and Company from September 16th 1858 at $600,000 per annum. The service to be performed in four horse coaches or spring wagons.

Route 8.911

St. Joseph, Mo. to Salt Lake City, Utah, advertised under Act of 29 May 1856 and let under date of 16 October 1856 to Hiram Kimball at $23,000 per annum: service to be monthly trips, in covered wagons.

On his [Kimball's] failure, it was accepted in October 1857 by S. B. Mills at $32,000 per annum.

Re-let, from May 1858, to J. M. Hockaday at $190,000 per annum for weekly service, in covered carriages or wagons.

April 14, 1859. Contractor ordered to reduce to 2 trips per month at $65,000 decrease in annual pay.

Route 10.615

Neosho, M[o] to Albuquerque, New Mexico: accepted by T. F. Bowler from October 1858 at $17,000 per annum – service, monthly trips in six mule spring coaches.

1859, 11th of May – Contractor, ordered to discontinue.

Route 8.076

San Antonio, Texas to San Diego, Cal[a]

Let - July 1st 1857: service, two trips per month on horseback - to James E. Burch at $149,800 per annum.

Transferred, January 1st 1858 to George H. Giddings at the same pay.

1858 – Octr. 27. Ordered to discontinue between El Paso and Fort Yuma at $59,131 deduction from annual pay; also to improve residue of route to weekly trips – leaving entire pay to stand at $196,448 per annum from the 1st of January 1859.

1859 April 14, Ordered to reduce to semi-monthly trips by taking off 28 of the weekly trips per annum] at a deduction of $76,448 per annum from June 7, 1859.

1860 Febry 1st: - Ordered to discontinue service between San Diego and Fort Yuma from 1st of April 1860 at $28,695 deduction from annual pay.

1860 March 12th - Ordered to discontinue service between Camanche Springs and El Paso, from 1st of May 1860 at a deduction of $37,599 per annum.

This order left the route a semi-monthly one from Camanche Springs to San Antonia – The pay to stand at $53,276 per annum from 1st May 1860.

[Memo - In this contract is "the express understanding that if any other route should be put under Contract that shall cover this in whole or in part, the Post Master General, reserves the power to curtail or discontinue the service on this route at his discretion"]

Contract expires on the 30th of June 1861.

Route 12,801

Salt Lake City, Utah to Placerville, Cal^a accepted by George Chorpenning - semi-monthly service from 1st July 1858 - at $65,000 per annum.

Ordered on 19 June 1858 to be improved to weekly trips at $65,000 per annum additional – making entire pay $130,000 per annum – service to be in 4 horse covered wagons or carriages.

1859 May 7. Reduce to semi-monthly trips at $50,000 decrease in the annual pay from July 1st 1859.

Route 15.050

Independence Mo. to Stockton Cal^a - accepted, from October 1858, by Jacob Hall for monthly trips in mule wagons at $79,999 -

Transferred, same date, to Barron, Porter & Crenshaw

1859 May 11 - ordered a discontinuance from August 1859

————Recapitulation————

Butterfield & Co - From Memphis, Ten. and St. Louis Mo, via Ft. Smith to San Francisco Cal - semi weekly $600,000

J. M. Hockaday = From St. Joseph Mo to Salt lake - semi monthly$120,000

~~J. F. Bowler From Neosho, Missouri to Albuquerque,~~
~~New Mexico, month trips $17,000 per annum. discontinued~~

Geo. H Giddings – From San Antonio Texas to San Diego Cala
Reduced - San Antonio to Camanche Springs

(originally 149,800 increased 196,000) now	$53,276
Geo. Chorpenning - From Salt Lake City to Placerville Cala semi-monthly, now	$80,000
~~Barron, Porter and Crenshaw - From Independence Mo to Stockton Cala 79,999,~~ discontinued	
Total paid per Annum	$853,274

Memo
Just one year ago:

for Panama Route with no limitation as to time of service	$738,000
For Tehauntepee Route, no time specified	280,000
Butterfield Route - in 25 days	600,000
Salt Lake - in 38 days	320,000
San Antonio - in 60 days	196,000
Albuquerque - in 60 days	90,000
	————
	$2,224,000

The last overland mail for St. Louis took away 10,197 letters. In February 63,030 were forwarded by this route form California and 38,674 received for San Francisco from St. Louis.

Memo

Steamers -	10	tons per mail Steamer
	275	Bags - 22,000 Letters or 20 Tons per month!!
	11,000	- Letters semi-weekly
	22,000	- Letters weekly
	44,000	- Letters each way monthly
		one ton per diem to Pacific Coast

Note by authors of *The Pony Express: A Postal History* by Richard C. Frajola, George J. Kramer, and Steven C. Walske, pages 149:

This document is marked on reverse folio as "Memoranda of the mail Routes to California, P.M. Genl running routes, Panama Route etc., Tehauntepec etc."

Please note that this report contains two mathematical errors.

On route #8.911 the math, as written out, yields a $125,000 per year while $120,000 is shown in recapitulation table.

Also, the recapitulation total, using the numbers present, yields $853,276 rather than $853,274 as listed.

———— **End Appendix J** ————

Appendix K

Report of the Postmaster General, Dec. 2, 1861
Selections from pages 7, 12-13, 28-29

POST OFFICE DEPARTMENT,
December 2, 1861.

Page 7

The entire California mail service was transferred from the Isthmus to the overland route on the 1st of July last ; but the Isthmus, Central and South American mails are still conveyed by the California line of steamers, under the existing law, which limits the compensation to the United States postages on the mails transported, Cornelius Vanderbilt, esq., the proprietor of the line, having consented "to carry them for the postages until Congress meets, and has the opportunity of making some more permanent provision." It is claimed by him that the postages on these mails fall far short of a fair and proper remuneration for the service performed in their transportation. In view of the importance of keeping up a direct mail communication with the Isthmus of Panama, and the countries on the Pacific coast of Central and South America, I respectfully recommend the subject to the early consideration of Congress.

OVERLAND CALIFORNIA MAIL. **Page 12**

By the 9th section of an act of Congress approved March 2, 1861, entitled "An act making appropriations for the service of the Post Office Department during the fiscal year ending June 30, 1862," authority is given to the Postmaster General to discontinue the mail service on the southern overland route, (known as the "Butterfield" route,) between St. Louis and Memphis and San Francisco, and to provide for the conveyance, by the same parties, of a six-times-a-week mail by the "central route;" that is, "from some point on the Missouri river, connecting with the east, to Placerville, California." In pursuance of this act, and the acceptance of its terms by the mail company, an order was made on the 12th of March, 1861, to modify the present contract, so as to discontinue service on the southern route, and to provide for the transportation of the entire letter mail six times a week on the central route, to be carried through in twenty days eight months in the year, and in twenty-three days four months in the year, from St. Joseph, Missouri, (or Atchison, Kansas,) to Placerville, and also to convey the entire mail three times a week to Denver City and Salt Lake; the entire letter mail to California to be carried, whatever may be its weight, and in case it should not amount to 600 pounds, then sufficient of other mail to be carried each trip to make up that weight, the residue of all mail matter to be conveyed in thirty-five days, with the privilege of sending it from New York to San Francisco in twenty-five days by sea, and the public documents in thirty-five days; a pony express to be run twice a week until the completion of the overland telegraph, through in ten days eight months, and twelve days four months, in the year conveying for the government, free of charge, five pounds of mail matter; the compensation for the whole service to be one million of dollars per annum, payable from the general treasury, as provided by the act; the ' service to commence July 1, 1861, and terminate July 1, 1864. The transfer of stock from the southern to the central route was commenced about the 1st of April, and was completed so that the first mail was started from St. Joseph on the day prescribed by the order, July 1, 1861. While the carriages have, it is believed, departed regularly since that time, the mail service has not been entirely satisfactory to the department. The causes of complaint, however, it is hoped. will be removed by the measures now in progress. The route selected is that by Salt Lake City, so that that office has now the advantage of a daily mail, and Denver City is supplied three times a week. The overland telegraph having been completed, the running of the pony express was discontinued October 26, 1861. By the terms of the law the contractors were required to convey only the California letter mail on each trip by the short schedule, and this they were to do whatever might be its weight; but by voluntary agreement they stipulated that in case it should fall short of 600 pounds on any occasion they would take other mails so as to make that weight. As the letter mails are seldom or never equal to

Page 13

600 pounds in weight, some papers are conveyed in connexion with the letter mails each trip by the short schedule, while others are necessarily delayed. This has occasioned complaint; and complaints have also been made of other delays, and that bags of printed matter have been thrown off *en route* for the admission of passengers and express matter. These charges are denied by the contractors; but while the conditions of the contract, fixed by law, allow a longer time for the transit of some mails than others, complaint and disappointment must of necessity occur.

At the commencement of threatening disturbances in Missouri, in order to secure this great daily route from interruption, I ordered the increase of the weekly and tri-weekly service then existing between Omaha and Fort Kearney to daily, and an increase of pay thereon of $14,000 per annum. By that means an alternative and certain daily route between the east and California was obtained through Iowa, by which the overland mails have been transported when they became unsafe on the railroad route in Missouri.

In sending them from Davenport, through the State of Iowa, joining the main route at Fort Kearney, in Kansas, the only inconvenience experienced was a slight delay, no mails being lost so far as known.

l have in a previous part of this report alluded to the refusal at the treasury to pay the appropriation for the overland mail service to California. It seems to me so evidently to have been the purpose of Congress to require the payment of the amount stipulated from the treasury, under the 9th and 11th sections of the act, that I again call the attention of Congress to the subject for such further legislation as may be required. It certainly cannot be supposed that a con-

Page 29

tract of that magnitude could be required by postal interests alone. The general interests of the country required it, and the compensation should therefore be made by a general appropriation from the treasury, as this department presumes to have been the intention of the law.

———————— **End of Appendix K** ————————

Montgomery Blair, Postmaster General, 1861-1864
*Image: The original of this image is at the National Library of Brazil
Created in New York by Edward Anthony, [about 1861 to 1876]*

Appendix L

Wording of the Central Route Butterfield Contract

Postal Appropriation Act of March 2, 1861

The contract for Route #10773, including compensation, were ordered by Congress in Sections 9 and 10 of the Post Office Department Appropriation Act approved on March 2, 1861 (12 Stat. 204):

Sec. 9. And be it further enacted, That . . . the Postmaster General is hereby directed to discontinue the mail service on route number twelve thousand five hundred and seventy-eight from Saint Louis and Memphis to San Francisco, California, and to modify the contract on said route, subject to the same terms and conditions only as hereinafter provided, said discontinuance to take effect on or before July 1, eighteen hundred and sixty-one. The contractors on said route shall be required to transport the entire letter mail six times a week on the central route, said letter mail to be carried through in twenty days time, eight months in the year, and in twenty-three days the remaining four months of the year, from some point on the Missouri River connected with the East, to Placerville, California, and also to deliver the entire mails tri-weekly to Denver City and Great Salt Lake City, said contractors shall also be required to carry the residue of all mail matter in a period not exceeding thirty-five days, with the privilege of sending the latter semi-monthly from New York to San Francisco in twenty- five days by sea, and the public documents in thirty-five days. They shall also be required, during the continuance of their contract, or until the completion of the overland telegraph, to run a pony express semi-weekly, at a schedule time of ten days, eight months, and twelve days four months, carrying for the Government free of charge, five pounds of mail matter, with the liberty of charging the public for transportation of letters by said express not exceeding one dollar per half ounce. For the above service said contractors shall receive the sum of one million dollars per annum; the contract for such service to be thus modified before the twenty-fifth day of March next, and expire July one, eighteen hundred and sixty-four.

Sec. 10. And be it further enacted, That the contractors on route twelve thousand five hundred and seventy-eight, shall be entitled to their present mail pay during the necessary time required to change their stock from their present route to the central route without performing the service, and shall be entitled also to two months' pay on their present contract as liquidated damages for such change of service if made by them in accordance with the terms of the preceding section.

————————**End Appendix L** ————————

Appendix M

Modification to the 1858 Postal Contract
in light of the March 2, 1861 Act of Congress

MARCH 12, 1861,—Route No. 12578, California, St. Louis, and Memphis to San Francisco semi-weekly, four-horse coaches. Overland Mail Company, E. S. Alvord, Superintendent,—$625,000.

Ordered: Pursuant to act of Congress, approved 2d of March, 1861, and the acceptance of the terms thereof by the Overland Mail Company. Modify the present contract with that company for route No. 12578, executed 16th of September, 1857, to take effect 16th of September, 1858, so as to discontinue service on the present route and to provide for the transportation of the entire letter-mail six times a week on the central route; said letter-mail to be carried through in twenty days' time, eight months of the year, and in twenty-three days the remaining four months of the year, from St. Joseph, Missouri, (or Atchison, in Kansas,) to Placerville, in California, and also for the delivery of the entire mail, three times a week each way, to Denver City and Great Salt Lake City; and in case the mails do not amount to six hundred pounds per trip, then other mail matter to make up that weight per trip to be conveyed; but in any event the entire Denver City and Salt Lake City mails, and the entire letter-mail for California, to be conveyed. The contracts also to be required to convey the residue of all mail matter in a period not exceeding thirty-five days, with the privilege of sending the matter semi-monthly from New York to San Francisco in twenty- five days by sea and the public documents in thirty-five days. And to be required also, during the continuance of their contract, or until the completion of the overland telegraph, to run a pony express semi-weekly at a schedule time of ten ;days, eight months of the year, and twelve days four months of the year, and to convey for the Government free of charge five pounds of mail matter, with the liberty of charging the public for transportation of letters by said express not exceeding $1 per half ounce. The compensation for the whole service to be $1,000,000 per annum, to take effect on or before the 1st of July, 1861, and to expire 1st of July, 1864. The number of the route to be changed to 10773 and the service to be recorded in the route register for Missouri.

In behalf of the Overland Mail Company the undersigned accept the above modification of their contract. 12th of March, 1861.

(Signed)

W. B. DINSMORE, President

E. S. ALVORD, Supt. O. M. Co.

———————**End Appendix M** ———————

Appendix N

March 16, 1861 The Overland Mail Co.
Sub-Contracts Eastern Portion of Central Route

CONTRACT FOR JOINT CARRIAGE OF MAIL BETWEEN
CENTRAL OVERLAND & PIKES PEAK EXPRESS
AND OVERLAND MAIL COMPANY

This Memorandum on Contract - Witnesseth - That, Whereas the last session of the 36th Congress a law was passed authorizing the Postmaster Gen'l. to make certain modification in the Contract for mail service on route 12,578 - among others changing their route to what is known as the Central or Salt Lake Route - to be accepted by the Contractors -

And whereas The Overland Mail Company now performing the service and the recognized Contractors on said Route have accepted said Modifications, and entered into a Contract with the Postmaster General for the performance of said service under Act of Congress - a copy of which Contract is hereto appended and made part of this agreement, And whereas it has been agreed that "The Central Overland California & Pikes Peak Company" shall perform a part of said service - Now these Presents Witness & duly Authorized by its Board of Directors, party of the first part, And the said Overland Mail Company Acting by Wm. B. Dinsmore its President, duly Authorized by its Board of Directors, party of the Second part, do mutually agree as follows.

1st Said first party agrees to perform the entire service between the Eastern terminus, and Salt Lake City, and to furnish facilities to accommodate the travel both "through" and "local" - The Second party to perform the balance of the service, and to afford like facilities, and to pay over to the first part quarterly as it shall be received from the Government & no sooner, Mail pay at the rate of Four Hundred & Seventy Thousand Dollars per annum, after deducting therefrom one half the amt. paid for Sea Service.

2nd The passenger business, and the Express business to be divided as follows - The through passenger business, and the Express business to be divided Equally - The local passenger & Express business of the first party to be divided Seventy percent to the first party - and Thirty percent to the Second party, And the local business of the Second party to be retained by them entire - Settlements are to be made quarterly and all accounts balanced - Business going only part way on both Divisions charged as local & price to be fixed by the parties.

3rd Each party is to pay all fines occasioned by failures on their respective Divisions - The Division of time to be as follows - On the 20 day schedule the first party has 12 days and 2nd party has 8 days. On the 23 day Schedule the first party has 14 days & the 2nd party 9 days - and a like ratio on the 35 day schedule.

4th The receipt from Pony Express to be divided Equally - Each party carrying the mail paying their own Expenses on their divisions -

5th A General Superintendent to be appointed by the Second party - and paid Equally by the two parties, Shall have general charge and Supervision of the Eastern line, so far as to see that the Service is properly performed, but is not to interfere with the management and detail of the first partys Division.

6th The Supt. or other authorized Agent of the Second party shall have the right to examine the Books of the first party in which are kept the accounts for this Division - And an Agent shall be kept at Ft. Kearney, paid Equally by the parties shall copy way bills & attend to the business of both parties.

7th The Second party reserves the right and privilege of making an Exclusive Contract for the Express business with Wells Fargo & Co. for all business going from the East to any point West of Salt Lake City, and for all business originating West of Salt Lake City going East - at a fair compensation. Said business shall be called through business and divided as such -

8th In case any change or modification by Congress or the P. M. Genl. of the said Contract so as to deprive the 2nd party of the mail pay then the 2nd party are not to be held liable or responsible for the first party.

9th Whenever either party reaches the Common Point of Salt Lake City - the other party shall proceed with the Mail at once without waiting for the Schedule time and it is understood that the whole trip is to be made as rapidly & promptly as possible.

10th It is further stipulated and agreed that in case the 1st party shall fail to perform their Contract, and a serious interruption should take place - and if it should become necessary for the 2nd party to assume the performance of the entire Service - then said Second party shall have the right to at once take possession of the entire Stock & Equipment at an appraised value Each party selecting an appraiser, and the two an umpire (whose decision shall be final) if necessary.

And it is further expressly stipulated that in case said 1st party shall fail as aforesaid and the second party be obliged to perform the service then said 1st party shall pay the sum of One hundred thousand Dollars - to the second party - which sum shall be liquidated damages - and paid without deduction or offset.

In witness whereof the Parties hereto have Subscribed their Names - this 16th day of March 1861 at the City of New York.

Interlineations on 2nd & 4th pages

Made before signing

In presence of Milton S. Latham

Wm. H. Russell Prest The C.O.C. & P.P.Ex.Co.

W. B. Dinsmore Prest

Overland Mail Co.

———————**End Appendix N**———————

Note: The above March 16, 1861 contract is found in The Pony Express: A Postal History by Richard C. Frajola, George J. Kramer, and Steven C. Walske, page 112-153 and is here likewise reproduced with original abbreviations and spelling errors.

Appendix O

We do NOT have any annual reports of Butterfield's Overland Mail Co. However, below is an annual report of *"The Central Overland California & Pikes Peak Company."*
Source: "War Drums and Wagon Wheels: The Story of Russell, Majors and Waddell"
by Raymond and Mary Lund Settle, Univ. of Nebraska Press, Lincoln, 1966, pp. 208-212.

The C.O.C.&P.P.Co. were sub-contractors selected by William Dinsmore and the Overland Mail Co. to operate the portion of the Central Route from St. Joseph to Salt Lake City (see blue portion of the route below). It is reasonable to expect that the Overland Mail Company had similar expenses on the red portion of the route that they operated.

The Central Overland Mail Route 1861 to 1869

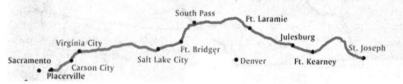

MS, Waddell Collection, Huntington Library.

The following *Estimates of Receipts and Disbursements* for thirteen months from May 1, 1861, to July 1, 1862, was made up in anticipation of the division of the Central Route between the Central Overland California & Pike's Peak Express Co. and the Overland Mail Co., which became effective July 1, 1861. It applies to the eastern half of that Route from St. Joseph, Mo., and Salt Lake City. It should be studied in the light of the contract of March 16, 1861, between the companies.

Estimates of Receipts & Disbursements

Supplies to be hauled for the road between Kearny & a point 300 miles of Salt Lake City, which embraces half the road based upon daily service & to last until July 1, 1862.

45,000 Bushels Corn	@ $0.50	$22,500
Hay for 50 Stations	@ $4.00	20,000
Rations for same district for say 150 men for 330 days		20,000

Quarterly Forage & Board from Kearny East—same period		36,000
Kearny East Western Division Corn average 3½ bushel, 22,500 Bus. Including Hay & Corn		98,350
Pay of 250 Drivers $325 each for 13 months	81,250	
5 Division Agents	4,500	
Extra Agents	2,500	
Office, Denver	5,000	
Do St. Joe	8,000	
Telegrams $2,500, Shops, Repairs $7,500	10,000	
Transportation of Grain 2,610,000 lbs 300,000 rations to Middle Division average 450 miles @ 5.62	$163,000	$476,642

Estimate of men is made for full daily service 13 months when it is only 11 months in fact & present service 2 months.

Estimate of Receipts
From 1st May, 1861, to 1st July, 1862

2 months Mail Pay		$24,000
12 ,, Daily Pay	$470,000	
Less bonus to Western Stage Co.	14,000	
	456,000	456,000
Passenger Receipts May & June estimating 6 trips pr week to and from Denver, two each way for Salt Lake weekly		31,600
Express Receipts each way during May & June		10,000
Pony Receipts		10,000
Daily Service through 12 months 8 through passengers daily, our half		249,600
To Denver 6 pr. day our 70% $140,000		92,280
Through Express		20,000
Express to and from Denver & Salt Lake our 70% $120,000		84,000
Pony Express our 70% $120,000		100,000
		$1,083,480
This estimate does not include Salt Lake Passengers for the 12 months Running Expense		476,642
		$606,838

Pony estimate is based upon 500 letters a trip after 1st July when reduced Tariff commences, as also Denver & Salt Lake Travel & Express estimates, besides we have a train of 29 wagons which will save several thousand in Transportation.

Wanted Prior to 1st July, 1861

Due on Road 1st April	$8,000	
Old Debts to provide for by 1st July	15,000	
Drivers & Agents 1st July	20,000	
⅓ Cost of Corn to start 1st June	7,500	
⅓ „ Rations „ „	6,700	
Western Division 1st July	20,000	
Eastern Division 1st „	10,000	
Incidentals	10,000	
	———	$97,200

Resources with which to pay

Mail Pay 1st July	$36,000	
Pony	10,000	
Passengers 2 mos to Denver & S. L.	31,600	
Express Receipts	10,000	87,600
	———	———
	Short	$9,400

At least $25,000 of the above will not be required till 1st August giving us the advantage of July receipts, which will exceed $50,000.

Wanted to 1st October 1861

Short 1st July	$9,400	
Grain $8,000 Hay $10,000	18,000	
Quarters Pay to Drivers	21,000	
Quarters Pay to Agents & Officers	8,500	
Quarterage East & West (Forage & Rations)	34,500	
Rations Middle Division	7,000	
Old Debt $30,000 & Transportation $50,000	80,000	$178,400
	———	
Bonus to Overland Co.	3,500	
17 Teams of „ „	10,000	$191,900
	———	

Resources with which to pay

Pony Pay	$25,000
Daily Mail	117,500

Quarters Passage & Exp.

Receipts	112,970	255,470

$63,570

Excess of Receipts of 1st October over outlay actually required.

Excess commencing 2nd Quarter	$63,570
Receipts for Quarter ending 1st January	255,470

$319,040

Disbursements for Quarter ending
31st December next.

Bal. Grain	$7,500	
2nd Quarter Pay Drivers, Agents, & Officers	29,500	
Hay	10,000	
Quarterage East & West Division	34,500	
Overland Company	15,000	
Western Stage Co. bonus	3,500	
Old Debt	50,000	
Transportation	50,000	
Contingent	20,000	220,000

$99,040

Receipts Quarter ending March '62, which I really esteem light for the winter	200,000

$299,040

Disbursements for that Quarter. Quarterage

East & West Division	$34,500	
Quarterage Drivers, Agts & Officers	29,500	
Overland Co.	10,000	
Western Stage Co. Bonus	3,500	
Bal. Old Debt	60,000	
Bal. Transportation	63,542	201,042

Excess 1st April out of debt	098,002
Recpts to 1st July	255,470

$353,472

Disbursements for Quarter ending 30 June 1862.

Quarterage Agts, Officers & Drivers	$29,500
Quarterage East & West Division	34,500
Western Stage Co. bonus	20,000

Contingent	$20,000	$87,500
Suppose you cut down Receipts estimated for the year from 30 June 1861 to 30 June 1862 one fourth say		$112,970
This gives you a surplus 30 June, 1862		153,002
Allow for replacing lost stock, wear & tear to place daily line in order for second year		53,002
		100,000
Excess end of last year		100,000
Mail 2nd year		470,000
Receipts predicated upon last year		457,880
Disbursements same as first year		476,642
		$545,238
Deduct estimate one fourth Receipts	$112,970	
Allow to replace stock	$32,628	145,238
Excess 2nd year		400,000
Receipts 3d year		921,880
Disbursements 3d year		$476,642
		845,242
Now add for reduction in cost of grain 2 years one fourth $35,000 and 3 years one half of $70,000		105,000
		$950,242
Property on hand 3d year worth		449,758
		$1,400,000
Cost without interest		200,000
		$1,200,000

MS, Waddell Collection, Huntington Library.

——————End Appendix O ——————

Appendix P

Report of the Postmaster General,Dec. 1, 1862
Selections from pages 126 - 127

REPORT

OF

THE POSTMASTER GENERAL.

POST OFFICE DEPARTMENT,
December 1, 1862.

CALIFORNIA OVERLAND MAIL.   **Page 126**

I regret to state that the overland mail service has not been satisfactory. It was assumed by Congress that this company could procure the transportation of much of the heavy matter by water, but no arrangement to effect this object was made till about the first day of July, 1862. To this cause of failure must be added the unprecedented floods of last winter and spring, and Indian depredations.

Arrangements having now been made by the company for the water carriage of periodicals, &c., and a new and more direct route having been started, less liable to interruption by the Indians, I hope for greater success than has yet been achieved. With a good road, and over a route which the special agents of the department, who have

Page 127

recently inspected it, think is now very safe, and can be made perfectly secure with a very slight increase of force upon it, future failures will be inexcusable. There have been irregularities on this line not excusable on any of the grounds above referred to, due measurably to mismanagement, and partly to the difficulties of the undertaking ; but I am disposed to believe that those now in charge of this great national undertaking are intent on making it successful.

Its importance, indeed, is becoming more and more manifest. Every day brings intelligence of the discovery of new mines of gold and silver in the region traversed by this mail route, which gives assurance that it will not be many years before it will be protected and supported throughout the greater part of the route by a civilized population. As an agency in developing these resources for the government the mail line is indispensable, and every needful protection and support should be given to the company, and some allowance made for failures in the beginning of the undertaking.

———— End of Appendix P ————

Appendix Q

Report of the Postmaster General, Oct. 31, 1863
Selections from pages 11 -12

REPORT .

OF

THE POSTMASTER GENERAL.

POST OFFICE DEPARTMENT,
October 31, 1863.

MAILS ON THE PACIFIC AND ATLANTIC.   **Page 11**

The floods on the North Pacific coast winter before last, and the insurrection in the South Atlantic States, interrupted the overland mails for a few months on the west coast, and continue to interrupt them on the east. In both cases I have had recourse to the routes by sea for the conveyance of mails between the ports in our possession. These were formerly the usual routes, and there is no law prohibiting the use of them by the department.

The Sixth Auditor has, however, refused to pay the contractors for this service, on the ground that contracts for service by sea between the ports of the United States are unauthorized by law, and illegal. He errs, I believe, both in the construction of the law and also as to the extent of his authority to revise and annul contracts made by the Postmaster General. It becomes necessary, therefore, for Congress to act on the subject to enable me to pay for the service already performed, and to continue it.

OVERLAND MAILS.

The contract on the overland route from St. Joseph, Missouri, to Placerville, California, authorized by the act of Congress of March 2, 1861, will expire by its own limitation on the 30th June, 1864. To continue the service I have divided the route into four parts, and issued invitations for proposals to convey the mails on these divisions as separate routes, the whole, however, being united by continuous schedules so as to form one route, as at present, but terminating at Folsom City, the intersection of the Sacramento Valley railroad, instead of Placerville.

The act of Congress directing one continuous route limits the duration of the service under it to June 30, 1864. To continue the service beyond that date I have fallen back upon the various enactments of Congress, covering the whole line as post roads in detached portions. This seems to me to be the preferable mode of letting the service, and most likely to secure the best terms. Legislation will therefore only be needed to secure the conveyance by sea of printed matter intended for the west coast, and for raising the rates of postage on such matter for intermediate places on the overland route. The last day for receiv-

12   REPORT OF THE POSTMASTER GENERAL.   **Page 12**

ing bids for these routes is, however, fixed for the 3d of March, 1864, allowing sufficient time for any action that Congress may deem best to adopt. The service on this route has been performed during the past year with commendable regularity and efficiency, and no accident, Indian hostility, or other casualty has occurred to prevent or retard the safe and prompt transmission of mails and passengers, the trips being, with rare exceptions, accomplished within the schedule time.

The contract for the service between Sacramento, California, and Portland, Oregon, and Olympia, Washington Territory, authorized by the act approved June 21, 1860, will expire on the 15th September, 1864, and as the route was but an aggregation of previously existing routes, it has become necessary to return to the original authority of the department over them, and invite bids for service on separate portions, as before. This has been done by advertisement dated on the 15th October.

——————— **End of Appendix Q** ———————

Montgomery Blair, Postmaster General, 1861-1864
Image Courtesy of The Gilder Lehrman Collection, New York

Appendix R

Report of the Postmaster General, Nov. 2, 1864
Selections from pages 12

REPORT

OF

THE POSTMASTER GENERAL

Page 12

POST OFFICE DEPARTMENT,
November 2, 1864.

Overland Mails

The contract for service on the route from the ~~Mississippi~~ river, *via* Salt Lake, to Placerville, California, under act of March 2, 1861, expiring on the 30th June last, an arrangement was made with the same parties for continuing the service on the same terms to September 30, 1864.

Under an advertisement dated March 22, 1864, inviting proposals for service from Atchison, Kansas, or St. Joseph, Missouri, to Folsom City, California, John H. Heistand, of Lancaster, Pennsylvania, was the lowest bidder, at $750,000 per annum; but his bid having been subsequently withdrawn, contracts have been made with Ben. Holladay, of New York, for the service between Atchison, or St. Joseph, and Salt Lake City, at $365,000, and with Wm. B. Dinsmore, president of the Overland Mail Company, also of New York, from Salt Lake City to Folsom City, at $385,000, making an aggregate of $750,000, per annum. These parties are believed to be able to fulfil their obligations. The contracts are from October 1, 1864, to September 30, 1868; the trips to be made in sixteen days eight months in the year, and in twenty days the remaining four months; to convey through letter mails only, mail matter prepaid at letter rates, and all local or way mails.

Paper and document mails for the Pacific coast are to be carried by sea, *via* New York and Panama, temporary arrangements having been made for their conveyance, within the sum named in the law of March 25, 1864, viz: $160,000 per annum, making the whole expense of territorial and Pacific mails not over $910,000 per annum, or $90,000 less than under the former contract.

Owing to Indian depredations, the overland service was much interrupted during the months of August and September last, and for a period of four or five weeks, the *whole mail* for the Pacific coast and the Territories was necessarily sent by sea from New York. ———— End of Appendix R ————

Appendix S

Summary of All Contracts of P.M.G. with Overland Mail Co. 1857-1864
Letter from The Postmaster General, January 13, 1881

46TH CONGRESS, 3d Session.	SENATE.	Ex. Doc. No. 21.

LETTER

FROM

THE POSTMASTER GENERAL,

TRANSMITTING,

In response to Senate resolution of the 11th instant, certified copy of contract with Overland Mail Company, statement of route as originally contracted for, the acceptance by the company to change of service, statement of route after change, and of all orders of record changing the service thereafter, or the pay of contractors, &c.

JANUARY 14, 1881.—Ordered to be printed.

POST-OFFICE DEPARTMENT,
Washington, D. C., January 13, 1881.

SIR: In response to Senate resolution, certified to me by you, on the 11th instant, I have the honor herewith to transmit to you,

1st. Certified copy of contract with "Overland Mail Company," statement of route as originally contracted for, the acceptance by the company to change of service as provided in act approved March 2, 1861, statement of route after change of service was effected, and of all orders of record changing the service thereafter, or the pay of contractors. The sums paid for service under said contract, and the several orders given, can be obtained from the Auditor of the Treasury for the Post-Office Department. It will be observed that contract for this service, by its terms, ended with June 30, 1864. There being no successor for the service prepared to take it July 1, 1864, the company continued the service, as far as Placerville, until September 30, 1864. The order of October 1, 1864, authorized payment for the same. The routes upon which, more than any others, "the overland mails" were carried, from October 1, 1864, to June 30, 1867, were routes No. 14260, Saint Joseph to Salt Lake City, and No. 14626, Salt Lake City to Folsom City.

2d. For contract and pay for service upon route 14260 you are respectfully referred to Ex. Doc. No. 211, a copy of which is herewith handed you.

3d. Certified copy of contract with "Overland Mail Company" for the service on route 14626, and of all orders of record pertaining to the service, are transmitted to you.

Respectfully,

JAS. N. TYNER,
Acting Postmaster-General.

Hon. JOHN C. BURCH,
Secretary of Senate, Senate Chamber, Washington, D. C.

2   CONTRACT WITH OVERLAND MAIL COMPANY.

POST-OFFICE DEPARTMENT,
Washington, D. C., January 13, 1881.

I, James N. Tyner, Acting Postmaster-General of the United States of America, certify that the annexed are true copies of the originals now on file in this department.

In testimony whereof, I have hereto set my hand, and caused the seal of the Post-Office Department to be affixed, at the city of Washington, the day and year above written.

[SEAL.]

JAS. N. TYNER,
Acting Postmaster-General.

Contract term from July 1, 1854, to June 30, 1858.

Route No. 12578.   From Saint Louis, Mo., and from Memphis, Tenn., converging at Little Rock, Ark., thence via Preston, Tex., or as near so as may be found most advisable, to the best point of crossing the Rio Grande above El Paso, and not far from Fort Fillmore; thence along the new road being opened and constructed under the direction of the Secretary of the Interior, to Fort Yuma, Cal.; thence through the best passes and along the best valleys for safe and expeditious staging to San Francisco, Cal.,   miles and back, twice *twice* a week, in good four-horse post coaches.

1857, July 2. The for'going route is selected for the overland mail service to California, as combining, in my judgment, more advantages and fewer disadvantages than any other. No bid having been made for this particular route, and all the bidders (whose were considered regular under the advertisement and the act of Congress) having consented that their bids may be held and considered as extending to, and applying to, said route. Therefore, looking at the respective bidders, both as to the amount proposed, and the ability, qualifications, and experience of the bidders to carry out a great mail service like this, I hereby order that the proposal of John Butterfield, of Utica, N. Y., Wm. B. Dinsmore, of New York City, Wm. G. Fargo, of Buffalo, N. Y., James V. P. Gardner, of Utica, N. Y., Marcus L. Kinyon, of Rome, N. Y., Alexander Holland, of New York City, and Hamilton Spencer, of Bloomington, Illinois, at the sum of $595,000 (five hundred and ninety-five thousand dollars) per annum, for semi-weekly service, be accepted. The contractors, however, to have the privilege of selecting lands under the act of Congress on only one of the roads, or branches, between Little Rock and the Mississippi River, the one selected by them to be made known and inserted in the contract at the time of its execution.

AARON V. BROWN.

1857, August 2nd. Modify the order of July 2nd, 1857, accepting John Butterfield and others as contractors, at $595,000 per annum, so as to fix the pay at $600,000 per annum, that being the true amount of their bid for the route, with branches both from St. Louis & Memphis, the smaller sum being for service only from one point on the Mississippi.

AARON V. BROWN.

1857, Sept. 11th. *Ordered,* That whenever the contractors and their sureties shall file, in the Post-Office department, a request in writing that they desire to make the junction of the two branches of said road

CONTRACT WITH OVERLAND MAIL COMPANY. 3

at Preston, instead of Little Rock, that the department will permit the same to be done by some route not further west than to Springfield, Mo.; thence by Fayetteville, Van Buren, and Fort Smith, in the State of Arkansas, to the said junction at or near the town of Preston, in Texas; but said new line will be adopted on the express condition that the said contractors shall not claim or demand from the department or from Congress any increased compensation for or on account of such change in the route from St. Louis, or of the point of junction of the two routes from Little Rock to Preston; and on the further express condition that whilst the *amount* of lands to which the contractors may be entitled under the act of Congress may be estimated on either of said branches from Preston to St. Louis, or Memphis, at their option, yet the said contractors shall take one-half of that amount on each of said branches, so that neither shall have an advantage in the way of stations and settlement over the other; and in case said contractors in in selecting and locating their lands shall disregard this condition, or give undue advantage to one of said branches over the other, the department reserves the power of discontinuing said new route from St. Louis to Preston, and to hold said contractors and their sureties to the original route and terms expressed and set forth in the body of this contract.

AARON V. BROWN.

1858, August 17. Change route so as to run from St. Louis by way of Springfield, Mo.; Fayetteville, Ark.; Fort Smith, Fort Belknap, Texas; Franklin and Fort Yuma, Cal., to San Francisco; also from Memphis via Little Rock to San Francisco. Contractors to include such other offices as may be designated from time to time by the department without change of pay.

Leave St. Louis and Memphis every Monday and Thursday at 8 a. m.; arrive at San Francisco in 25 days.

Leave San Francisco every Monday and Thursday at 8 a. m.; arrive St. Louis and Memphis in 25 days.

1858, Dec. 3rd. Direct contractors to supply on the road from Saint Louis to San Francisco. Springfield, Mo.; Fayetteville, Ark.; Fort Smith, Sherman, Texas; Fort Belknap, Fort Chadbourn, El Paso, Tucson, N. Mex.; Fort Yuma, Cal., and Los Angeles.

1859, August 1st. Supply Camp Stockton next after Fort Chadbourn, being on the route.

1859, Sept. 9th. Supply Jacksboro' between Sherman and Fort Belknap, if on direct route.

1859, Oct. 8th. Supply Isleta between Camp Stockton and El Paso, if on direct route.

1860, Dec. 21. Locate Boggy depot, Ark., between Fort Smith and Fort Sherman and direct contractors to supply, the office being on the direct route.

1860, Dec. 31. Instruct P. M. of St. Louis, Memphis, and San Francisco to send mails for way offices in two bags, those for Fort Smith, Sherman, Fort Chadbourn, Fort Davis, El Paso, and Tucson; the other, those for the residue of said offices.

1861, Jan. 9th. Route-book clerk will restate the route as on next face.

Overland route to California.

Route 12578. From Saint Louis, by Springfield, Mulloy's Station, Fayetteville, Fort Smith, Boggy Depot, Sherman, Fort Belknap, Clear

4   CONTRACT WITH OVERLAND MAIL COMPANY.

Fork, Fort Chadbourn, Camp Stockton, Fort Davis, San Elizario, El Paso, Mesilla, Tucson, Casa Blanca, Fort Yuma, Temascal, Ternacula, Los Angeles, Fort Tijou, Visalia, Kingston, Fresno City, Firebaugh's Ferry, Gilroy, San José, and Redwood City to San Francisco.
2883
320 branch.

3203 miles and back, twice a week.

Overland Mail Company,
(E. S. Alvord, Supt.)

$600,000 4 h. c.
12,000

612,000

1861, Jan. 10. Accept proposition of contractors to convey from 1 April next the printed matter between Fort Yuma & San Francisco (789 miles), and to supply San Diego 1 a. w. by side supply, on horse, at $12,000 additional per annum, with privilege of changing their road between Los Angeles & Gilroy, so as to run by the way of Santa Barbara, San Luis Obispo, and San Juan, omitting present offices.

1861, March 12. Ordered that overland mail service on route 12578 be discontinued.

1861, March 13. Allow one month's extra pay, $50,000, on order to discontinue service.

(The 10th section of the act of Congress of March 10, 1861, allowed two months' extra pay, the claim to which was relinquished by the company; but the above payment was ordered. Claim for the other month made and declined by the Postmaster-General. April 10, 1866. See his letter to J. J. Tracey.)

The contract is as follows:

No. 12578.]   [$600,000 per annum.

This article of agreement, made the sixteenth day of Sept., in the year 1857, between the U. S. (acting in that behalf by their Postmaster-General), and John Butterfield, of Utica, N. Y., William B. Dinsmore, of New York City, William G. Fargo, of Buffalo, N. Y., James V. P. Gardiner, of Utica, Marcus L. Kinyon, of Rome, N. Y., Alexander Holland, of New York City, and Hamilton Spencer, of Bloomington, Ills., and Danford N. Barney, of the city of New York, Johnston Livingston, of Livingston, N. Y., David Moulton, of Floyd, N. Y., and Elijah P. J. Williams, of Buffalo, N. Y.,

Witnesseth, That whereas John Butterfield, William B. Dinsmore, William G. Fargo, James V. P. Gardiner, Marcus L. Kinyon, Alexander Holland, and Hamilton Spencer, have been accepted, according to law, as contractors for transporting the entire letter mail, agreeably to the provisions of the 11th, 12th and 13th sections of an act of Congress, approved 3d March, 1857 (making appropriations for the services of the Post-Office Department for the fiscal year ending 30th June, 1858), from the Mississippi River to San Francisco, California, as follows, viz:

From St. Louis, Missouri, and from Memphis, Tennessee, converging at Little Rock, Arkansas, and thence via Preston, Texas, or as near as may be found advisable, to the best point of crossing the Rio Grande above El Paso, and not far from Fort Fillmore; thence along the new road being opened and constructed under the direction of the Secretary of the Interior, to or near Fort Yuma, Cal.; thence through the best passes and along the best valleys for safe and expeditious staging to San Francisco, California, and back twice a week, in good four-horse post-coaches or spring wagons, suitable for the conveyance of passengers as well as the safety and security of the mails, at six thousand dollars a year for and during the term of six years, commencing the sixteenth day of September, in the year one thousand eight hundred and fifty-eight, and ending the fifteenth day of September in the year one thousand eight hundred and sixty-four: Now, therefore, the said John Butterfield, William B. Dinsmore, William G. Fargo, James V. P. Gardner, Marcus T. Kinyon, Alexander Holland, and Hamilton Spencer, contractors, and Danford N. Barney, Johnston Livingston, David Moulton, and Elijah

CONTRACT WITH OVERLAND MAIL COMPANY.   5

P. Williams, their sureties, do jointly and severally undertake, covenant, and agree with the U. S., and do bind themselves—

1st. To carry said letter-mail within the time fixed by the law above referred to, that is, within twenty-five days for each trip, and according to the annexed schedule of departures and arrivals.

2d. To carry said letter-mail in a safe and secure manner, free from wet or other injury, in a boot under the driver's seat, or other secure place, and in preference to passengers, and to their entire exclusion if its weight and bulk require it.

3d. To take the said letter-mail and every part of it from, and deliver it and every part of it at, each post-office on the route, or that may hereafter be established on the route, and into the post-office at each end of the route, and into the post-office at the place which the carrier stops at night, if one is there kept; and if no office is there kept, to lock it up in some secure place at the risk of the contractors.

They also undertake, covenant, and agree with the United States, and do bind themselves jointly and severally as aforesaid, to be answerable for the persons to whom the said contractors shall commit the care and transportation of the mail, and accountable to the United States for any damages which may be sustained by the United States through their unfaithfulness or want of care; and that the said contractors will discharge any carrier of said mail whenever required to do so by the Postmaster-General; also, that they will not transmit, by themselves or their agent, or be concerned in transmitting commercial intelligence more rapidly than by mail, other than by telegraph; and that they will not carry out of the mail letters or newspapers which should go by post. And, further, the said contractors will convey without additional charge the special agents of the department, on the exhibition of their credentials.

They further undertake, covenant, and agree with the United States, that the said contractors will collect quarterly, if required by the Postmaster-General, of postmasters on said route, the balances due from them to the General Post-Office, and faithfully render an account thereof to the Postmaster-General, in the settlement of quarterly accounts, and will pay over to the General Post-Office all balances remaining in their hands.

For which services, when performed, the said John Butterfield, William B. Dinsmore, William G. Fargo, James V. P. Gardner, Marcus L. Kinyon, Alexander Holland, and Hamilton Spencer, contractors, are to be paid by the United States the sum of $600,000 a year, to wit: Quarterly in the months of May, August, November, and February, through the postmasters on the route, or otherwise, at the option of the Postmaster-General of the United States; said pay to be subject, however, to be reduced or discontinued by the Postmaster-General, as hereinafter stipulated, or to be suspended in case of delinquency.

It is hereby also stipulated and agreed, by the said contractors and their sureties, that in all cases there is to be a forfeiture of the pay of a trip when the trip is not run; and of not more than three times the pay of the trip, when the trip is not run and no sufficient excuse for the failure is furnished; and a forfeiture of a due proportion of it when a grade of service is rendered inferior to the mode of conveyance above stipulated; and that these forfeitures may be increased into penalties of higher amount, according to the nature or frequency of the failures and the importance of the mail; also, that fines may be imposed upon the contractors, unless the delinquency be satisfactorily explained to the Postmaster General in due time for failing to take from or deliver at a post-office the said letter mail, or any part of it; for suffering it to be wet, injured, lost, or destroyed; for carrying it in a place or manner that exposes it to depredation, loss, or injury, by being wet or otherwise; for refusing, after demand, to convey a letter mail by any coach or wagon which the contractors regularly run, or are concerned in running, on the route, beyond the number of trips above specified; or for not arriving at the time set in the schedule; and for setting up or running an express to transmit letters or commercial intelligence in advance of the mail, or for transporting knowingly, or after being informed, any one engaged in transporting letters or mail matter in violation of the laws of the United States, a penalty may be exacted of the contractors equal to a quarter's pay; but in all other cases no fine shall exceed three times the price of the trip. And whenever it is satisfactorily shown that the contractors, their carrier, or agent, have left or put aside the said letter mail, or any portion of it, for the accommodation of passengers, they shall forfeit not exceeding a quarter's pay.

And it is hereby further stipulated and agreed by the said contractors and their sureties that the Postmaster-General may annul the contract for repeated failures; for violating the post-office laws; for disobeying the instructions of the Department; for refusing to discharge a carrier when required by the Department; for assigning the contract or any part of it without the consent of the Postmaster-General; for setting up or running an express, as aforesaid; or for transporting persons carrying mail-matter out of the mail, as aforesaid; or whenever either of the contractors shall become a postmaster, assistant postmaster, or member of Congress; and this contract shall in all its parts be subject to the terms and requisitions of an act of Congress passed on the 21st day of April, in the year of our Lord 1808, entitled "An act concerning public con-

6   CONTRACT WITH OVERLAND MAIL COMPANY.

tracts." And the Postmaster-General may also annul the contract whenever he shall discover that the same, or any part of it, is offered for sale in the market for the purpose of speculation.

It is hereby further stipulated and agreed that if obstacles, such as the want of water or feed, or physical obstructions, should be found between the points herein designated, so that time cannot be made, and a better line can be found between these points, the Postmaster-General may vary the route to such better line.

And it is also further understood and agreed that the contractors shall have all the rights of pre-emption, whatever they may be, secured by the twelfth section of the act of Congress aforesaid, approved 3d March, 1857, on either of the lines, from the Mississippi River to the point of their junction with the main stem, but not on both. The election to be made by them at any time within twelve months after the date of the execution of this contract.

In witness whereof, the said Postmaster-General has caused the seal of the Post-Office Department to be hereto affixed, and has attested the same by his signature; and the said contractors and their sureties have hereunto set their hands and seals the day and year set opposite their names respectively.

[SEAL.]

AARON V. BROWN,
Postmaster-General.

Signed, sealed, and delivered by the Postmaster-General in the presence of—
WM. H. DUNDAS.
REVERDY JOHNSON.
And by the other parties hereto in the presence of—
REVERDY JOHNSON.
ISAAC V. FOWLER.

JOHN BUTTERFIELD.	[SEAL.]
W. B. DINSMORE.	[SEAL.]
WM. G. FARGO.	[SEAL.]
J. V. P. GARDNER.	[SEAL.]
M. L. KINYON.	[SEAL.]
ALEX. HOLLAND.	[SEAL.]
H. SPENCER.	[SEAL.]
D. N. BARNEY.	[SEAL.]
JOHNSTON LIVINGSTON.	[SEAL.]
DAVID MOULTON.	[SEAL.]
ELIJAH P. WILLIAMS.	[SEAL.]

I hereby certify that I am well acquainted with Danford N. Barney, Johnston Livingston, David Moulton, and Elijah P. Williams, and the condition of their property, and that, after full investigation and inquiry, I am well satisfied that they are good and sufficient sureties for the amount in the foregoing contract.

ISAAC V. FOWLER,
Postmaster at New York, N. Y.

Ordered, that whenever the contractors and their securities shall file in the Post-Office Department a request, in writing, that they desire to make the junction of the two branches of said road at Preston instead of Little Rock, that the Department will permit the same to be done by some route not further west than Springfield, in Missouri; thence, by Fayetteville, Van Buren, and Fort Smith, in the State of Arkansas, to the said junction, at or near the town of Preston, in Texas; but said new line shall be adopted on the express condition that the said contractors shall not claim or demand from the Department, or from Congress, any increased compensation for, or on account of, such change in the route from St. Louis, or of the point of junction of the two routes from Little Rock to Preston; and on the further express condition, that whilst the amount of lands to which the contractors may be entitled under the act of Congress may be estimated, on either of said branches, from Preston to St. Louis or Memphis, at their option, yet the said contractors shall take one-half of that amount on each of said branches, so that neither shall have an advantage, in the way of stations and settlement, over the other; and in case said contractors, in selecting and locating their lands, shall disregard this condition, or give other undue advantage to one of said branches over the other, the Department reserves the power of discontinuing said new route from St. Louis to Preston, and to hold said contractors and their securities to the original route and terms expressed and set forth in the body of this contract.

AARON V. BROWN,
Postmaster-General.

11th September, 1857.

CONTRACT WITH OVERLAND MAIL COMPANY. 7

MARCH 12, 1861.—Route No. 12578, California, St. Louis, and Memphis to San Francisco semi-weekly, four-horse coaches. Overland Mail Company, E. S. Alvord, Superintendent.—$625,000.

Ordered: Pursuant to act of Congress, approved 2d of March, 1861, and the acceptance of the terms thereof by the Overland Mail Company. Modify the present contract with that company for route No. 12578, executed 16th of September, 1857, to take effect 16th of September, 1858, so as to discontinue service on the present route and to provide for the transportation of the entire letter-mail six times a week on the central route; said letter-mail to be carried through in twenty days' time, eight months of the year, and in twenty-three days the remaining four months of the year, from St. Joseph, Missouri, (or Atchison, in Kansas,) to Placerville, in California, and also for the delivery of the entire mail, three times a week each way, to Denver City and Great Salt Lake City; and in case the mails do not amount to six hundred pounds per trip, then other mail matter to make up that weight per trip to be conveyed; but in any event the entire Denver City and Salt Lake City mails, and the entire letter-mail for California, to be conveyed. The contractors also to be required to convey the residue of all mail matter in a period not exceeding thirty-five days, with the privilege of sending the latter semi-monthly from New York to San Francisco in twenty-five days by sea and the public documents in thirty-five days. And to be required also, during the continuance of their contract, or until the completion of the overland telegraph, to run a pony express semi-weekly at a schedule time of ten days, eight months of the year, and twelve days four months of the year, and to convey for the Government free of charge *five* pounds of mail matter, with liberty of charging the public for transportation of letters by said express not exceeding $1 per half ounce. The compensation for the whole service to be $1,000,000 per annum, to take effect on or before the 1st of July, 1861, and to expire 1st of July, 1864. The number of the route to be changed to 10773 and the service to be recorded in the route register for Missouri.

Note at bottom of this order:

"In behalf of the Overland Mail Company the undersigned accept the above modification of their contract.

"12th of March, 1861.

"(Signed)

"W. B. DINSMORE, *President.*
"E. S. ALVORD, *Supt. O. M. Co.*

Route 10773. From St. Joseph by Troy, Lewis, Kinnekuk, Goteschall, Log Chain, Seneca, Gautard's, Marysville, Cottonwood, Rock House, Rock Creek (Lodi P. O.), Virginia City, Big Sandy, Millersville, Kiowa Station, Liberty Farm, 32 Mile Creek, Sand Hill, Kearney Station, Fort Kearney, Platt's Station, Garden, Plum Creek, Willow Island, Midway, Gilman's, Cottonwood Springs, Cold Springs, Frémont Springs, Dansey's Station, Gills, Diamond Spring, Frontz Station, Julesburg, 9-mile Station, Pole Creek No. 2, Pole Creek No. 3, Mud Springs, Court-House, Chimney Rock Station, Scott's Bluff, Horse Creek, Cold Springs, Verdling's Ranch, Fort Laramie, 9-mile House Station, Horse Shoe, Elk Horn, La Bonta, Bed Tick, Lapierelle, Box Elder, Deer Creek, Bridger, North Platte, Red Butte, Willow Springs, Horse Creek, Sweet Water, Plants, Split Rock, Three Crossings, Ice Springs, Warm Springs, Rocky Ridge, Rock Creek, Upper Sweet Water, Pacific Springs, Dry Sandy, Little Sandy, Big Sandy, Big Timber, Green River, Ham's Fork, Millersville, Fort Bridger, Muddy, Quaking Aspen, Bear River, Needle Rock, Head of Echo Cañon, Half Way, Weber, Wheaton Springs, East Cañon, Mountain Dale, Salt Lake, Traders' Rest, Rockwell, Dug Out, Camp Floyd, Bush Valley, Point Lookout, Simpson's Springs, Dugway, Fish Springs, Willow Springs, Deep Creek, Antelope Springs, Shell Creek, Egan Cañon, Bates', Mountain Springs, Ruby Valley, Jacob's Wells, Diamond Springs, Sulphur Springs, Robert's Creek, Camp Station, Dry Creek, Simpson's Park, Reese, Dry Wells, Smith's Creek, Edwards' Creek, Cold Springs, Middle Gate, Sand Springs, Sand Hill, Carson Sink, Desert Station, Fort Churchill, Clugage's, Nevada, Carson City, Genoa, Friday's, Yank's, Strawberry, Webster's, Moss, Sports-

8   CONTRACT WITH OVERLAND MAIL COMPANY.

man's Hall, Placerville, Duroc, and Folsom (by rail) to Sacramento, —— miles and back, six times a week, supplying Denver City and Great Salt Lake City three times a week each way, and run pony express semi-weekly in 10 days 8 months, and 12 days 4 months of the year—to convey for government 5 lbs. matter free of charge.

Overland Mail Co., $1,000,000. Wm. *B. Dinsmore, Pres't, New York.*
E. S. *Alvord, Sup't.*

1861, July 10. P. M. St. Joseph's reports commencement of service by Overland Mail Co. from his office on the 1st July, 1861.
1861, Aug. 7. Permit the Overland Mail Company to start the "pony express" from Ft. Kearney (the present western terminus of the Magnetic Telegraph) instead of St. Joseph, provided they make the time through from St. Joseph to Placerville as provided by their contract, viz, in *ten days 8 months, & twelve* days 4 months of the year.

SCHEDULE.

(See order of 21 Jan., '64, in regard to schedule.)

Sept. 12, 1861.—Leave St. Joseph daily, ex. Sunday, at 8 a. m. Arrive at Placerville in 20 days 8 months, & in 23 days 4 months, by 8 a. m.
Leave Placerville daily ex. Sunday at 12 m. Arrive at St. Joseph in 20 days 8 months & in 23 days 4 months, by 12 m.
(In pencil on the margin:) Arrive at Salt Lake City in 12 days and Denver City in 6 days from St. Joseph.
1862, May 17.—Authorize the P. M. at Fort Kearney to procure a suitable room for storing the overland mail matter accumulating at his office in consequence of the interruption of the overland mail service, at reasonable rates of compensation, the expense to be made chargeable to contractors.
1862, July 7.—Permit change of route so as to leave present road and keep along the South Platte and Cherokee trail *via* Bridger's Pass and intersect present route at Fort Bridger, shortening the distance 100 miles, provided the offices on the present route, omitted by the change, be supplied with the mails once a week.

M. BLAIR.

1863, Nov. 24.—Instruct Overland Mail Company to supply office at Virginia City, Neb. Territory, 15 miles east of Carson City and immediately on route without increase of pay.
1864, Jan. 21.—The Overland Mail Company having provided for the conveyance of the mails by railroad between St. Joseph and Atchison, instruct inspection office that the schedule time of said company is to be calculated from the hours of departure from and arrival at Atchison instead of St. Joseph.

M. BLAIR.

1864, Oct. 1.—Recognize service of the Overland Mail Company (Wm. B. Dinsmore, of New York, pres'd't), in conveying the mails from 1 July, to 30th September, 1864, between St. Joseph, Mo., and Placerville, California, at rate of $840,000 per ann., and refer to Auditor to adjust and pay subject to fines and deductions.

WM. DENNISON.

——————End Appendix S ——————

Appendix T

Report of the Postmaster General, Nov. 15, 1865
Selections from pages 9

REPORT

OF

THE POSTMASTER GENERAL.

POST OFFICE DEPARTMENT,
November 15, 1865.

Overland Service   **Page 9**

The overland mail service from the Missouri river to California is performed under two contracts, one from Atchison to Salt Lake City, and the other from the latter place to Folsom City. On the western division the service has been performed with reasonable regularity, while on the eastern portion it has been more or less irregular, owing, as alleged by the contractors, to high water, bad roads, and hostilities of the Indians, disappointing the expectations of the department as to the value of the service.

——————— End of Appendix T ———————

Alexander W. Randall, Postmaster General
1866 - 1869

Appendix U

Report of the Postmaster General, Nov. 26, 1866
Selections from pages 4

POST OFFICE DEPARTMENT,
November 26, 1866.

Overland Route to California   Page 4

By a recent order of the department, the overland mail route to California, of which Atchison, Kansas, had been the initial point, has been changed so as to have two points of departure—one from Junction City, Kansas, on the Union Pacific railroad route, (eastern division,) running from Wyandotte, Kansas; and the other from Fort Kearney, Nebraska, on the Union Pacific railroad route, running from Omaha City, Nebraska. The lines from these two points meet at Denver City, in Colorado Territory.

The Junction City road connects at Wyandotte with the Pacific railway from St. Louis, Mo., making a continuous railway connection with the eastern cities. By this route the stage travel is diminished one hundred and sixty-eight miles, and the time occupied in the transit should be proportionally reduced. The mails to and from California, which before were sent via Chicago and St. Joseph, were consequently ordered, on the 15th of August last, to be sent via St. Louis, Wyandotte, and Junction City. The reports so far received of the actual running of the mails since the change took effect do not show the average diminution of time in the performance of the through trip which the department was led to expect, though the capacity of the route for superior expedition is proved by the fact, that in one or two instances the mails have been received at New York in nineteen days from San Francisco, a day less than the shortest time ever made previous to the change. Subsequently, however, the extension of the Chicago and Northwestern railway to Omaha City, which is necessary to form a continuous line by rail to Fort Kearney, has become so nearly completed, that, on the 13th of November instant, orders were issued to forward via Chicago, Omaha City, and Fort Kearney, all mails destined for the overland route from the distributing offices at Portland, Boston, Hartford, Albany, New York, Philadelphia, Pittsburg, Buffalo, Cleveland, and Detroit—the expectation being that mails from that portion of the country represented by these distributing offices will find their quickest transit by the northern route.

—————— End of Appendix U ——————

Sources

Sources for images are listed under image itself, and are not in this list.

Ahnert, Gerald T., "Butterfield Makes Southern Overland Trail His Own," Overland Journal, Spring, 2020, and his numerous other articles.

Birkinbine II, John, Collection of Arizona and New Mexico Postal History, Robert A. Siegel Auction Galleries, Inc. Sale – 1189, October 23, 2018

Brewer, William H. his journal description of Camptonville, California

Butterfield, John, Report to Overland Mail Company Board of Directors, August 2, 1858

Butterfield, John, Letter dated December 2, 1858, published in the Arkansas True Democrat, January 5, 1859

Butterfield Overland Mail, by Waterman Lilly Ormsby, edited by Josephine M. Bynum, Lyle Henry Wright, Huntington Library, 1942.

Butterfield Overland Mail, Vol. 1, Conkling, Roscoe, page 223

Butterfield Overland Mail Co. Articles of Association, 1857, New York

Butterfield Overland Mail Record Book, Smithsonian National Postal Museum

Butterfield Overland Mail Minute Book, Wells Fargo Museum, San Francisco, CA

Congressional Globe for the 36th Congress, Appendix, p. 2461

Courier-Journal, Louisville, Kentucky, Friday, April 12, 1861 mentions Jennie Whipple ends service

Crossman, Bob, Butterfield's Overland Mail STAGECOACH Route Across Arkansas: 1858-1861, 2021

Crossman, Bob, Butterfield's Overland Mail Co. use of STEAMBOATS to Deliver Mail and Passengers Across Arkansas 1858-1861, 2022

Crossman, Bob, Butterfield's Overland Mail Co. as REPORTED in the Newspapers of Arkansas 1858-1861, 2023

Daily Missouri Republican, June 18, 1865, list of unclaimed letters

Daily Missouri Republican, Sunday, June 2, 1861, mentions sale of Jennie Whipple

Find-a-grave, images of headstones of senders and recipients

Frajola, Richard, George J. Kramer, and Steven C. Walske, The Pony Express: A Postal History, The Philatelic Foundation, 2005

Frajola, Richard, Postal History of the Western Overland Routes, sale 2018

Gamble, James, Wiring A Continent: The making of the U.S. transcontinental telegraph line, The Californian magazine, 1881

Godfrey, Anthony, Historic Research Study Pony Express National Historic Trail, page 68, 86-87

Hamilton Historical Records, by Phillip Hamilton and A History of New California, 1903, page 173-ff, biography of cover recipient Henry Coe

Holiday, J. H., The World Rushed In: California Gold Rush, pages 310-311

Kramer, George, Butterfield Overland Mail National Telegraph, exhibit

Kramer, George, The Butterfield Overland Route, exhibit

Laws of the Territory of New Mexico, 18550 1856, Santa Fe, 1856, p.142-144.

Legends of America.com, history of Wells Fargo & Co.

Louisville Daily Courier, Thursday, December 16, 1858, mention of Jennie Whipple's purchase

Marysville Daily Appeal, Marysville, CA, April 6, 1861, Saturday, page 2 mentions Russell's sub-contract with Overland Mail

McArthur, Priscilla, Arkansas in the Gold Rush, 1986, page 126

Memphis Daily Appeal, Sunday, August 6, 10 and 28, 1859, and Sept. 14, 1859 mentions Jennie Whipple aground in Indian Territory

Milgran, James W., Stampless Cover Editor for The Chronicle of the Classic United States Postal Issues, email January 6, 2023

Nathan, M C. and W. S. Boggs, *The Pony Express*, Collectors Club Handbook No. 15, 1962

Nelson, Dr. Gordon, professor at Florida Tech in Melbourne, Florida, and recipient of the Basil C. Pearce Award from the Western Cover Society. He was honored in 2021 with the completion of the Gordon L. Nelson Health Sciences Building. Dr. Nelson is a frequent contributor to *Western Express Journal of Western Mails*.

Online Archive of California, biography of the recipient, James L. Martel

Overland Mail 1849-1869 by LeRoy R. Hafen, 1969, AMS Press

Overland Stage to California: Personal Reminiscences and Authentic History of the Great Overland Stage Line and Pony Express, Frank Albert Root, 1901

Portsmouth Athenaeum Library in Portsmouth, New Hampshire, they have letters written by cover recipient Robert Harris

Post Office Appropriation Bill of March 2, 1861, ending southern route

Postal Contract modification of March 12, 1861

Postal Contract and sub-contractors, March 16, 1861

Red Bluff Beacon, Red Bluff, California, May 9, 1860, page 1, falsely reports Butterfield deposed because of his southern Pony Express plans

Report of the Postmaster General, 1859, 1860, 1861, 1862, 1863, 1864, 1865, 1866 , and Contract Office letter, March 22, 1860, Letter of PMG to the Senate, Jan. 13, 1881; letter of the PMG Dec. 16, 1868

Resolutions of the Legislature of California, Senate Miscellaneous Documents, 33rd Congress, First Session, No. 49; and 34th Congress, First and Second Sessions, No. 2 and No. 57, pages 1-2.

Sacramento Bee, Sacramento, California, April 14, 1860, page 2, mention of Butterfield's desire to start a southern Pony Express

Sacramento Daily Union, California, June 11, 1861, Letter from Salt Lake, From our Special Correspondent

San Francisco Alta, correspondent writing from St. Louis May 5, 1860, mention of Butterfield's desire to start a southern Pony Express

San Francisco Alta, August 13, 1860 advertising new Pony Express rate

San Francisco Alta, May 8, 1861, description of new Pony Express pre-printed franked envelopes

San Francisco Evening Bulletin, June 26, 1861, ad by Butterfield's Pony Express, William Buckley, Superintendent

Sacramento Bee, Sacramento, California, July 6, 1981, on Pony Express

Sanitary Reporter, 1864, April, 1864 report of recipient C. W. Christy's Soldier's Lodge in Memphis

Scott Specialized Catalogue of United States Stamps & Covers

Smithsonian Libraries and Archives, Baasil Wilder, Librarian, Washington DC

Smithsonian's National Postal Museum, Manda Kowalczyk, Accessions Officer, Washington D.C.

Stimson, Alexander Lovett, History of the Express Companies, 1858

Trepel, Scott R., Wells, Fargo & Company 1861 Pony Express Issues, 2005

Van Buren Press, March 8, 1861 report of Overland Mail ending

Vicksburg Daily Whig, Tue., Dec. 21, 1858, mention of Jennie Whipple's purchase

Walske, Steven C. and Frajola, Richard C., Mails of the Westward Expansion, 1803 to 1861, Western Cover Society, 2015

Wikipedia, numerous articles relating to people and towns named on the covers shown in this volume, including "Central Overland Route," "Butler Ives," "John Butterfield" and "Visalia."

Dr. Robert O. "Bob" Crossman has lived within a few hundred feet of Butterfield's Overland Mail Co. stage route across Arkansas most of his adult life in Russellville 1968-1971, Morrilton 1972, Brightwater 1977, North Little Rock 1977-78, Pottsville 1979-1981, Prairie Grove 1981-1988, and since 1988 in Conway.

He is a member of several philatelic groups including the American Philatelic Society, State Revenue Society, American Revenue Association, Pinnacle Stamp Club of Little Rock, Carriers and Locals Society, U.S. Philatelic Classics Society, U.S. Stamp Society, Civil War Philatelic Society, U.S. Cancellation Club, Western Cover Society, The Postal History Foundation of Tucson, and the American Association of Philatelic Exhibitors.

He is also a member of the Butterfield National Historic Trail Association, Southern Trails Chapter of the Oregon-California Trails Association, Faulkner County Historical Society, Arkansas Historical Association, Shiloh Museum of Ozark History, and Old Colony History Museum.

After graduating from Russellville High School, Dr. Crossman received a B.A. from Hendrix College in Conway, Arkansas, and received graduate and post-graduate degrees from SMU in Dallas, Texas.

He is the author of three additional books on the Butterfield:
• *"Butterfield's Overland Mail Co. STAGECOACH TRAIL Across Arkansas"* 2021
• *"Butterfield's Overland Mail Co. Use of STEAMBOATS Across Arkansas"* 2022
• *"Butterfield's Overland Mail Co. as REPORTED in the Newspapers of Arkansas"* 2023

His postal history published articles include: *"I Lived on The Butterfield Mail Route for Decades and Didn't Know It,"* The American Philatelist, Jan. 2023, and *"Walter Arndt Elected Postmaster General of McDonald Territory,"* The American Philatelist, Dec. 2008.

He has also authored several Butterfield articles including: *"Fort Smith's Connection to the Butterfield's Overland Mail Co.: Stations Between Memphis and Fort Smith"* in the Fort Smith Historical Society Journal, Fall 2021, p. 25-43; *"The Butterfield Overland Mail Company: Faulkner County Connection"* in the Faulkner County Facts & Fiddlings, Fall 2021, p. 24-32; and *"Dardanelle's Connection to Butterfield's Overland Mail Co."* in the Yell County Historical Society Journal, Fall 2021.

Before retiring as a national and state staff member of The United Methodist Church, he wrote several additional books including:
Living Generously / Giving Generously, Ingram Spark Press, 2020
Preach Grace: 480 Sermons from a New Church in Conway, Arkansas, 2020
New Church Handbook: Planting New Churches in the Wesleyan Tradition, 2018
Committed to Christ: Six Steps to a Generous Life, Abingdon Press, 2012

Dr. Bob Crossman • bcrossman@arumc.org
8 Sternwheel Drive, Conway, AR 72034-9391

© 2023 Robert O. Crossman

I just couldn't resist including photos of my family.

Bob & Marcia Crossman

Paul Crossman & Louis Lefebvre

Jessica, Blake Charles, Grayson
with Bob & Marcia Crossman

Owen, David, Cooper & Marlie
Crossman

Fred Borck, Raquel Borck, Brooks Bachamp,
Bailey Bachamp, Dylan Bachamp & Sherry Borck

Gracie & Maggie Mae
Crossman

My Golden Anniversary Edition
of the 1929 Model A

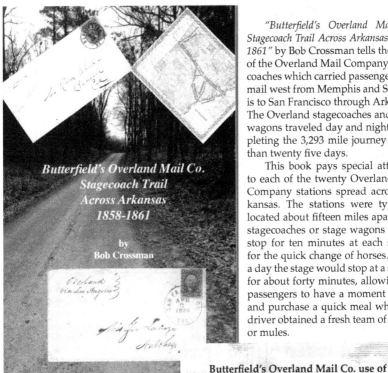

Butterfield's Overland Mail Co.
Stagecoach Trail
Across Arkansas
1858-1861

by
Bob Crossman

"*Butterfield's Overland Mail Co. Stagecoach Trail Across Arkansas: 1858-1861*" by Bob Crossman tells the story of the Overland Mail Company stagecoaches which carried passengers and mail west from Memphis and St. Louis to San Francisco through Arkansas. The Overland stagecoaches and stage wagons traveled day and night, completing the 3,293 mile journey is less than twenty five days.

This book pays special attention to each of the twenty Overland Mail Company stations spread across Arkansas. The stations were typically located about fifteen miles apart. The stagecoaches or stage wagons would stop for ten minutes at each station for the quick change of horses. Twice a day the stage would stop at a station for about forty minutes, allowing the passengers to have a moment of rest and purchase a quick meal while the driver obtained a fresh team of horses or mules.

Butterfield's Overland Mail Co. use of
STEAMBOATS
to Deliver Mail and Passengers Across Arkansas
1858-1861
by Bob Crossman

"*Butterfield's Overland Mail Co. use of STEAMBOATS to Deliver Mail and Passengers Across Arkansas 1858-1861*" explores the untold story of John Butterfield's use of STEAMBOATS to carry the Overland Mail over portions of the Fort Smith to Memphis route of Butterfield's Overland Trail.

While the purpose of my research of the Overland Mail was to satisfy my personal curiosity, hopefully this collection of my research will also make a contribution to the efforts of officially recognizing the route of Butterfield's Overland Mail Co. as a National Historic Trail.

Arriving in Little Rock, this letter departed on John Butterfield's steamboat "Jennie Whipple," on May 6, arriving at Memphis, Tenn. on May 9, 1859.

– 351 –

Butterfield's Overland Mail Co. as REPORTED in Arkansas Newspapers of 1858 - 1861
by Bob Crossman

In this volume, the newspapers of Arkansas do an amazing job of covering the news around Butterfield's Overland Mail Company. Frequently the newspaper editors would draw their information from their exchange of newspapers across the country to bring to their subscribers the most accurate and comprehensive description of facts as possible.

In this book I have let the newspaper reporters tell the story in their own words. It has been difficult, but I have limited my interpretive comments to a brief title I've assigned each article. In this way, today's reader can immerse themselves into the world of the citizens of Arkansas.

This new full color book reports on the mail carried by Butterfield's Overland Mail between September 1858 and March 1861 on the Southern Ox Bow Route, and beginning in July of 1861 on the Central Route. Also, to include additional information and artifacts from US transcontinental mail carried immediately before and immediately after the existence of Butterfield's Overland Mail Co.

In most instances within his previous three books on Butterfield's Overland Mail Co., he focused primarily on the Arkansas route. This volume, by contrast, expands to focus on the entire route of the Butterfield. Also, by contrast, this volume focuses on Butterfield's presence on the Southern Ox-bow Route and later on the northern Central Route. In addition, this volume covers the entire time period of the Overland Mail Company's contract with the postal system: 1858-1864.

While the purpose of this research of the Overland Mail was to satisfy his personal curiosity, he is hopeful that summary of Butterfield Postal History will also make a contribution to Butterfield's Overland Mail Co. new status as a National Historic Trail.

POSTAL HISTORY of John Butterfield's Overland Mail Co. on the Southern & Central Routes including Butterfield's Pony Express 1858-1864
by Bob Crossman

 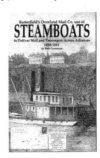  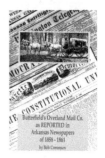

© 2023 Robert O. Crossman

REVIEWS

"The book offers a complete story of the Overland Mail, both Ox Bow and Central Routes, complexities not always understood. Relationships to the Pony Express and Wells Fargo are clarified. Lots of full color illustrations. Lots of contemporary articles and ads. The book gives life to a difficult subject."
Dr. Gordon Nelson, Florida Tech, Melbourne, Florida

"Bob Crossman's latest book, Postal History of John Butterfield's Overland Mail Co. on the Southern & Central Routes including Butterfield's Pony Express 1858-1864, is an indispensable resource to any collector or historian seeking to understand the challenges and triumphs of mail delivery in the western United States during the middle of the 19th Century.

Profusely illustrated with numerous, detailed route maps, contemporary photographs, drawings, original source documents, colored and black and white engravings and - to delight of postal history collectors - a wide variety of domestic and international covers carried "Via Overland Mail", Crossman's book is both a gold mine of American and philatelic history and a pleasure to read." **Don Chenevert, Jr., APS Life Member**

"Bob Crossman has compiled a large number of original documents into a fascinating collection, providing an in-depth understanding of the history and operation of the Butterfield Overland Mail Company's stage line and other components of the postal service prior to the completion of the transcontinental railroad. It's a resource I'm pleased to have on my bookshelf." **Susan Dragoo, Oklahoma Historian**

"This book is well written and the use of color adds much to the pleasure of readers. Bob has researched and published yet another book packed with great graphics, thoroughly documented sources, and an in-depth look into his topic.

The best part of these books? They are INTERESTING to read. Between the color, maps, sketches, photos etc, reading them is almost like having a great lunch buffet"
Teresa Harris, Ouachita County, Arkansas historian
Co-Editor of the Ouachita County Historical Society Quarterly
Administrator, Ouachita County Historical Society Facebook Page

"Bob Crossman explores the audacious history of John Butterfield's Overland Mail Co. with lively prose and vivid narrative. The comprehensive history is delightfully detailed with copious illustrations and newly published research. This fascinating, accurate and exciting book should be of interest to all US western postal history researchers and enthusiasts." **Joe Cody, President, Arizona & New Mexico Postal History Society**

"Bob Crossman's chapter on The Overland Mail Company's Pony Express is informative. Unlike most histories of the Pony Express, it does not rely on sentimental or romantic notions of the service. Rather, it sticks to the facts, quoting extensively from primary and secondary sources. It is a good source of information for anyone who wants to learn more about this aspect of the famous enterprise." **Scott Alumbaugh, Author,**
"On the Pony Express Trail: One Man's Journey to Discover History From a Different Kind of Saddle"

"Thoroughly researched and filled with attractive illustrations and informative and entertaining quotes and excerpts, Bob Crossman has given us an important contribution to the literature on early communication and transportation in the American West. This book is appropriately timed with the recent Congressional designation of the Butterfield Overland National Historic Trail. I look forward to owning my own copy."
Patrick Hearty, Historian/National Trails Liaison
National Pony Express Association

Printed in the USA
CPSIA information can be obtained
at www.ICGtesting.com
LVHW021204211023
761739LV00001B/6